For
Marge,

Jack Smith

# The Big Orange

# THE BIG ORANGE

## JACK SMITH

**WARD RITCHIE PRESS • PASADENA, CALIFORNIA**

First printing

Library of Congress Catalog Card Number: 76-4628
ISBN: 0378-04956-9

This book is based on the author's series
**A Day in the City** in *Westways* magazine.

Printed in the United States of America.

*For Frances, Dave, and Larry*

# Contents

Introduction    **9**
Hollywood Boulevard    **15**
Homes of the Stars    **23**
Movieland Wax Museum    **31**
Sister Aimee's Temple    **39**
Carroll Avenue    **47**
Will Rogers State Park    **55**
Chinatown    **63**
Santa Anita and the Arboretum    **73**
The Huntington Library    **79**
The Pike    **87**
Elysian Park    **97**
Avalon    **105**
Venice    **113**
Watts Towers    **121**
Disneyland    **127**
The Lake Shrine    **135**
El Mercado    **143**

CONTENTS

Descanso Gardens    **151**
Lion Country Safari    **159**
The Swap Meet    **167**
Marineland    **175**
MacArthur Park    **183**
The Bicycle Path    **191**
Farmers Market    **201**
The Watts Festival    **207**
Rodeo Drive    **215**
Busch Gardens    **223**
Pierce College Farm    **229**
The J. Paul Getty Museum    **239**
Santa Monica    **247**

# Introduction

Gertrude Stein, in one of her more lucid moments, said "There is no there there." Contrary to popular inference, she was speaking of Oakland, not Los Angeles.

But her felicitous phrase seemed to fit Los Angeles so well that it has been claimed for this city, especially by people from San Francisco and New York and probably Oakland.

Los Angeles has also been called The Nowhere City, Double Dubuque, and Forty Suburbs in Search of a City, though it is more like eighty suburbs now. These old metaphors are only a few of the many invented by outsiders, and insiders, too, who have tried to define, explain or apologize for a place they seem more inclined to criticize than to leave. In that sense, living in Los Angeles is something like being married.

Writers from out of town have a hard time trying to get Los Angeles down on paper. Photographers have it even harder. Whatever it is that gives Los Angeles its peculiar character, it can't be verbalized or photographed.

New York has its skyline. San Francisco has its bridge. Paris has its Eiffel Tower. The only pictures I can think of that instantly identify Los Angeles are Grauman's Chinese Theater and our strange City Hall, with that Greek temple at the top.

I think I know how they feel, those writers who have been responsible for the epithets we endure. I understand the distaste they must feel for Los Angeles when they wake up the morning after their arrival and draw the curtains in their hotel room and look out and don't see anything. They are overcome by a sense of blah. They feel literally lost. It is a feeling close to panic, I imagine, and the only thing they can think of to do is call room service. And while they're waiting for the day's first bloody mary or tequila sunrise they sit at their portables and bat out a few paragraphs to reassure the more sophisticated

9

folks back home that Nathanael West was right; that their correspondent is in the city of broken dreams at this very moment, wasting his talent on boors and philistines and mindless suntanned beach girls.

I've been there. I've often tried to write something about a strange city. New York and Paris, and San Francisco, of course. Even Hannibal, Mo., and Sauk Center, Minn. As far as I know I've never written anything about them but cliches, since that's all I had time to see. All I could hope for was that I had the buildings on the right streets and the streets in the right town.

Once, to tell the truth, I wrote that I had seen Grant's Tomb in Washington, D.C., but that was during the war and it was only on a postcard I wrote to my wife explaining why I hadn't been writing. I was too busy sightseeing. Those were heady days. I was about to depart for the Pacific. I wasn't getting much sleep in Washington, and when I did get some sleep I dreamed. So I had either dreamed I saw Grant's Tomb in Washington, or I had actually been to New York and seen Grant's Tomb but couldn't remember having been to New York.

I hope there are no misplaced Grant's Tombs in this book, but there may be one or two. Readers to whom accuracy is more important than truth may find a few such errors here, but I suggest that they ignore them. For example I may mention a particular landmark, and you may happen to pass it every day and know that it isn't there anymore. Well, that's exactly the way it is with Los Angeles. A writer has no defense against the wrecking ball. Tomorrow is out of date as soon as it becomes today.

I am more to be believed, in any case, than the New Yorkers who come to Los Angeles and search about, in the tradition of De Tocqueville, all their critical faculties alert, for those quick unerring insights that make even the natives see their city more clearly than before.

A few years ago a writer for a national magazine, a man who evidently had never been west of the Hudson, tried to describe downtown Los Angeles. "At dusk," he wrote, "they position themselves in the shadow of the city's tallest, busiest building and are simultaneously bee-swarmed by the swish of traffic, smell of bagels, whistles of cops and honking of cabs, while they wait to feel the electricity of the place coming right through their shoe soles from the neon-sparkly sidewalk."

Now that may very well describe the scene at dusk in the shadow of the city's tallest, busiest building in *New York*. But not in Los Angeles.

Not long after I read that fantasy I stood at dusk in the shadow of our tallest building. It wasn't busy at all. The building was new and not fully occupied yet, for one thing, and most of the tenants had already bugged out for the suburbs. I listened in vain for the whistle of cops. Los Angeles cops don't whistle. I listened for the honk of cabs. Los Angeles cabs don't honk. I sniffed the early evening air for bagels. Alas, whatever the scent of downtown Los Angeles is, bagels it isn't.

I would like to be able to say that here at last is the definitive book about the real Los Angeles, but of course it isn't and it doesn't even pretend to be. The *real* Los Angeles is invisible. It is to be found in such abstract qualitites as newness, space, openness, freedom, variety and the weather.

This book is more about the *visible* Los Angeles, which is of course unreal, like the nylon alligators out at Disneyland. It is about the visible entertainments of this place which Will Rogers affectionately called cuckooland. There is nothing behind the scenes here, no doors are opened that the reader can't enter. There are no discoveries here that the reader can't make for himself.

This is simply a very personal and impressionistic account of some little journeys I have taken into the visible Los Angeles, and the very minor adventures I've had.

If nothing else, I hope it helps to free us of the notion that there's no here here, and sends it back to Oakland, where it came from.

11

# The Big Orange

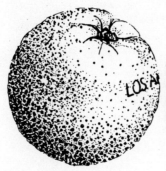

# Hollywood Boulevard

*Look! Betty Grable's leg!*

Clara Bow, it is said, used to ride down Hollywood Boulevard in an open Kissel with half a dozen chow dogs to match her hair. It is a legend as pretty as a balloon, and I would hate to see it exploded.

Today, though, the It Girl of the Twenties would turn few heads. The boulevard is peopled by exotics beside whom the flamboyant Miss Bow would attract no more attention than a nymphet from Hollywood Hi, a species that is also seen in abundance.

The boulevard, like Hollywood itself, has been defined many times, but never with much success.

It would be perfectly correct to say that Hollywood Boulevard is the main street of a small community, near the heart of Los Angeles, with churches, a college, schools and banks, a gung ho chamber of commerce, hospitals and legitimate theaters, and several hardware stores where one can buy the *other* kind of screwdriver.

It would also be correct to say that Hollywood Boulevard is the weirdest street in Southern California. A bizarre bazaar indeed. A rut of pornography and decadence. Western terminus of the sawdust trail and winter headquarters of the speed freaks, the Jesus freaks and the motorcycle freaks.

Many locals are frightened by the boulevard these days, as the Roman citizens must have been frightened when the sidewalk cafes on the Via Veneto were overrun by brutish Teutons. They

15

lament the days when the street was frequented by recognizable movie extras, and now and then a star could be made out behind her shades.

Among the fixtures of the night are the Hare Krishna, chanting mindlessly on the sidewalk in front of Diamond Jim's, swaying back and forth in their orange robes in an involuntary kind of rhythm, as if moved by forces outside themselves, like sea plants at the bottom of the ocean deep. Harmless, unless it frightens you to be hustled for a dollar to "feed the poor."

And a block or two to the east a dozen motorcycles in full armor wait against the curb like medieval war steeds. On the sidewalk their riders hold council in denim, leather and spangles, like Vandal chieftains plotting the depredation of a convent. They stand in the apelike stance affected by men whose lifestyle requires them to look tough and dangerous—feet apart, shoulders hunched, necks outthrust, arms hanging loose, elbows out. One must be careful not to tease them.

At first the mode of dress on the boulevard seems extraordinary and outlandish, but it soon becomes evident that denim pants and tank shirts aren't a mark of individuality but of conformity, faithful to a code as rigid as that which decrees jackets and neckties on the upper floors of the Arco building.

It would also be correct to say that Hollywood Boulevard remains a fascinating, walkable street, full of vitality and outrageous vulgarity, comedy, and dreams—old and new. The danger, like everything else about Hollywood, is more illusory than real. Some of the locals who fled when the hippies came in the 1960s have come down from the hills again and learned to adjust. All it takes is a bit of protective coloration.

And the tourists love it.

The boulevard is unique. Empty of people, it might be Main Street of any Southern California suburb. But once the cast is called onstage and the show begins, there is no mistaking it for El Monte or Glendale or Santa Ana.

The Garden Court Apartment Hotel, on the north side of the boulevard near La Brea, stands like a temple to nostalgia. It is an old wedding cake, French Renaissance, I would guess—a four-story palace with Atlas-like figures holding up the top three stories, and a cherub fountain in the forecourt. It is no longer the most glamorous address in Hollywood, though it is still in business as a déclassé apartment house and "motel," and not long ago I saw a bearded young man sitting out on one of the upper balconies with his portable typewriter, perhaps some would-be Nathanael West, pecking out the new definitive novel of the Hollywood Dream Factory and seeking inspiration from the famous boulevard below.

The grand old name—*GARDEN COURT APARTMENT HO-TEL*—is still faintly visible under a bad paint job over the elegant entrance.

I walked up the steps circling the fountain, long since gone dry and planted to geraniums, and entered the genteel lobby, French windows opened on the storied courtyard. The palm trees and potted plants looked seedy; the ornamental pool was dry.

There was an elderly lady at the desk.

"Can I help you?" she asked.

"I guess some of the big stars lived here once," I said.

"Oh, my yes." She looked off beyond me. "My, yes. Mae Murray lived here, you know. And Mack Sennett lived here for years. And Valentino . . . There were some lively times . . ."

I remembered some of the stories. The times became so lively at one point that the manager planted cactus around the ground floor windows to discourage the lotharios from climbing into the chambers of their lady loves.

Down the street and east of the Garden Court stands Hollywood's premier shrine—the Grauman's Chinese Theater. Indeed it has changed hands and is now Mann's Chinese Theater, but that is an affront to history, and need be treated only as a footnote.

In this capital of make believe and eclecticism, it seems fitting that the one structure which most universally symbolizes Hollywood should be a bastardized Chinese pagoda, nine thousand miles from home and utterly unsuited to its homely midwestern environment.

As I neared the theater two buses rolled up and began disgorging tourists. They streamed out, rushed to the celebrated forecourt and began hunting among the handprints, footprints and signatures of the Great in the cement squares.

17

"Here's Gloria Swanson!"

"Dick Van Dyke!"

"Look! Betty Grable's *leg*!"

Most of the stars had left only their handprints and footprints and signatures, with a greeting to the late Sid Grauman. *"To my pal Sid—George Raft."* But some had lowered themselves into the wet cement to give posterity a crude intaglio of their most famous anatomical features. Thus, Betty Grable's leg, John Barrymore's profile, and Al Jolson's kneecaps (from which, in 1927, he had blasted movies out of their silence forever).

It is not true that the only people captivated by the old Hollywood are survivors of that era. I stood nearby as a young couple, evidently newcomers to America, looked down at the Jolson slab. They spoke in Chinese, something that made them laugh, and then the man got down on his knees in the kneeholes left by Jolson. He clasped his hands together and looked around mischievously at his wife. I held my breath, hoping to hear him shout "Mammy!" But he merely giggled and stood up. How disappointing. I would never know what "Mammy" sounded like in Chinese.

Jean Harlow had left her marks on September 29, 1933, and her feet, from the size of the prints, must have been tiny. It was a shame, I thought, that Miss Harlow hadn't left something more symbolic of herself, in the spirit of Barrymore and Jolson. Then I saw that a nickel and two pennies had been imbedded in her square. A man got down on one knee and tried to pry the nickel out with a fingernail. It held.

"You know she only had seven cents when she was discovered," said a man at my side. He wore a black billed cap and a red coat and turned out to be the tour dispatcher. "Carfare. That's all she had. She'd given up on Hollywood and was waiting for a streetcar to take her home."

"I'd have thought those coins would be stolen by now," I said.

"Oh, they were. Long ago. I put those in myself. With glue."

An usher in a red uniform began haranguing the tourists over a loudspeaker. "The tour begins in six minutes! See the inside of the world famous Grauman's Chinese! Thousands of people from all over the world tour this theater every week!"

The price of the tour was the price of a souvenir booklet, the one price being good for the whole family. I bought a booklet and got in line. Inside the lobby another usher aimed a flashlight down at the lush rug, from which a Chinese dragon glared up at the tourists.

"Please form a circle around the dragon," the usher said.

It was only a ten-minute tour, restricted to the lobby, because a movie was being shown and people were sitting in the darkness under the extravagant chandelier, surrendering to some other fantasies than ours.

Along Hollywood Boulevard pedestrians are often seen walking with heads down, as if looking for lost coins. They are looking at the stars. Some years ago, worried that the boulevard was losing its glamor, the Chamber of Commerce conceived the idea of imbedding the names of the film industry's celebrities in the sidewalks. By the end of 1975 there were more than sixteen hundred names thus enshrined underfoot, from Francis X. Bushman to Elton John, from Mary Pickford to Carol Burnett.

The names are set in brass letters in the center of coral-colored terrazzo stars. Many of the imbedded stars are of course still nameless. They await the convergence of their destiny with that of some yet undiscovered nova.

The famous Montmartre is gone, but the building is still there, on the north side of the boulevard just east of Highland, and some old-timer could point out the stairway to the upstairs cafe where the stars gathered to dine, dance to the music of Jackie Taylor or Xavier Cugat and drink bootleg booze. You might have heard Bing Crosby and the Rhythm Boys at the Montmartre. On the dancefloor you might have bumped into Ricardo Cortez and Vilma Banky or Jack Oakie and Alice White. And on Friday it was a good bet that Joan Crawford would win the Charleston contest again.

The Pickwick Bookstore, at McCadden Place, is said to do the biggest paperback business in the west, a phenomenon that tends to discredit the notion that Hollywood people read nothing but *Variety,* the *Daily Reporter* and the *Racing Form.* The prosperity of the Pickwick is especially gratifying to those who remember that the premises once were occupied by a tailor, and the lofts in which today's customer finds marked-down art books and prints of the masters were once the scene of the town's premier non-stop crap game.

This whole block, in fact, reflects a quiet, contemplative underground. There are book shops that survive without dealing in pornography, unless it happens to be old and rare; stores specializing in motion picture memorabilia; and stamp and coin shops, including one that has been in business on the boulevard for thirty years.

The distinguished Musso & Frank's is in this neighborhood, a classic restaurant with wooden booths, white tablecloths, gentleman waiters, and an extensive continental-American menu that has served Hollywood and the film industry since 1919.

Elsewhere along the boulevard or on its side streets one finds cafes offering Greek, Mexican, French, Hungarian, Italian, Polynesian, Viennese, Chinese and Turkish cuisine, in varying degrees of quality and authenticity, as well as hot dogs, tacos and hamburgers. And there is always the Brown Derby, which still caters to genuine stars.

A mere anachronism should not come as a surprise in Hollywood, but the Janes house, where Hudson deadends into the boulevard, seems too much—a put-on more improbable than the Chinese Theater. There it stands, a turn-of-the-century manse, a grimy, dark green gingerbread, far back from the sidewalk behind two scruffy old palm trees, stuck between the Greek Village (exotic dancing, bouzouki music) and a four-story apartment.

The house was left to the two Misses Janes by their father, who built it when the boulevard was a muddy lane, a nickel trolley ride from downtown Los Angeles.

"Their daddy told them never to sell," I was told, "and they never did."

I saw a woman emerge from the shaded porch of the house, elderly but agile. One of the Misses Janes. She pottered about the yard, oblivious to the stream of life on the boulevard, like any grandmother tending her roses in the suburbs.

It might be said that Miss Janes pottering in her garden is a symbol of the boulevard's tendency to live and let live. It is a street where the individual may give free expression to his artistic tastes and impulses without censure. The clothing on the boulevard may be outlandish, shocking or only silly, but the general effect is entertaining. I did see one woman who may have gone too far. She was tall and suntanned, with stringy blond hair, and as far as I could tell she was attired in nothing but a T-shirt.

Serious shoppers can find anything they want in Hollywood. Guru shirts, wigs, chalk Aphrodites, moccasins, beads, Persian rugs, and possibly the widest variety of underwear and false appurtenances this side of Paris. "We carry D-cups," said a sign in one window.

As I walked I kept checking the stars on the sidewalk. Most of the names meant nothing. Elton Britt, Ernest Tubbs, Pee Wee Hunt. But now and then I spotted a great one—Buck Jones, Charlie Chase, Helen Twelvetrees . . . Then I almost stepped on the greatest of them all—W. C. Fields. The old misanthrope's star was planted right in the doorway of a saloon. Good. I was glad they hadn't immortalized Fields in front of the Christian Science Reading Room.

Hollywood and Vine is one of the half dozen most famous corners in the world, a mecca to millions of movie worshippers. It must be a letdown to those who finally make the pilgrimage. It is the main corner of Anyplace, U.S.A. A department store, a couple of stolid office buildings, a restaurant. A block north on Vine, though, the Capitol Records Building rises thirteen stories, cylindrical in shape, giving Hollywood a new landmark.

The stars in the sidewalk turn the corner at Vine, scattering their names south to Sunset, passing the Brown Derby on the way. The Derby has not changed much in thirty years; only the faces at the tables. It is still the home of the four-martini lunch hour, where press agents parade their clients, reporters interview succulent not-yets and faded has-beens, and you're nobody if they don't page you or plug a telephone into your booth.

I stood in front of the Derby a while, hoping to catch the arrival of someone like Katharine Hepburn, or at least Raquel Welch. A teen-age girl with an autograph book in one hand eyed me uncertainly from a distance. Finally she made her move. She marched up, gave me her book and asked for my autograph.

I signed my name. She examined it. She looked up at me. "You're not *really* Jack Smith," she said. It wasn't a question. She knew I wasn't the one she'd seen on television.

"No," I agreed. "It's only a stage name."

Many years ago, when the first bank was built on Hollywood Boulevard, Cecil B. DeMille said he had been in doubt that there would ever be a bank in this city of false fronts and make believe. Today, at Sunset and Vine alone, there are three.

The old green NBC building, once the heart of the upstart television industry, is gone. In its place stands a monumental money temple erected by the Home Savings and Loan Association. It was at this corner, more than half a century ago, that a man from the East, Jesse L. Lasky, rented a barn from an orange grower and shot the first feature film ever made in Hollywood. It was called "The Squaw Man," and its director, a stubby, energetic man in puttees, was Cecil B. DeMille himself.

The new Home Savings building reveres this heritage. On its facade a dozen beloved stars are depicted in mosaic, heroic in size, in their most memorable roles: Bill Hart, Charles Laughton, Clara Bow, John Barrymore and Dolores Costello, Douglas Fairbanks, Chaplin and Jackie Cooper . . .

Inside, a brilliant stained glass window, called "The Chase," re-creates some of film's most enduring moments—the Keystone Kops in slapstick pursuit, Harold Lloyd clinging to the face of a clock above a city street, Captain Ahab after Moby Dick; the Marx Brothers, the chase across the ice and the pursuit of the Phantom of the Opera.

Across the street stands the Hollywood home of Los Angeles Federal Savings, an eighteen-story tower whose pinnacle is the "Room at the Top," a restaurant that serves vin rosé with brunch and provides Hollywood with its greatest height and most panoramic view.

As I started back up Vine I caught a familiar name in the sidewalk. Oliver Hardy. His star seemed perilously close to the curb. A cliffhanger.

Good old Ollie. He always liked to leave us laughing.

# Homes
# of the Stars

*There goes Zsa Zsa Gabor's car!*

"I saw Cary Grant coming down this street one day," our driver said.

There were six passengers in the black Fleetwood limousine as he tooled it slowly past miles of wooded estates in the hills west of Hollywood. At the moment the sinuous street was empty of traffic, and in the silence that followed the driver's revelation I knew we were all trying to cope with the knowledge that Cary Grant himself had been here.

"I was so surprised," the driver went on, "that I said, 'Oh, folks—it's Gary Cooper!' "

We all laughed at this perfectly understandable mistake, and the spell was broken. Cary Grant was gone; our eyes strained for the next apparition.

As far back as I could remember, these tours of the movie stars' homes had been one of our institutions. Vendors stood on street corners along Sunset Boulevard selling maps to the mansions where the stars actually ate and slept and had parties and children and dogs, and sometimes, to most everyone's disbelief, denied their immortality by dying.

Being a native, I had naturally never bought one of those maps to seek out the abodes of the demigods, nor taken one of the guided tours I had seen departing in endless relay from in front of the Chinese Theater. Guided tours of the stars' homes were for newlyweds from Salt Lake City and vacationing data processors from Denver, who didn't keep up with the new journalism and didn't know that the star system and Hollywood both were dead.

There is one aspect of a city that its own residents rarely see, and that is the city as seen by the tourists. In New York City this common syndrome keeps locals from climbing the Statue of Liberty; in Los Angeles it keeps us from going to Forest Lawn, for example, until we must.

As a newspaper reporter I have enjoyed a privileged access to many of our city's inner sanctums, but Hollywood was never my beat, and I rarely intruded beyond its fringe, if anything that is *all* fringe can be said to *have* a fringe. I had drunk coffee with Charlton Heston in his kitchen the morning after he won an Oscar. I had interviewed Debbie Reynolds once in the palace she shared with husband Harry Karl; and back in the Thirties, when I worked for Cannell & Chaffin, I had helped carry a lacquered liquor closet, I believe it was, into the house of Ronald Colman, through the back door.

So I was just about as big a rube as the tourists who had streamed off the buses at the Chinese Theater that morning to contemplate this most famous piece of Los Angeles architecture and wonder at the strange graffiti left in the cement of the forecourt by the most famous people the world has ever known.

And it was a first for me, too, when I bought my ticket and climbed aboard the limousine for this cruise among the homes of the stars.

Sid Grauman himself had started the tours back in the early Thirties for his own pleasure. He was a gregarious man with many friends, as the inscriptions in the forecourt attest, and he used to have his chauffeur drive him around the hills to see their houses and say hello. Soon Grauman's friends from the East were demanding the tour. In time the chauffeur began operating daily from the theater and started charging for the tour to pay expenses. Today, about five million people visit the forecourt every year, and one hundred thousand take the limousine tour of the stars' homes, most of them from out of town.

Some of the limousines hold eleven passengers and look like centipedes. The one I took held six, with two sitting in pulldown seats. As I was a single the dispatcher put me in front with the driver, a debonair young man named Joe, who turned out to be an aspiring singer. Most of the tour guides are in show business or trying to get in.

A party of three, looking like a married couple and a mother-in-law, took the back seat. A couple of obvious newlyweds took the pulldown seats.

"All here and accounted for?" said Joe, looking around. "Okay, we're off."

The electric windows slid up and the air conditioning came on and we moved out into the traffic stream on Hollywood Boulevard.

"Where are you all from?" Joe asked.

"Hawaii," said the newlyweds.

"Pennsylvania!" said the mother-in-law, with spirit.

"I'm from Los Angeles," I said, wondering why it struck me as ridiculous to be from Los Angeles.

"That's the Yamashiro restaurant up on top of that hill to your right" said Joe, ignoring my confession. "It was built in 1913 as a private palace. They filmed *Sayonara* there."

We turned south on La Brea, Joe not failing to point out the Hungry Tiger restaurant. "Up ahead, see that rainbow on the roof? That's the old Charlie Chaplin studio. I believe it was built in 1923."

We turned west into Sunset Boulevard and passed an old house that had been turned into a School of Massage with a large sign that said *LEARN MASSAGE ON A NUDE GIRL.*

"Sunset Boulevard has gone through many changes," said Joe with an enigmatic little laugh. He was a buoyant type, and his own amusement kept his patter from flattening out into singsong, the curse of tour guides.

"Schwab's drugstore," he announced, "on your left. It is said Lana Turner was discovered there, eating an ice cream soda."

I liked the tone in which he delivered this bit of canon. An edge of skepticism, not untinged with reverence. We need not believe all we were about to hear, but it was to be accorded at least the respect due any established mythology. In the back of the limousine there were murmurs of recognition. A woman said, "Oh, yes." The mother-in-law. We were not a garrulous

25

group, it appeared, perhaps being fearful of overtalking our guide and missing some evanescent scrap of revelation.

"The Body Shop," said Joe as we passed that landmark. "Where they don't fix cars."

"Dino's place," he went on. "Dean Martin doesn't own it any more but he gets ten percent for the name."

It was those minuscule facts and insights, I discovered, that gave substance and authenticity to Joe's narration.

"Cyrano's . . . I saw Rudy Vallee sitting out on the patio one day, in short pants . . ."

We observed Alfi's, where Peter Falk was sometimes to be seen; the Scandia, very expensive; and the City National Bank building, in which Dean Martin's agent had his office.

"We are now in Beverly Hills," said Joe as we left the Strip behind and turned up into ivy-covered hills with narrow roads that wound through forests of oaks, palms and jacarandas, hydrangeas, geraniums and bougainvilleas. Here and there could be glimpsed a gabled roof or a palatial doorway. Sometimes stone walls parted for driveways with wrought iron gates through which could be seen great English cottages, French chateaux, Mediterranean villas and Frank Lloyd Wright imitations soaring out over dropaway lots on the arms of cantilevers.

"There's lots of wildlife here," said Joe. "Rats and snakes. Possums. Oh, yes. This ivy gives good cover. You'll see deer day and night. Skunks. Quail. Doves."

Through a gate we saw a big car with an MA 5 license plate, a Nevada plate in blue and white. "That's Morey Amsterdam's place. 'The Dick Van Dyke Show.' That's his car."

Maybe Morey Amsterdam wasn't a really big star, but that MA license plate seemed to confirm that it was his place, all right, and if *that* was true then everything could be true.

"That's Danny Thomas's place up there on top," Joe said, looking up at a stone rotunda perched out on a spur of the mountain high above us. It looked as inaccessible as Camelot. "We're going up there now."

Up the street on our left a maid in a yellow uniform was out at the mailbox. It was Groucho Marx's house, so this was Groucho's maid, fetching Groucho's mail. "Last of the Marx brothers," Joe said.

As we climbed, a break in the foliage revealed the city below us in the summer fog. "Take my word for it," Joe said. "You can see Santa Monica from here, and Catalina Island out there—twenty-six miles away . . . There's a dove."

We came to the house that Elvis Presley had moved out of three years previously. "He moved out, but the girls are still coming up here. They stole his mailbox and his street numbers. They even stole bricks right out of his wall. See those missing bricks?"

Danny Thomas's house was a luxurious villa with a fountain in the front courtyard and a view of the coastal plain. There were cries of appreciation in the limousine, and the click of camera shutters.

"I had a chance to get an invitation to that house," said Joe, without a note of irony. "I knew his mother-in-law. But she passed away."

We were in the Mother Lode of movie star homes now. One after another they showed through the greenery. Dean Martin's first wife's house. Carol Burnett's, with seven children and seven cars . . . Pat Boone's behind a pure white wall . . .

"I met Katharine Hepburn driving down this street once . . . Also Jane Wyman and Sheldon Leonard . . ."

We circled the pink Beverly Hills Hotel, where Paul McCartney, the Beatle, was said to be holding court at that moment in a very expensive cottage. "Charlie Chaplin used to stay there, and now Colonel Sanders, the Kentucky Fried Chicken man." Across the street was the home of Gloria Swanson—"seventy-four years young and still going strong"—and next door was Uncle Miltie.

Sometimes, Joe said, you would see Glenn Ford out working in his garden, but he wasn't there today. "He used to be married to Eleanor Powell, the dancer, but they're divorced. He's been linked up with Debbie Reynolds and Hope Lange and Johnny Carson's ex-wife," he added, which seemed to explain why Glenn Ford wasn't out working in his garden.

"There's an orange tree on the right . . ."

There was a white wall around the eight-acre Pickfair estate, where little Mary Pickford, once Gladys Mary Smith, was still living in seclusion with that Buddy Rogers lad. But the gates were open and we could see that the driveway ran right through the house and came out on the other side of the estate.

"You can see her Oscar up there in that window," Joe said. We all peered up at a high uncurtained window with an object in it that might have been an Oscar. "She won it in 1928, the second year."

Sammy Davis Jr.'s house seemed to loom above us like a white ocean liner on the crest of a great green wave. "He's got two Stutzes," Joe informed us. "See the lemon tree over there?"

We observed Fred Astaire's house, where at seventy-two the master still danced every day . . . Danny Kaye's . . . Polly Bergen's . . . Rosemary Clooney's . . . Jeanne Craine's . . .

"There's Lucille Ball's place on the left. Three years I've been driving, I've never seen Lucy. Across the street there, that's the nicest man on the block. He brings his neighbors corn and tomatoes from his garden. Jimmy Stewart."

"Oh," cried the mother-in-law at the back of the limousine. "He's from our *state,* you know. Pennsylvania."

Warner Baxter . . . Oscar Levant . . . Of course stars moved, like other people, and they died, but ninety-five percent of the listings on the tour were as up-to-date as they could be.

"Now we leave Beverly Hills and get into Bel-Air," Joe said as we turned off Sunset Boulevard again.

Soon we were at the outer gate of the new house in which the beleaguered Elvis Presley had taken refuge, apparently to no avail. "They come up here and kiss the wall and have picnics and litter the place. See those no-dumping signs? They've got the numbers and the mailbox, too."

Messages had been chalked on the gate: "I love you Elvis . . . Elke was here."

"He's forty and still going strong," said Joe. We passed a secluded school for girls whose alumnae include Shirley Temple, Elizabeth Taylor and Judy Garland. "The girls drive those little sports cars you see, and the teachers are the ones to drive the Volkswagens."

A blue Rolls Royce overtook and passed us, going down the hill. "There goes Zsa Zsa Gabor's car!" Joe said. Electrified, we strained our eyes at the driver, but it appeared, alas, to be a man.

28

Later we came to Ms. Gabor's former house, which was said to have had a special kitchen beside her bedroom, for her personal preparation of Hungarian dishes. "Zsa Zsa is a very good housekeeper," said Joe. "Every time she gets a divorce she keeps the house."

This jest had hardly sunk in before we were passing by Ms. Gabor's current house, a chateau with a copper mansard roof and a view of the canyon, the city and the Pacific. Whatever the state of Zsa Zsa's career, she certainly didn't seem to be moving down.

We crossed over into Holmby Hills and added to our list, like birdwatchers, the home of Henry Mancini; the forty-five-room castle built by William Randolph Hearst for Marion Davies, now occupied by the philosopher-publisher Hugh Hefner and his sybaritic retinue; the Harry Karl mansion so recently vacated by Ms. Reynolds; the Buddy Hackett house, with the concrete white elephant its occupant had placed out front when he found out he had a leaky roof and backup plumbing; the house from which George Burns, now seventy-seven, drove every day to the Hillcrest Country Club for cards and lunch with his cronies; the nice white house from which that nice doctor, Marcus Welby, set out on his house calls . . .

"This is where I saw Jack Benny walking down the street . . ."

The house owned in "happier days" by Sonny and Cher, heaved into view above its jungled grounds, a huge Mediterranean extravagance which during the Bono occupation had sheltered two bodyguards, five watchdogs, a Jaguar, a Rolls-Royce, an Audi, a Porsche and a Datsun, at least, and was modestly know as the Bono Hilton.

"Here's a girl likes yellow," Joe said as we neared an attractive yellow house of a size closer to the human scale. "Likes bicycle riding. Likes dogs. And sings. *Que sera, sera!*"

"Doris Day," the mother-in-law guessed.

We turned down a street whose relatively small homes told us we had descended to a lesser galaxy. "There's an actor in this house here," Joe said, "can't think of his name, he always waves and says hello. You know, he's in *Hogan's Heroes*. German general."

There were two men in the yard standing by a Mercedes and

29

one of them saw us and waved. He was a short man with a shock of black hair and a formidable belly.

"That's *him*," Joe exclaimed, vindicated.

"That's him, all right," said the man in the back seat, evidently a *Hogan's Heroes* fan.

The crowd had grown in the forecourt since we left the theater. There were two buses out front and two limousines, and Joe said he would be taking off with a new group as soon as he had a cup of coffee.

It had been a bargain. Not only had we seen a part of Los Angeles that most natives never see; we had also seen Groucho Marx's maid and Zsa Zsa's Rolls Royce and that German general, what'shisname, from *Hogan's Heroes,* and I wouldn't be surprised if we had just missed Jimmy Stewart walking over to Lucy's place with a basket of corn and tomatoes.

I would like to have seen Doris Day on her bicycle, but you can't ask for everything. *Que sera sera.*

# Movieland
# Wax Museum

*Why is the red carnation in
Gloria Swanson's hand a real
carnation and not wax?*

Perhaps the Movieland Wax Museum is another good starting
point for an exploration of the visible entertainments of Southern California. We live with illusions here as comfortably as
people in Pittsburgh live with steel mills and people in Iowa
live with corn; and the wax museum is an illusion of an illusion;
a mirrored image of a mirror; an echo of an old sound track.

Drive east on the Santa Ana Freeway past the Assyrian palace
rubber factory to Beach Boulevard, then go south on Beach until
you come to an eighteen-foot replica of Michelangelo's *David*.
Unless they have changed their attitudes in Orange County,
he will be wearing a fig leaf.

The David stands in front of what appears to be a Buddhist
temple and to one side of what might be the portal of some
fashionable mausoleum. Unless you have taken a wrong turn
and fetched up at some previously unmapped outpost of Forest
Lawn, you will be at the Movieland Wax Museum and Palace
of Living Art.

There is a large parking lot whose spaces are reserved for
movie stars, past and present. It's all right to take one. Parking
in John Gilbert's place, for example, is just a part of the atmosphere.

I parked in Greta Garbo's place and walked past the towering
*David* to the entrance of the wax museum, which is the building
with the white façade. The lobby is plush and gilded. The rest

31

rooms are marked *Actors* and *Actresses,* a device designed, I imagine, to stir an illusion of personal involvement.

A girl who looked a little like Alice White took my ticket and nodded me through a doorway into what turned out to be a labyrinth of mirrors, broken every few steps by a lighted set in which wax figures are caught in some memorable scene from the movies.

The spell is cast by the first set. It is a scene from *The Taming of the Shrew,* with Douglas Fairbanks and Mary Pickford. Doug stands at the well, grinning up at Mary, a horsewhip in his hand. "As they were 45 years ago," a small sign says, and below it a legend is chalked in on a shooting blackboard, fixing the moment:

> *THE TAMING OF THE SHREW*
> *Mary Pickford*
> *Douglas Fairbanks*
> *Universal Pictures 1929*
> *Scene No. 49. Take No. 6*

The pervasive mood of the museum is nostalgia. One is not enlightened, but one is drawn back and down into a whirlpool of memories, into an illusion of time past that is not dispelled by a wax Nancy Sinatra jumping onto a chromeplated motorcycle.

The corridors are dim. The walls are mirrors, so that images are repeated, as many as half a dozen times, and songs and dialogue from sound tracks mingle faintly as one drifts through this maze of make-believe, parting one from a sense of being in Orange County, U.S.A., only a stone's throw from such material institutions as Disneyland and the home of the California Angels.

Down the first hall from *The Taming of the Shrew,* a Keystone Kop stands smiling at the customers. They realize only gradually that he is wax.

"Gosh," a woman exclaimed, "he looks real!"

"Don't he though!" said her companion.

Most of Movieland's figures were made of beeswax in Spain by modern masters of a very ancient art. The Egyptians made wax gods to put in their graves; the Greeks made wax dolls and dieties; Roman patricians kept wax images of their ancestors; Spaniards made wax effigies of the saints for their churches in the Middle Ages; and many of the great masters of the Italian Renaissance modeled in wax. In modern times the art has been preserved mainly by such notorious exhibitions as Madame Tussaud's, in London, and its imitators, of which Movieland is probably the most remarkable and successful.

Movieland runs from *The Taming of the Shrew* to *Bonanza,* but the accent is on the movies and stars of the 1930s and 1940s, when Hollywood was mining its great mother lode and all America loved the flickers. The Marx Brothers, Laurel and Hardy, Gable, Garbo, Wayne and Harlow.

I came upon Jean Harlow stretched out in a white satin negligee on a white *chaise longue* beside a white French telephone. It is a scene from *Dinner at Eight,* 1933. Her smile is expectant but arrogant, with that curl of cupid's bow lip that drove men mad. Obviously someone has just entered her boudoir, and it is not the maid. Edmund Lowe? John Barrymore? There is a green Lucky Strike package on the table and a scatter of popular magazines. *Liberty, Collier's, Judge, American.* They are all gone now, along with Miss Harlow, who was to die in four more years, at only twenty-seven.

Two middle-aged women were gazing at the effigy of the departed siren, the star for whom the phrase "sex symbol" probably was coined.

"Remember," one said, "Jean's father had his office right there in Kansas City where I worked."

"Yes," said her friend. "We used to drive right by the house."

They moved on, possibly reflecting on the compensations of staying home in Kansas City instead of running off to Hollywood to burn with a platinum flame and die in your twenties.

I heard Gary Cooper before I saw him, that spare but eloquent diction that a generation of men unconsciously imitated as pure American. He stands in the doorway of the bleak hotel in *High Noon,* looking out into the hostile day. Grace Kelly sits tensely in a chair behind him. Over Cooper's shoulder the hands of the tall oaken clock stand at four minutes to noon. Miss Kelly says something unintelligible. She is overwrought. Cooper speaks:

33

*"I'm not trying to be a hero. If you think I like this, you're wrong. But, honey, this is my town . . ."*

"I thought she was prettier than that," a man said, gazing at Miss Kelly.

"Well," his wife said, "she's over forty now, you know."

Down the corridor I found Sophia Loren on her knees under the wrecked altar of a war-torn church where she and her daughter have been raped by soldiers. She holds the bruised and bloodied girl in her arms, looking up in terrible anguish out of those enormous green eyes.

*"Do you know what they have done!"* she cries. *"Those heroes that you command! Do you know what they have done in a holy place, under the eyes of the Madonna! They have ruined my little daughter forever!"*

It was quiet in the broken church a moment, and then another voice came out of the mirrors, distant but unmistakable:

*"I'm not trying to be a hero. If you think I like this, you're wrong. But, honey . . ."*

Illusion. All is illusion.

Halfway through the maze one comes upon a wax effigy of Frankenstein's monster, seated in front of a camera operated by a peppy young lady.

"Come on, folks," she invited. "Have your picture taken with Frankie, here! A souvenir photo in sixty seconds!"

A man and wife, each pushing the other, shuffled into the booth to have their pictures taken with the most beloved of monsters. The woman flung a leg over "Frankie's" knees and crooked an arm around his neck.

"Say whiskey!" the photographer ordered.

"Whiskey," said the man and wife.

There was a flash and the couple stepped out, grinning, and two women took their place. I noticed a look of pained forebearance on Frankie's face. He seemed to be thinking, *"Oh, heavens, this is monstrous."* It was, after all, the monster's dignity that set *Frankenstein* apart from other horror films.

Bill Powell and Myrna Loy are "as they were 40 years ago" in *The Thin Man*. The arm of a dead body dangles from a day bed. He doesn't matter. The essential quality is the lightness, the air of fey sophistication in the demeanor of Powell and Miss Loy.

Powell's expression is not an easy thing to bring off in wax, I imagine. As many other leading men of the era knew, it was not an easy thing to bring off with a real face. The artist in Spain, perhaps more used to saints, has done amazingly well with this unsaintly man.

If the movies of the twenties taught the young to Charleston, neck and drink, the comedies of the thirties taught them to face adversity with *sangfroid,* or at least a wisecrack. A generation of newlyweds tried to copy the domestic badinage of Bill and Myrna, without benefit of script. Who knows? Maybe it helped a few marriages through the straits of the Depression.

Somewhere in the back of Movieland one emerges into a snack bar set out with garden tables and canvas chairs bearing the names of Janet Gaynor, Gregory Peck and the like. I got a cup of coffee and sat in a chair named Joan Crawford, next to a table at which the management had seen fit to seat a group of three wax dummies, looking like customers eating ice cream sodas.

I was sitting there under the domed ceiling, lighted by yellow marquee bulbs, looking off to a wall at a poster for *Sign of the Cross* and thinking of the desirability of Elissa Landi, who played the Christian girl, as I remember, when suddenly I became aware that a man and woman had stopped quite still and were staring at me.

I raised my cup. The woman threw a hand to her mouth.

"Oh, my goodness!" she squealed. "I thought he was . . ."

They hurried on. I realized that for a moment I had become a part of the whole insidious machine, my own wax image.

*"As they were 23 years ago . . ."*
*Katharine Hepburn*
*Humphrey Bogart*
THE AFRICAN QUEEN

Miss Hepburn can not be done in wax. She is not made of flesh, but of style. Her essence is in the tone of her voice, the flick of her finger. She does not look her high-strung self as she sits on the stern of Humphrey Bogart's riverboat. It was a wonderful movie, though, and an echo of that improbable love affair

35

escapes from the sound track tape. You hear it faint and also indistinct:

> *"You ever get homesick, Miss?"*
> *"Only on Sunday afternoons."*
> *"On Sunday afternoon I was always sleeping one off."*
> *"I beg your pardon?"*
> *"Nothin', Miss."*

In a scene from *Sunset Boulevard,* Gloria Swanson, holding a red carnation, alights from a gold Rolls Royce on the arm of William Holden. The Rolls is real and so is the red carnation. Why a real carnation, I wondered, among this wax?

*"Why is the red carnation in Gloria Swanson's hand a real carnation and not wax?"* a woman was reading aloud to her husband from a sign beside the Rolls. *"Because, Miss Swanson has carried one with her through her fascinating career, and to further enhance her fabulous good fortune, Movieland perpetuates the symbol here. Every day at two o'clock this lucky charm is presented to one of the ladies in the audience and is replaced with a new red carnation."*

The woman looked quickly down at her watch and shrugged. Only 11:30 a.m. It was not her lucky day.

Shirley Temple and Edward G. Robinson, like Sophia Loren and Gary Cooper, are close enough together in the museum that their sound effects intrude upon each other.

Miss Temple stands on the deck of a boat that carries a cargo of all-day suckers and ragamuffin animals and sings her song, over and over, in that dimpled voice:

> *On the good ship Lollypop*
> *It's a nice trip,*
> *Into bed you hop . . .*

And then you hear the snap of gunfire and hurry down the hall a few steps to find that Eddie Robinson has just rubbed out a man in a shop window and is wounded in the arm. The scene is animated. It is quite sudden. *Rat-a-tat-tat.* The man in the window dies. Mr. Robinson turns to flee, clutching at a bloodstained coat sleeve.

*. . . Into bed you hop*
*And dream away,*
*On the good ship Lollypop!*

With Miss Temple's theme song in my heart I left Movieland and went next door to the Palace of Living Art. One ticket is good for both.

The Palace of Living Art is not a palace, and perhaps its objects are not art, living or dead. The genre is eclectic. It combines copies of the world's best known works of art, from ancient to modern times, enhanced by a third dimension borrowed from the "Living Masterpieces" of the Laguna Art Festival and an ostentatious piety borrowed from the creations of Forest Lawn.

From the shadow of *David* the visitor walks through the temple door and into a dark room in which Jesus is at the Last Supper with His disciples. On one wall is a reproduction in oil of Leonardo da Vinci's sanctified painting, and beyond it a lighted set of the kind seen in Movieland, in which the figures of *The Last Supper* are reproduced in beeswax, at a real table. A plangent voice, heavy with reverence, comes out of the walls:

*"Welcome to the Palace of Fine Arts . . . one of the most interesting and daring experiments in the history of art presentation . . ."*

Turning to *The Last Supper* in wax, the voice instructs us that at the moment Jesus is saying, *"One of you will betray Me,"* and invites us to see if we can detect the treacherous Judas.

In another chamber we see not only a copy of the *Mona Lisa* in oil, but also a wax Leonardo painting his masterpiece in his studio, where a wax Mona Lisa sits for him, trying to duplicate the celebrated smile. Evidently Mona Lisa's expression is harder to catch in wax than Jean Harlow's, because this Mona Lisa is not enigmatic; she is crafty and ambitious, and if I'm not mistaken, cruel. She might well be her notorious contemporary, Lucrezia Borgia.

The collection betrays a happy taste for the voluptuous, as well as the sacred. A marble copy of the *Venus de Milo,* big as life, stands beside a garden in which her "living" double, in wax—with both arms in place—steps into her bath, as nude as a Playboy pullout.

There is also a copy in oil of Jean Ingres's creamy nude, *La*

37

*Grande Odalisque,* with her duplicate in wax; of Reni's painting of Salome with the head of John the Baptist on a plate; and a rare, perhaps unique copy of *Leda and the Swan,* carved by Ammanati from a design by Michelangelo. This is an exquisite and erotic work. I wondered, as I watched a number of visitors examine the *Leda* casually, and then walk on, whether the catalogue ought to explain just what Leda and the swan are up to. Perhaps not.

The most popular display in the palace is the Vincent van Gogh, a three-dimensional reproduction of Van Gogh's stark room at Arles, with the artist himself sitting in it in wax. *"After you've looked at his self-portrait,"* the leaflet notes, *"step closer and look at the right side of the figure, which shows part of his right ear missing. Following a quarrel with Gauguin, Van Gogh sliced off part of his ear, wrapped his head in a towel, and delivered the severed ear to a girl in a brothel . . ."*

But the most dramatic staging is saved for the last. The room is momentarily dark and silent as the visitor steps in. Then a light fades in, like a dawn, revealing a wax Jesus, praying in the garden of Gethsemane.

The voice of *The Last Supper,* even more sepulchral now, describes this scene. The light fades over the praying figure and dawns on a wall of stones—authentic stones, we are told, over which Christ's shadow once passed. Then the light fades from the wall and rises over a replica of Michelangelo's poignant masterpiece, the *Pietà.*

The management may be applauded for restraining itself from conjuring up a wax *Pietà.* Perhaps it was thought that procuring an exact replica, carved in Michelangelo's home town, of marble from his own quarry, was provoking the angels far enough.

It has been my fortune to see the *Pietà* in its niche in St. Peter's, and I rather prefer it there, but it would be graceless to deny that this splendid copy, in a dark room in Buena Park, exposed to its eternal cycle of dawns and sunsets, is beautiful and touching.

People stand silently in the room, or sit on benches beside the Garden of Gethsemane, listening to the voice, and then, as the voice falls silent and light dims over the body of the dead Christ in His Mother's arms, they go out into the real world, only half a mile from Knott's Berry Farm.

38

# Sister Aimee's Temple

*Sweet was her victory over evil.*
*But the police were unhappy.*

Nearly half a century ago the readers of Outlook magazine were given a tip on how, for the price of a street car ride, they might enjoy one of the beautiful scenic hideaways of Los Angeles and at the same time behold one of its stunning architectural wonders.

"Take the Edendale car out of Los Angeles some Sunday afternoon toward five o'clock," the magazine advised. "Ride for a bit less than half an hour and alight at Echo Park. Here are much shade, cool green water, pleasant grassy glades, and, beyond and above it all, looming stark, ugly, bloated, a huge gray, concrete excrescence on this delightful bit of nature. It is Angelus Temple, citadel of Aimee Semple McPherson and the Foursquare Gospel."

The Edendale car is gone. Today one takes the Hollywood Freeway and drives for two minutes and exits at the Echo Park offramp, and there it is, the same scene, as unchanged as an old picture postcard found in a trunk.

"Here are much shade, cool green water, pleasant grassy glades . . ."

Few ever take the off ramp to investigate this mirage. The park is blessedly uncrowded. It is visited mostly by people of the neighborhood: old men playing cards, young couples boating, mothers sunning infants, small boys fishing.

I took the off ramp one morning and parked near the old boathouse and walked around the lake over the asphalt path. As I walked I found my tempo slowing. I stopped to watch two boys fishing from the south bank. One had a crooked branch with a string and a safety pin.

"I got it," he said. He raised a tin can, muddy and dripping. He looked into the can through the small triangular hole in one end and shook the mud out and looked in again.

"Nope," he said, and tossed the can back in the lake.

"What are you trying to catch?" I asked.

"Crabs," he said. "Like this one here."

He pointed to a small live crustacean twitching on the bank. It looked like a crayfish.

"You catch those with a hook?"

"You gotta hook the cans. They're inside the cans."

I wondered how the crayfish got into the cans through those small holes, the kind made by a beer opener.

"Their mother puts them in there," the boy said, "when they're babies, and they grow up inside."

"I see," I said, and walked on, wondering at the adaptability of life.

The lake was formed a hundred years ago to supply water for a downtown woolen mill. The natural basin in the hills was dammed up, and water came in through a ditch at the north end and out through a canal to the mill at Fifth and Figueroa streets. In time the mill failed and became an ice plant, and that failed too, according to a wry historian of the day, when "competition froze it out."

Near the turn of the century the city took the lake over and made it into a park. It was an English landscape architect, hired to lay the park out, who named it. He shouted to an assistant one day, and got only an echo.

The Echo Park district is one of the older neighborhoods of Los Angeles. The hills around the lake have a look of the 1920s, of Raymond Chandler's Los Angeles, with their shingle bungalows and stucco courts, and some of the streets are still ornamented by the jigsaw houses of the 1890s. The ethnic character has changed. On Sunset Boulevard, a block or two from the park, the delicatessens have given way to Mexican restaurants and taco stands; and the district has been cut off from the old European culture of Temple Street by the freeway, a Red Sea that will not part.

As long ago as 1915 a writer spoke of Echo Park's "turbid waters." The waters are indeed turbid, below the "cool green" surface. The bottom seems a murky trash dump, uglified by shoes, cans, bottles and other by-products of the waste-maker society. Above this hideous underwater landscape, though, the park is clean and pretty. Its trees are old. The palms have grown tall and spare and bearded, like old patriarchs. There are old oaks and eucalyptus trees and pines.

Men with something of the quality of the old trees sit in the sun at their card games, and others play a game of bowls on the grass, shouting and arguing over this quaint old pastime in some cryptic alien tongue, as if the outcome mattered as much as the Super Bowl.

I walked around to the boathouse. A warped sign sags over the doorway:

*FORGET YOUR WORRIES*
*TAKE A BOAT RIDE*

The boathouse is old and neglected. There is a sandwich counter inside, smelling of popcorn and mustard, a couple of pinball games and worn steps leading down to the boat landing, to which a flotilla of faded green boats is tied, offering escape from anxieties and pressures. A tall man in levis and a yellow shirt and a cowboy hat led a woman with a baby down to the landing and rented a boat. They got in under the striped canvas canopy and set out on the lake alone, scattering ducks.

"It's good on Sundays," the boatman told me. "Sometimes we have all the boats out. Especially in summer."

From the boathouse the view is surprisingly pleasant. The lake is a mirror. Squadrons of ducks are out on maneuvers. Flights of sea gulls rise from the lake like small gray clouds. The little island with its brown banks and fence of palm trees looks tranquil and exotic enough for Gauguin.

"*. . . and beyond and above it all, looming stark, ugly, bloated, a huge gray, concrete excrescence on this delightful bit of nature . . .*"

One need not accept all the epithets heaped upon Angelus Temple by its critics to grant that it is not the most beautiful structure ever erected in God's name. It looks like an egregious wedding cake, decorated along the bottom layer with vaguely

41

Doric columns and arched doorways. This layer is topped by another, all square windows, and this by a great dome, on which stands a lighted cross. A marquee overhangs the sidewalk, spelling out the day's events in movable letters, and above these appears the permanent legend:

*ANGELUS TEMPLE*
*Aimee Semple McPherson*
*Founder*
*CHURCH OF THE FOURSQUARE*
*GOSPEL*

A separate structure, also with a circular facade, sits next door behind a small lawn and a wall. It vaguely resembles a French chateau, of perhaps the eighteenth century; but here it seems pretentious and out of place. This was the residence of the founder. However undistinguished these buildings may be as architecture, I can think of no others in Los Angeles that have served as the theater of more flamboyant dramas.

In the 1970s thousands of motorists who daily rush by Angelus Temple over Glendale Boulevard may never have heard of Aimee Semple McPherson, or, if they have, think of her only as some kind of notorious woman of the gaudy 1920s, like Texas Guinan. Gaudy and notorious she was, but Sister Aimee was also adored by tens of thousands of her followers as the personal handmaiden of God. As an evangelist she was bold, inventive, tireless and courageous, and these were qualities that served her with abundance in the great crisis of her life.

Sister Aimee was born in rural Canada of a Salvation Army lassie and a Methodist farmer. In her teens she was converted and wed by an itinerant Holy Roller with whom she hit the sawdust trail. They sailed to China to save souls, and there Robert Semple died, leaving his bride stranded and expecting. When her child was born Aimee returned to America. In a year or two she married Harold McPherson, a grocer. But Aimee had the call. After a son was born, she divorced McPherson and set out with her two children to spread the Gospel.

With incredible will and energy she barnstormed the nation, doing the work of a roustabout as well as shouting the glory of God.

"I sometimes look back upon those years with amazement," she wrote later, "and wonder just how the Lord enabled me to go into new cities, without even an invitation or any earthly backing, search out a piece of vacant land, erect a tabernacle, swing the sledge hammer, drive the stakes, tie the ropes, build the seats, erect the platform, distribute handbills on the streets and paste posters in the windows, hold several street meetings each day and conduct two or three tent services, play the piano and lead my own singing between each testimony, lead in prayer, preach the Gospel, give the altar call, pray for the converts, dismiss them, put out the lights, put the babies to bed and cook our own late supper over the campfire . . ."

Inevitably the Lord led Sister Aimee to Los Angeles, where He bade her build a temple, she revealed later, and inspired her with a text from Joshua: *"Shout, for the Lord hath given you the city."*

"I was definitely led to a specially beautiful property with a circular frontage," she wrote, "facing the entrance of peaceful Echo Park. Surely no other location could have been so ideally located, near the center of the city, adjacent to the principal car lines, yet so restfully quiet and apart.

"The placid lake, the shady trees, the picnic tables . . . make the park an ideal place for our congregations to spend the hours between services in meditation and prayer . . ."

If it was this tranquility that drew Sister Aimee to Echo Park, she was soon enough to shatter it. Here, in 1922, she built her temple, with seats for five thousand, and added a Bible school and the chateau and started radio station KFSG (Kall Four Square Gospel) with the third radio license ever issued in Los Angeles. All was paid for with those "dollars for the Lord" that Sister Aimee's spellbound followers dropped into her collection plates at her rousing services. In return they got a show that had the effect of a three-ring circus featuring Sousa's band, a Wagnerian opera and the burning of Joan of Arc.

Angels descended. Cardboard waves crashed against cardboard lighthouses. The Devil appeared in person. Heaven and Hell were rolled in from the wings. And the singing, wrote a contemporary critic, was "stupendous, cataclysmic, overwhelming."

"It is the most successful show in the United States," wrote a reporter from *Harper's*. "She knows no equal. She is playwright, producer, director and star performer in one. It is not a famous prima donna . . . It is not a world-renowned tragedienne, or a queen of the flying trapeze. It is she who outstrips all of these. It is Sister. In this unique house of worship the Almighty occupies a secondary position."

Sister Aimee was indeed the star, standing front and center in her satin robes, her auburn hair effulgent in the spotlight, clutching her white leather Bible and her bouquet of red roses, shouting God's praise in that brassy and strangely exciting voice.

"She is a beautiful woman," wrote the very man who had deprecated her temple, "seen from the auditorium, with the soft spotlight shining upon her. Let no man venture to deny it."

I entered the temple and took the stairs to the first of the two balconies and looked down into the arena of Sister Aimee's extravaganzas. The chamber is enormous. Red carpets run down through the rows of opera seats to the pulpit where Sister stood, flanked by two praying angels, under the legend:

*JESUS CHRIST*
*The Same Yesterday*
*Today and Forever*

It was in this setting that Sister preached the Gospel, exorcised the Devil, converted and baptized and healed the multitudes, and harangued the "forces of darkness" in the hour of here severest trial.

It began on May 18, 1926, the day Aimee Semple McPherson vanished; it ended, officially at least, nearly eight months later when the Los Angeles Superior Court reluctantly dismissed the criminal charges against her for conspiracy to corrupt morals and obstruct justice. On that May day half a century ago Sister Aimee disappeared while swimming, supposedly, at Ocean Park. Her mother, the redoubtable Minnie (Ma) Kennedy, a partner in her temple affairs, announced to the world that "Sister is drowned. She has gone to the arms of Jesus."

For the next five weeks Ocean Park was the scene of a macabre carnival. Thousands came down to see where Sister had gone into the sea. A human chain, miles long, kept vigil on the sands around the clock. Boats and airplanes searched for Aimee's body. At night searchlights played over the water. Divers probed the pilings of Lick Pier. At least two men were drowned.

At one o'clock on the morning of June 23, Sister Aimee reappeared in the Mexican village of Agua Prieta, across the border from Douglas, Arizona. She told a fantastic story of being kidnapped and held captive in an adobe shack, and of escaping and walking twenty miles across the Sonoran Desert to Agua Prieta. Sister Aimee's disappearance had been merely a sensation; her reappearance was hailed as a miracle. It struck the nation like news of the Second Coming. At first, even those who later doubted were too dumbfounded to be skeptical.

Sister Aimee returned to Los Angeles in triumph. Fifty thousand people met her at the railroad station. The Fire Department band played "Praise God from Whom All Blessings Flow" and the temple choir sang "Wonderful Savior!" One hundred thousand people lined the streets from the station to Echo Park; seven thousand were jammed into the temple; ten thousand stood in the street outside her home.

Sweet was her victory over evil. But the police were unhappy. They could find no adobe shack. Sister's shoes were unscuffed. Her clothes were not soiled. She had not asked for water. Detectives began to wonder about a handsome young man named Kenneth Ormiston. He had been the temple's radio engineer. Ormiston was as elusive and ubiquitous as a ghost. The day Mrs. McPherson vanished he had been seen with a woman in the Clark Hotel. Later he had been seen with a woman near Santa Barbara. He had lived with a woman in a cottage at Carmel. Gradually, as more and more witnesses came forth, the police were convinced the mystery woman was Sister Aimee.

At length District Attorney Asa Keyes, whose victories were all to turn to ashes, made the public accusation: Sister Aimee's story was untrue. There was no kidnapping. She had been with Ormiston, at Carmel and elsewhere, and had been driven across the border for the staging of her "escape." Thus Asa Keyes drove the first nail.

No other story in Los Angeles history, before or since, has held the front page so long. The press was delirious. The nation

45

was scandalized, or bewildered, or at any rate vastly entertained by this titanic struggle between God and the Devil in Los Angeles, where at least one of them was presumed to reside.

Throughout, Sister Aimee was indomitable. She spent grueling days in court, confronting her tormentors, and exuberant nights at her pulpit, rallying her flock, comparing her ordeal favorably with the Crucifixion, shouting her innocence before God and acting out hilarious lampoons of her antagonists. Night after night these parodies of her prosecution were played with standing room only at the temple and broadcast to the millions over Aimee's airwaves.

The preliminary hearing lasted an unprecedented five weeks, after which Aimee, her mother, Ormiston and a third woman were held to answer to the charges. Two months later the charges were dismissed. There was no trial.

In the end Sister Aimee prevailed. She had crumpled a grand jury, broken a deputy D.A., driven a police captain into early retirement, ruined a judge, enriched the newspapers and had risen triumphant in her temple, clutching her roses and her Bible, looking wan but beautiful in her spotlight, shouting "Praise the Lord" while the faithful made the temple tremble with "Jesus Let the Sunshine In."

Mrs. McPherson's remaining years were fraught with conflict, public and private. She died in 1944 in an Oakland hotel room. Her son Rolf K. McPherson took her pulpit and carried on, in his quieter way.

Angelus Temple no longer lights the night with the garish flame of Sister Aimee; but it still burns with her evangelistic fervor, and Sister's Foursquare Gospel still resounds from the temple and the bible college throughout the world, as if on the waves of her inexhaustible energy.

I walked back to the park and looked again at the temple. It is indeed a prosaic structure. But beauty, perhaps, is in the eye of the believer.

# Carroll Avenue

*Only the sheet music on the piano*
*seemed too modern for the mood.*
*It was "Avalon."*

Professor Robert Winter and I had agreed to meet at the house at 1321 Carroll Avenue, but we never did, because the house wasn't there. It had been torn down.

It was an ominous beginning for our tour of the 1300 block of Carroll Avenue, that nostalgic street of late nineteenth-century houses which somehow have escaped "modernization" or the wrecker.

Carroll Avenue is only two blocks long, and most of its remaining period houses are in the easterly block, three on the north side of the street, six on the south. It is this concentration of vintage houses in one block that makes Carroll Avenue unique in Los Angeles, and precious.

Bunker Hill is gone. Like Carthage it has been ploughed under, and salted with the tears of those of us who learned too late to cherish its exuberant old houses as irreplaceable museum pieces and charming reflections of the taste and aspirations of our grandfathers, or more truly, perhaps, our grandmothers.

Carroll Avenue is the nineteenth century's last stand in Los Angeles. Fortunately, up to now, it hasn't been in anyone's way. The street is near the top of Angelino Heights, an old déclassé residential neighborhood on the hill just north of the Hollywood Freeway and east of Echo Park.

Professor Winter was standing on the sidewalk looking at a vacant lot when I drove up. It was a cold morning, windy and

47

sharp; an excellent morning for looking at old houses. Robert W. Winter is professor of history at Occidental College, and he has an affectionate as well as academic interest in Southern California houses of the late nineteenth and the early twentieth centuries.

"This has to be 1321," he said, looking speculatively at the vacant lot as if a Queen Anne house might appear at any instant in a puff of smoke. The lot wasn't quite vacant. There was an old granite retaining wall and steps leading up to the ploughed ground. A few trees stood neglected, like sentries that had failed.

"We're too late," I said.

It had been only yesterday, it seemed, that the Cultural Heritage Board had sponsored a walking tour of the street and given out a mimeographed tour guide with a description of each house. I still had a copy, and 1321 was the first house on the list:

"1321—Carl Laux, druggist, chose the Modern Quaint Style when he built this house in 1889. The rounded corners and high roofed porches were thought to harmonize with the much-publicized semi-tropic weather of Los Angeles . . ."

And now "modern quaint" was dead; buried in this vacant lot.

We walked down to the corner to look at 1300. This is the largest house on the block, except for one across the street which has been "modernized" with stucco. The house at 1300 had been well preserved. It was probably built in 1887, like most of its neighbors, and was a good example of the ornate Queen Anne-Eastlake style that was the rage of the 1880s.

"I'd say," Winter declared, "that it's Queen Anne going on Eastlake."

It is futile, trying to classify any house of the period as truly this style or that. "Victorian" is used, but it is correct only in the sense that it was indeed the Victorian era, and we call everything of the era Victorian. At the Philadelphia Centennial Exposition in 1876, however, America had rediscovered Queen Anne, and at the same time discovered Japan, so recently opened up by Commodore Perry. With its abundance of timber, America adapted the Queen Anne style to shingles and two-by-fours, added Japanese ornamentation and concepts of interior space, improvised and elaborated with such new toys as the scroll saw and power lathe, and then corrupted this entire eclectic package by applying the prescriptions of Sir Charles Eastlake, an eminent English interior decorator, to the *exterior* of the house. Sir Charles had published a little book called *Hints on Household Decoration,* which had a modest vogue in England, but was seized upon by Americans eager to refine a frontier culture and to recall its origins.

"Americans," said Winter, as we studied the porches and gables of the 1300 house, "transferred his interior designs to the exterior. When Eastlake got wind of this he deplored what he had done. Horrors! *Mea culpa!*"

He pointed out the spindly machine-carved pillars holding up the fanciful gable over the porch. "That's a beautiful example of using dining table legs as columns for the front door."

He laughed, shaking his head. But it was a laugh of wonder and affection, rather than scorn. However vain and ridiculous these architectural concoctions might seem, they still have a vivacity, a joie de vivre, that delights the spirit.

"It's partly nostalgia," Winter said. "There's no getting around it. By almost any standards of Greek, or Gothic, or Renaissance taste, all these would fail. They wouldn't make it. But you just have to have a different base."

The house had an improvised look, bulging here, soaring there, hinting at an interior full of inviting spaces and surprises. It was a sort of free form made possible by the American "balloon frame" of light lumber.

"The big house and the picturesque layout appeal to people," Winter said. "It has a sort of hang-loose quality. There's a beginning in these things of a kind of interior sculpture. And notice the windows, compared to the earlier Victorian style. They're larger. The idea was to open the room to the light. The Japanese effect again."

We walked on up the sidewalk to the driveway of the house at 1316. The driveway ran back past an Eastlake two-story bay of the house proper, past a stand of eighty-year-old palm trees, to the nineteenth-century carriage house at the rear.

"Isn't that a *gem,*" said Winter. "The old weather vane is still there. I don't know the social history of this area, but it must have been forgotten for a while. It's salutory neglect."

49

Further on, it was evident that salutory neglect was no longer in effect at 1324 Carroll. The house was newly painted and roofed, its general character unchanged, but the front door was a heavy Spanish type, and there was an elaborate new brick patio in the back yard with a Spanish fountain. It was Queen Anne gone California hacienda.

Next door, at 1330, we looked at the house with the best credentials on the street. It was built in 1888 for Charles Sessions, a dairyman, by the prominent J. Cather Newsom, a San Francisco architect who built the fantastic Carson house in Eureka and some of the vanished mansions on Bunker Hill. The house was substantial in its Queen Anne shapes and angles, but lightened with Moorish curves and towers and lacy Oriental lattices. Two carved Chinese dogs, hideously painted, guarded the porch.

"Boy," said Winter, admiring the dogs, "would I like to get to work with some paint on those!"

It was at the rooming house stage of its long life cycle, no longer a private residence, so we stepped into the entry hall, and out of the twentieth century. The hallway was almost intact. There was a wall panel of carved or "gouged" leather. The newel post had survived unbroken, and a soft colored light fell on the main stairway from a perfect stained glass window. There was a temptation to knock on a large door to what surely was the front parlor, but its transient tenant had a right to what little privacy a rooming house affords. People who live in houses that others cherish as museums do not invariably share that enthusiasm.

The Newsom-Sessions house was probably started in 1887, and it seemed to reflect a substance and stability that was not universal in that peak year of the Southern California land boom. It was a year of inflationary madness. The scene had been set when the Southern Pacific connected with the East, giving Los Angeles its second transcontinental railroad and igniting a price war so unrestrained that at one point tickets from Missouri River towns to Los Angeles were a dollar.

The results, like most great human events, seem predictable, now that we can look back on them. Tens of thousands of visitors poured in from the East and Midwest, arriving at the best time of year, when the mountains were in flower and the air was perfumed with orange blossoms. They hurried home, sold out and came back to Southern California to live.

When they arrived, they found whole new cities waiting for them, from San Bernardino to the sea—Carlton, Nadeau, Manchester, Santiago and even a place called Chicago Park. The cities were nothing but vacant tracts, though jerry-built hotels stood here and there to accommodate the crowds of buyers. But few people ever actually saw the lots they bought. Dazzled and exhilarated by brass bands, free lunches and excursions, extravagant handbills and columns of purple prose, they couldn't wait to get to the promised land. They stood in line to buy lots, and some sold their places in line. Lots were sold not only once but several times a day, the price inflating with each transaction.

When Azusa was first opened to this avaricious horde, the second man in line sold his place for $1,000 and at the end of the first day the sales added up to $280,000, and not one in ten of the buyers and sellers had ever been to Azusa or intended to go.

In 1887 the total value of land sales in the county was at least two hundred million dollars. By the time the balloon deflated, in 1889, no less than sixty towns had been laid out, most of them only on paper, without inhabitants. Chicago Park, with two thousand and eighty-nine lots, had one inhabitant—the watchman hired to take care of its "leading hotel."

At the center of this speculative hurricane, however, the Angelino Heights Tract was laid out by respectable developers for respectable citizens, business and professional men who wished to live close to downtown, but raise their families and attend to their social obligations away from the hubbub of downtown.

Pat Adler, researcher for the Cultural Heritage Board, notes that many of the upper middle-class families who built in Angelino Heights were listed year after year in the Blue Book of Southern California's social life. "A remarkable stability prevailed here, in contrast to the restlessness of Los Angeles society generally, as prominent families moved from Bunker Hill to University Place to the Adams district and westward."

It must have been a pleasant life for the residents of Carroll Avenue. Their houses were spacious and handsome, according to the taste of the day, with views across the plain to the sea, and they stood beside each other in harmony.

One could imagine the city councilman and shoe merchant, Daniel Innes, coming home in his carriage to the house at 1329, across the street from the Sessions house. It looked substantial behind its wall of granite blocks, almost severely dignified with its vertical "stick style" lines, despite the "table leg" Eastlake columns on the front porch and the edging of colored glass around the windows. The Innes family occupied this house for thirty years, and happily, it still looked livable.

We walked down the sidewalk from the Innes house to look at 1345, which had plainly been abandoned to its fate. It was not doing well. For reasons I couldn't define, I found it more appealing than any of the others. It was slightly atilt, like an old lady's hat, and as bare of paint as a piece of driftwood. The wooden steps were broken and askew. But the house had a vigor and dignity and an air of inviolability, from its red brick foundation to the wrought iron belvedere at the top. It was hanging in there.

"It's a crime there's nobody to care about a house like that," said Winter. "At least come and give it a paint job. That dilapidated porch. It's the original. That beautiful tree. It's probably as old as the house."

"What do you think about that house?"

It was a man calling to us from the front yard of the house across the street.

"We were saying," I told him, "that it's too bad nobody cares about it."

He was Alan Wheatley, and he had been living for seven years at 1344 Carroll, across from the house we were looking at. His place was called the Gay Nineties house, having been built in 1895 and reflecting some of the ornamental conceits of that period. Wheatley said he had recently bought the run-down house across from his and liked it so much he was hoping to fix it up and move in.

"I really like that old house," he said. "It's good and sturdy. I want to get it painted and get the steps repaired."

He invited us to look at the Gay Nineties house. He said he worked in movies and had bought the house because he liked the location and the atmosphere. He had taken care, it was evident, to sustain that atmosphere, inside and out, right up to the *HOME SWEET HOME* on the wall. Only the sheet music on the piano seemed too modern for the mood. It was *Avalon.*

"There's a maid's room and bathroom upstairs," he said. "The maid had the best view. But there wasn't much to look at."

Actually, in 1895 the maid's view might not have been so bleak. Downtown was growing south along Broadway and was lighted with electroliers at night. The streets had recently been paved and electric cars had replaced the horse-drawn trolleys. Mr. Doheny had reached oil near downtown with pick and shovel, and there were derricks all the way out to Westlake Park. And on a clear day, she could have seen Catalina.

"This street's a showcase," Wheatley said, "but it's a mess. Nobody cares."

But somebody does. The block has been declared a Historical-Cultural Landmark by the Cultural Heritage Board. This means that before any houses can be demolished the board will have a year of grace in which to seek its rescue.

Walking back to our cars we looked at the street as a whole, talking about what a good thing it would be to preserve it intact, as a park, rather than wage those last-ditch fights to save each house, by itself, and move it someplace where it looked unhappy.

How wonderful it would have been, Winter said, if a few houses could have been spared on Bunker Hill, to lend an exciting and historic contrast to the concrete towers rising forty or sixty stories above them.

"We need this," he said. "It gives us a thrill. Often people who get interested in these things are sort of little old ladies in tennis shoes who love them just because they're old. It seems to me that history should be used for variety, for spice, because it is so *different.* That's what makes it good."

Our tour ended where it had begun, in front of a set of old steps leading up to some lonely trees on an empty lot.

# Will Rogers State Park

*They don't like to have you drink
on the premises, folks. You know.
This is a shrine.*

"You must judge a man's greatness," Will Rogers once said, "by how much he will be missed."

On August 15, 1935, the eve of the long Arctic night, a red monoplane, with two men in it, sputtered, nosed over and crashed into a shallow stream in the tundra near Point Barrow, northernmost tip of America.

The men were killed. One, the pilot, was a one-eyed aviation pioneer named Wiley Post. His passenger was a part-Cherokee folk genius named Will Rogers.

The only witness to the crash was an Eskimo seal hunter. He ran fifteen miles to the town of Barrow with the news that was to plunge the nation into gloom.

Post and Rogers were authentic American heroes. Will Rogers was the best loved American of his time, perhaps the best loved of his century, excepting, for one incandescent moment, his young friend Charles Lindbergh.

It was soon evident how much Rogers would be missed. When a man dies a silence fills his house. When Rogers died a silence filled the nation.

For nearly twenty years, since World War I and its doomed peace, Will Rogers had been letting the air out of the over-blown American balloon, poking holes in the pompous, the venal and the greedy.

Five presidents had roasted on Will's spit, sometimes laughing as they burned. Through his daily words in three hundred newspapers, and on network radio, Will kept a wry diary of the wonders and follies of his beloved "Cuckooland."

*"America is just like an insane asylum,"* he said. *"There is not a soul in it will admit they are crazy."*

His homely wisdom fell on the nation as true and welcome as rain. Then it stopped. The daily box vanished from the front page. That amiable drawl vanished from the air. A light went out in forty million homes.

In 1935, when he crashed with Post, Will Rogers was living with his wife Betty and their children, Will, Jim and Mary, in the ranch house Rogers built on three hundred and forty-five acres in the Santa Monica Mountains. After Mrs. Rogers died in 1944, the family deeded half the land to the state of California, including the house, stables and polo field. This is now maintained as Will Rogers State Historic Park.

It lies on the west of Rustic Canyon, between Bel-Air and Pacific Palisades, up a curving narrow road half a mile above Sunset Boulevard. Probably few who drive by its two entrances even know the park is there. From the busy boulevard the road is lost in eucalyptus and brush. The house stands on a vast lawn, looking out over the plain to the sea. Below it lies the green polo field, three times as long as a football field, and the only one left between Palm Springs and Santa Barbara.

The house Rogers built in the late 1920s is a pale yellow frame construction, comfortable looking but unpretentious. It is a house a man could wear boots in and a horse could stand outside of.

A silver-haired guard stood inside the main door. At the moment I was the only visitor. About three hundred thousand persons visit the park every year, but half of these come in the big sightseeing buses, mostly middle-aged out-of-staters who remember Will Rogers well.

Rogers obviously built the big living room for his cronies. It has rough redwood panel walls, a plank floor, open rafters with a wagon wheel, an ox yoke and a doubletree for chandeliers.

"Those chandeliers came off his father's ranch in Oklahoma," the guard assured me.

The furniture is western rough-hewn by Barker Brothers. But the Navajo rugs on the floor are the real thing, and so are

56

the Charles Russell paintings and bronzes, and the steer's head over the stone fireplace.

"That steer's head," the guard said, "that came from the old Buckhorn saloon in San Antone. Got a spread of seven feet four inches."

I guessed it had heard a lot of lies. It was here, in front of the fireplace, that Will Rogers would have talked horses, flying, politics and show business with such old-timers as Bill Hart, Irvin S. Cobb, Fred Stone, Wiley Post, Tom Mix and Florenz Ziegfeld.

Some of Will's polo trophies and movie memorabilia are kept in a room off the back. A few of his most familiar sayings are spelled out on the walls.

*"Americans are getting too much like the Model A Ford. They all have the same upholstery and they all make the same noise . . .*

*"We are all ignorant, but not about the same things . . ."*

And the best known of all, the sly credentials Will offered when he challenged the high and mighty—

*"All I know is what I read in the papers."*

There is a photograph of Will climbing out of a plane with Post, and a copy of the telegram he sent to his daughter Mary from Fairbanks before his last flight.

"Great trip. Wish you all were along . . . Going to Point Barrow today. Furthest point of land north on whole American continent. Lots of love. Don't worry. Dad."

A scrapbook is open to a clipping from a Fairbanks newspaper of August 16, 1935, by Will's friend, novelist Rex Beach:

"When the news of the crash in the chill fog of the Arctic tundra was made known the entire population of the territory was stricken dumb. I have never seen a people so completely stunned . . ."

There is an alcove off the main room with a large window looking out on the city.

"Mr. Ziegfeld had that put in," the guard said, "on account of Mr. Rogers liked the view so much from there. When it isn't so cloudy you can see all the way to Catalina."

There was a stuffed calf in the alcove, too, standing on a Navajo rug, looking lonely and weatherbeaten. His ears were in shreds.

"Mr. Rogers and Mr. Fred Stone used to rope that calf," the guard explained. "They'd stand there by the hour, talkin' and ropin' that calf, seein' who could do the best."

It was his way with a horse and rope, and not his wit, that got Will out of the Oklahoma Territory and into the bright lights. Will was never a poor boy. He was born in a two-story house on his father's prosperous ranch between Claremore and Oologah.

*"My father was one-eighth Cherokee and my mother one-fourth Chero-kee, which I figure makes me about one-eighth cigar store Injun."*

Will learned to ride and rope as a boy. His father sent him off to school, but Will was never broke to book learning. As a youth he rode a cattle train to Chicago with his Uncle Clem, saw Buffalo Bill's Wild West Show and was bit forever by wanderlust and show business.

Later he shipped out for Argentina on a cattle boat, rode as a cowpoke with the gauchos, worked his way to Africa, joined a traveling show, did Europe and England, and then came back to star, eventually, in vaudeville, the Ziegfeld Follies and the movies.

As I left that part of the house, the guard was reproaching a couple who had come to the door with bottles of soda pop in hand,

"They don't like you to drink on the premises, folks," he said. "You know. This is a shrine." There was no irony in his tone.

I crossed the flagstone patio, with its bougainvillea and hanging fuchsias, wondering what Will Rogers would have said if he knew that the house where he took his boots off and ate his beloved chili was regarded by another generation as a shrine.

There is a parlor in the family wing that reflects, even more than the big room, the simple tastes of the Rogers family—a vintage radio, a mandolin, family pictures, a few books. Among them, handy on a table, is Irvin Cobb's *Exit Laughing*. The only grand thing in the house is the piano in this room.

"That belonged to Mrs. Rogers," a younger guard told me. "She was a piano teacher before she married Will."

I climbed a plain stairway to the bedrooms and the small room that was Will's study, hardly big enough for a Model A Ford. If the park is a shrine, then this is its inner sanctum.

The room is rude in its simplicity: a handmade desk with a leather chair, and beside it a chair made from an old barrel, with a polo mallet leaned against it and a helmet on its cushion.

There is also a high-back red plush chair, looking pompous and out of place.

"That was the chair Mr. Rogers sat in," the guard said, "when he was mayor of Beverly Hills."

He had been elected in his absence as honorary mayor of this rich new town full of movie stars and real estate men. When he arrived on the Santa Fe Chief, half the town was waiting at the station. Billie Dove gave him a key to the city, trimmed with carnations.

They paraded through Los Angeles and out to the Beverly Hills Hotel, where Will stood on a platform with Tom Mix, Bill Hart and Douglas Fairbanks, and the Boy Scout band played *Home Sweet Home.*

*"This is a unique town,"* the new mayor told them. *"We've got two swimming pools to every Bible . . .*

*"I think I can run this town in the evening, when it needs running, and work at something else in the daytime . . .*

*"As to my administration, I won't say it'll be exactly honest, but I'll agree to split fifty-fifty with you, and give the town an even break . . ."*

By the desk is a large world globe, its colored seas and continents dulled by years and dust. A line is marked on the globe from Los Angeles to the tip of Alaska.

"Mr. Rogers and Wiley Post charted their course on that globe," the guard said, "before the last flight."

Will Rogers had been flying's preeminent passenger and booster. He had crisscrossed the nation in every kind of crate and weather. He had climbed out of wrecks and back into airplanes twice in one day. He had befriended Billy Mitchell and scolded the military for its blindness to airpower's future.

*"The nation in the next war that ain't up in the air is just going to get something dropped on its bean . . ."*

The relic that evokes Will's presence more than any other in the house is the old black Remington portable in its open beat-up case on top of the desk.

On this machine, here and all over the world, in cold Asian hotel rooms, in cramped cockpits, on Siberian trains, backstage at the Follies, Will typed out the daily insights, jokes and aphorisms that were read at every breakfast table in America from Oologah to Pennsylvania Avenue. On that little typewriter he ranged over the whole gaudy fabric of American society and its awkward relations with foreigners.

Will loved peace but he didn't trust it. From Versailles on, he saw the next war coming.

*"Peace is like a beautiful woman. It's wonderful, but has been known to bear watching."*

During the Depression he told an isolated America:

*"There is more in the wind than just our little local condition over here . . . You can't pick up a paper that don't prophesy that Prosperity is just around the corner. But let me tell you that war is nearer around the corner than prosperity is."*

A photograph on the wall shows Will dressed like a British lord at Ascot for a movie role. It is Will Rogers out of character, which is how he often felt in his early movies. It wasn't until the talkies that Will Rogers came over on the screen. Then he was Number One at the box office. But he had no more illusions about the movies than he had about the U.S. Senate.

*"The movie business is a cuckoo business made by cuckoo people for cuckoo audiences, and as about eighty percent of the world is cuckoo anyway they fill a spot that nothing will ever replace unless somebody invents something more cuckoo."*

Did Will foresee TV?

There is a back stairway down from the study and a path runs up a furlong to the handsome stables where the Rogers family kept their horses. The twenty stalls are rented out now to the Will Rogers Polo Club.

The stables area was alive with teenage girls and even younger ones; saddling horses, feeding horses or cantering and walking horses in the exercise ring. The men of the Polo Club, I learned, maintain the field and the stables and have an amiable arrangement with the budding equestriennes to exercise and ready their horses for the Saturday afternoon matches.

One of the players explained to me: "Boys don't like horses so much. Girls fall in love with them."

A hiking trail winds up the hill a mile to Inspiration Point. I toiled up it, breathing the scent of eucalyptus. All structures were soon out of sight. There are deer and coyotes in the park, and every year, I was told, the tracks of a mountain lion are found.

Ed Earl, area manager for the state, saw this protected rusticity as the main value of the park.

"An island of peace," he said. "That's the best expression I've heard for it."

Later I sat on the grassy bank by the polo field and watched a chukker. It is the noblest of sports, this ancient game of horses and men.

The Will Rogers Polo Club has thirty members, mostly businessmen who are wealthy enough to keep a string of half a dozen horses and fit enough to ride hard in six or eight seven-and-a-half-minute chukkers twice a week. Not even the rich could afford polo in Los Angeles if it were not for the Rogers bequest. It isn't the horses that cost too much; it's the land.

"Nice play by Baker . . ." The voice of a polo wife came over a loudspeaker from across the field. "That takes the ball into Malibu territory . . ."

There was a thundering, a rush and clash of shining horseflesh and white breeches and red and blue jerseys, and then a sprint downfield toward the goal posts, and the whack of a mallet against wood ball, the breath of excited horses and the sharp shouts of the riders.

"It looks good!" cried the loudspeaker. "It *is* good! And Malibu leads."

I was quite ignorant of the rules, but I remembered that everybody is ignorant, only on different subjects.

I wonder what Will Rogers would have to say today—about television, Watergate, detente. Maybe it is all too complex now for the Cherokee Kid and the little black Remington.

But I would like to hear that voice in Cuckooland again.

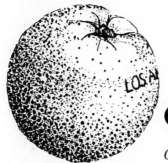

# Chinatown

*Chinatown good. No worry.*
*Chinatown okay.*

Fong See does not go back as far as Confucius; not quite. He was a Chinese merchant in Los Angeles. He died in the 1950s, at the age of ninety-nine. He had been a shopkeeper in Chinatown for three-quarters of a century.

In 1949, when the wrecking ball was about to demolish the old brick building, near the Plaza, in which he had spent a normal man's lifespan selling curios and works of Chinese art, Fong See was asked by a newspaper reporter for his thoughts on this seeming disaster.

"Allee time change," said Fong See. "Allee time city glow and change. Move many time. Allee time people think change sad. Not sad. Change must come."

Since leaving China, Fong See had gone first to San Francisco, then Sacramento, then Los Angeles. He had set up shop in the old Chinatown here in 1881 and moved in the 1930s when most of that section was torn down for the new Union Terminal. At the age of ninety-four, he moved again; this time to the new Chinatown that had been built on North Broadway.

Fong See is with his ancestors now, but the house of Fong See is still in business in New Chinatown, on Chung King Court. The lettering on the window reads: *F. See. Importing.*

It has been four or five years now, I suppose, since I first walked into the shop. A small bell rang when I opened the door. It was quiet inside. The air was incensed. There were two or three customers. They walked carefully among the antique vases and screens and Buddhas, talking softly, as if their very sound waves might shatter something precious.

A young Chinese came toward me.

"Can I help you?"

A tranquil but not humorless face, with eyes magnified by glasses. I wondered if he could be a Fong.

He smiled. "No. You want to see Mr. Fong?"

The question startled me. "You mean his son?" I asked. "Or grandson, perhaps?"

He smiled. "His brother."

By now, I calculated, Fong See would have been something like—what?—115 years old? Could he possibly have a living brother?

"Come," the young man said. "I'll show you." He led me to the door and pointed down Chung King Road to a red sign over another shop.

### FONG'S JEWELRY

"You may find Fong Yun there," he said.

"Incredible," I said. "How old is he?"

"Fong Yun is very old."

I walked down Chung King Road to the house of Fong Yun. The door was locked. There was a sign in the window with a clock face, showing the hour the proprietor would return. I determined to come back.

Chung King Court was noisy. It is always noisy in the afternoon when school is out and the small boys and girls who live in the apartments over the shops are out playing. They have a fiendish love of firecrackers, an abominable invention for which their ancestors must eternally be held to account.

From the open doors of garment-making shops on Chung King Road came an orchestra of Cantonese voices, the newly arrived women, chattering as they worked their sewing machines.

I escaped into the serenity of The Jade Tree, where I browsed among ivory sculptures and Coromandel lacquerwork and inspected a great gilt screen, carved in wood and inlaid with silver. A woman came out of a back room.

"Yes?"

"I was wondering about the screen?"

"It is from Canton," she said. "Of the eighteenth century."

"How much is it?"

"It is seven thousand dollars. It is very rare."

The bazaars of New Chinatown cater to an astonishing range of pocketbooks and taste. You will find magnificent silk scrolls and lovely carvings of jade and rosewood next door to shops hawking the most egregious novelties and souvenirs.

Since the days of the old Chinatown, with its dark alleys, its mysterious back rooms, its old men passing time in contemplation, its tinny music and rude chop suey houses, there may have been more changes than old Fong See might have accepted with equanimity.

A loudspeaker hanging above a gift shop door blared a stream of rock music into the afternoon. The Chungking Photo Shop invited you to come inside and have your picture taken with a grotesque prop, one dollar. In the windows were vulgar jokes and mottoes and tawdry works of gilded plaster sculpture. Which culture was corrupting the other? I decided to blame the Oriental for the firecrackers and the Occidental for the rest.

People were tossing coins into the wishing pool, aiming at tiny shrines, Christian and pagan, scattered over its miniature mountains: *Good Health, Success, Happiness,* the little signs promised, and near the summit a Christian crèche offered the ultimate reward for generosity and marksmanship: *God Bless You.*

Despite the kitsch and schlock, there is the flavor of an alien and ancient culture. It is pervasive, like the aromas of incense in the shops and Cantonese cooking on the air. It is a culture of such antiquity, purity and strength that it has survived the most terrible blows and hostility in this raw and distant land, America.

To enter one of the good art shops is to be transported far away in place and time. There is a scent of sandalwood. Serene landscapes decorate the walls. Heathen gods surround you. Buddhas in brass and stone and ivory; fat little gods, laughing and wanton; Kuan Yin, the goddess of mercy, graceful and pure in white porcelain.

Most of these treasures may be fresh off the boat from Hong

Kong, but they are the fruits of skills that date back through the dynasties into ancient times, before Buddha, before Christ. Shelves teem with exquisite small carvings, in jade and agate, carnelian and teak; you see humans and animals and fruits and trees and fishes, all revealing an ancient and creative people's mystic love of life and form.

The first Chinese came to California in the 1850s, lured by tales of easy gold and brought over by greedy captains of virtual slave ships. Duped and empty-handed, they turned to ancient trades and coolie labor, cooking, washing the white man's clothes and building his railroads.

Hated for their yellow skin and heathen ways, they were persecuted for half a century; discriminated against, robbed, terrorized and even massacred. On one dreadful night in 1871 in Los Angeles, nineteen or twenty Chinese were hanged or otherwise murdered by a white mob.

The Chinese survived, building their own communities within the cities, only to be vitiated and all but obliterated by an alien exclusion act that until only recently kept immigration to a trickle.

Again and again they were uprooted. Old Chinatown was razed for the terminal; then the remnant structures around the Plaza were torn down for the spreading Civic Center. A new China City was erected just north of Olvera Street, only to be destroyed by fire one night in 1938. Despite that disaster, many Chinese returned to China City, and today a stepchild of that ill-starred venture thrives along one block of North Spring Street from Ord to Macy.

This Spring Street settlement remains undiscovered, I suspect, by most of those who visit the New Chinatown on Broadway. It has good restaurants of its own but is most appealing for its markets. Here is where the *Chinese* buy their meats and vegetables and exotic canned goods. Shelves are stocked with such staples as dried shark's fin, dried lotus root and white jelly fungus, hot turnips, sweet sesame pudding and fried pond fish, bean curd and ginger. I found dried squid from Hong Kong, dried sliced bêche-de-mer (sea slugs) from Fiji, canned *fukujinzuke* (pickled vegetables) and preserved eggs from Taiwan, canned abalone from New Zealand and curry powder from Bombay.

Also in this busy block is the Sing Lee Theater, which regularly shows Chinese movies and which once presented the genuine Foo Hsing Opera Company of Taiwan. Though this event went unnoticed by the general public, it was virtually an affair of state in the Chinese community, with a first night attended by the Consul General of the Republic, as well as a music critic from the *Times,* who found the opera's "sheer wash of exoticism superbly refreshing."

Besides theaters, there are two or three old herb shops. They do not cater to the non-Chinese, but I found myself pushing into one, after looking into a window that was bare except for a few dusty jars and some dishes containing minute dried mounds of herbs.

It was dark inside, and still. No keeper responded to my entrance. In the dimness I saw a long, glass-topped case, like a display case in a museum. In it were more dried herbs and powders in small dishes. A bank of mahogany drawers climbed the wall from floor to ceiling. The room might have been like this for years, undisturbed by human presence. Then I heard a voice. I peered into the back of the room and saw an ancient man, with a short white beard, like Confucius, sitting against the wall in a wooden chair. Near him sat another man. He spoke in Chinese. The old man answered. They did not seem to be aware of me.

In what is left of the old Chinatown, I was told later, there are a few places like that, a few quiet retreats, filled with old familiar sights and odors and sounds, where old men sit and talk, in the easy tongue of their youth, or play mah-jongg, growing old in their chairs, with nothing but memories to mark their days.

I walked back to Broadway and up to New Chinatown, past the Chinese modern facade of the Chinese Consolidated Benevolent Association, looking through an open portal into an assembly room with high-backed, leather chairs, where the elders sit, under heroic portraits of George Washington, Sun Yat-sen and Chiang Kai-shek.

Just inside the gateway to New Chinatown is a solemn statue of Sun Yat-sen, seated, and under it, in Chinese and English, the inscription.

*"Dr. Sun Yat-sen, founding father of China . . . one of the greatest figures in China's long history . . ."*

Dr. Sun seemed a suitable patron for this community, which had held on so tenaciously in the face of an often perverse fate.

Unlike San Francisco's venerable Chinatown, our own is not a hodge-podge. It did not just grow, a tumble of brick piles and crooked alleys, but was built to an enlightened plan, with broad lanes, green islands, ceremonial gates and pagoda-like facades. It is open and airy; a place to take the family and walk. What it lacks is an atmosphere of sin. You look in vain for evil. An occasional gambling scandal is the only illicit excitement to surface since the days of slave girls and opium dens.

Still, Dr. Sun is not the only patron saint of New Chinatown. The Chinese character is not all that ascetic. Also near the Broadway gate you will find another hero painted on the wall, a jolly fat man idling under a tree with a jug of wine. This is Li Po, the great drunken poet and leader of the Eight Immortals of the Wine Cup, whose dissolute likenesses, carved in rosewood, you can buy in any art shop.

Li Po's disciples can find a dozen cozy cocktail lounges tucked away in New Chinatown, with dark coves and bare-thighed waitresses, with chanteuses or piano stylists, or at least jukeboxes. The cocktail hour finds them swinging with refugees from the Civic Center, where the old oases are being rapidly buried under asphalt and concrete by the grand design of our righteous elders.

But the essential lure is food. It was Cantonese cooking, the great culinary art, that made it possible for the Chinese to survive on this hostile shore. It was his food, succulent, salubrious and digestible, that subdued the native barbarians. Chinese cooking did more than any other imported art to refine the Yankee taste and civilize the American West.

Every other door in New Chinatown is a restaurant. The air is heavy with that sweet and pungent aroma from their kitchens. It drifts through Gin Ling Way and down the side lanes and out into the traffic on Broadway and Hill, tantalizing even the homeward-bound motorists racing toward the Pasadena Freeway.

Like the art shops, many of New Chinatown's restaurants are family enterprises going back a generation or more. The opulent

Grand Star was started by Him Gin Quon as a penny arcade and now is run by his widow and their sons. Man Gen Low, better known as General Lee's, is run by the four Lee brothers, who grew up in their father's old chop suey house, who grew up in *his* father's chop suey house. The Lees have been in Chinatown for ninety years.

Man Jen Low has been acclaimed nationally for the excellence of its fare. I was savoring a bowl of winter melon soup at Man Jen Low when one of the four sons stopped by my table. He was Walter, the debonair Lee, with longish, wild hair and a rakish scarf at his throat. I had always wondered, I told him, where the name General Lee's had come from, a few years back, suddenly supplanting the traditional Man Jen Low.

"Was your father once a general?" I asked. "Or maybe your grandfather?" Chinese history was not short of generals.

Walter Lee laughed. The name, he told me, had been thought up by Paul Coates, the late newspaper columnist.

"People had a hard time remembering Man Jen Low," Walter Lee recalled. "Paul Coates said, 'Why don't you call it General Lee's?' "

"We said, 'But, Paul—none of us Lees was ever a general.' Paul said, 'So Mike Romanoff isn't a prince, either, or even a Romanoff.' It worked great. Now everybody knows General Lee's."

He laughed and left the table, leaving me alone with my fortune cookie. I broke it open and extracted the fortune:

*You are in for a pleasant change.*

It was time to look in on Fong Yun.

I found the door of Fong's jewelry shop unlocked. There was a youngish man inside, too young to be Fong Yun or even a son; a grandson, I guessed.

"Is Mr. Fong in?" I asked. "Fong See's brother?"

He hesitated. "I'll see if my father's busy," he said. He went to the back of the shop and drew a curtain aside. He spoke in Chinese. He beckoned to me.

Fong Yun was working at a table. He held a carved wood figure in one long, thin hand, a paintbrush in the other. The

69

skin of his hand was silken and translucent over the bones and knuckles. He looked up and laughed. His eyes were bright under the folds. His face was porcelain. One tooth was missing, a comical gap. He wore a plain, gray wool *chong sam,* or long-coat.

Yes, he said, nodding and smiling. He was indeed the brother of Fong See On, who had died many years ago at the age of ninety-nine. Fong Yun had come from Canton when he was thirty, and worked for his older brother in old Chinatown. Then, when Chinatown was torn down, Fong Yun had built a place of his own in the new China City, on Main Street. It was destroyed in the fire.

"Oh, I lose everything," said Fong Yun, laughing at this excellent joke.

"Everything," his son said. "Nothing was insured. But his credit was good. He started all over again. It was like a second life."

Fong Yun nodded, laughing, putting a hand over his mouth to hide the missing tooth.

Now he was retiring. His sons were taking over. He pointed to one ear. "No hear good. No hear customers. But like work. Keep busy."

Fong Yun came to work every day, his son said, to make intricate bamboo kites, a lost art; paint screens; repair figurines.

"Mr. Fong," I said, "how old are you?"

Fong Yun smiled mischievously. "How old? Not very old. Ninety-seven?" He looked at his son and laughed. "Okay. Ninety-eight. Not old. But no hear good. Make mistakes."

I stood up to leave. Fong Yun extended a hand. I thought I knew why Chinatown had survived.

"Chinatown good," said Fong Yun, shaking my hand. "No worry. Chinatown okay."

Recently, on a blustery night when business was slow in Chinatown, I found myself on Chung King Court again and saw the *OPEN* sign in the door at Fong's. I entered and saw Fong Yun's son sitting alone at his desk. He rose and came toward me, alert and smiling. I recalled my earlier visit, and the conversation with Fung Yun.

"Ah, yes," he said, remembering. "My father has passed on."

"I am sorry," I said. "How old was he?"

"He was ninety-eight." He smiled. "But the Chinese are generous. They gave him a hundred."

Fong Yun was with his ancestors, but his son was watching the store, and one of the old man's last works, an elaborate kite in the form of an eagle, hung from the ceiling.

Not sad. Change must come.

# Santa Anita and the Arboretum

*"By gad, this is paradise!*
*I'm going to buy it!"*

It can be nippy, even in Arcadia, at eight o'clock on a winter day, when they bring the thoroughbreds out of their green stables at Santa Anita Park for morning workouts on the big track.

It was nippy the morning my wife and I went out, determined to make a day of it, but the sun was up, warming the horses and the exercise boys and the railbirds and quickening the whole lush landscape.

At Santa Anita the public is free to watch the workouts, from eight to ten daily, a privilege once unheard of. Visitors can park on the big lot and walk to the rail just west of the grandstand.

The atmosphere is clubby. I felt like a novice at a secret rite. One stands at the rail, sipping hot coffee from a plastic cup, watching the horses run and gallop. They are almost close enough to touch. One hears their breath and the plunk of their hoofs. Even a man who never laid a bet or saw a thoroughbred up close is somehow touched by the excitement and mystique of racing. For a moment he rubs elbows with jockeys, owners and maybe the ghost of Lucky Baldwin.

It was a fine way to begin a day in Arcadia, a day to be divided between the tensions of the racetrack and the leafy tranquility of the State and County Arboretum, just across the street.

These may seem an odd match—horse racing and horticulture—but both are the legacy of Elias Jackson "Lucky" Baldwin,

73

the Indiana grocer who came West, made millions in the Comstock Lode and bought the eight thousand-acre Rancho Santa Anita for his private Eden.

Baldwin was riding toward Bear Valley to look for gold when he first laid eyes on this lotus land in the San Gabriel Valley. It is said that he exclaimed, "By gad, this is paradise! I'm going to buy it!"

And that he did, in 1875. He paid two hundred thousand dollars in cash, counting out the bills from a tin box in which, it was reported, he had a million more. Here Baldwin built and planted, ranched and wenched, entertained his famous friends, and bred thoroughbreds until he died, in 1909, at eighty-one.

What is now the Arboretum was the heart of Baldwin's estate. And the racetrack is only a furlong or two from the track he built in 1907.

We watched the workouts half an hour, then drove north on Baldwin to the Arboretum gate.

We picked up a map at the office and read a sign: "These grounds serve as a human sanctuary from the sound and noises of urban living." No radios or musical instruments are allowed.

An asphalt walk led us toward the South African and Australian sections. We passed orchid and begonia houses, then found ourselves on a small plateau, like a bit of the African high veld. Civilization was out of sight.

Off the main walk, paths wander among the plantings: South African daisies with flowers of cream and lavender; strange aloes, birds of paradise and the butter-yellow *Gazania uniflora*. Thanks to the metal tags, even an urbanite can spot an *Olea africana,* a Cape chestnut, a pompon or a Kaffir plum.

There was a peacock in the *Olea africana.* He flopped down to the path and gave me a gimlet eye. It was our first encounter with one of the Arboretum's three hundred peafowl, though soon enough we seemed to have met them all.

This hardy flock is descended from a single pair of Indian birds (*Pavo cristatus*) imported by Lucky Baldwin to decorate his Eden. They are seen everywhere, adding a touch of fantasy to the landscape. Now and then a cock takes flight, screaming and clawing the sky like something prehistoric.

The walk horseshoes through the Australian section among numerous species of eucalyptus, that graceful gum tree from Down Under. The air is scented with their oil. Here also we saw a kurrajong tree, and the white peacock. That was a good omen. There is only one white peacock in the flock, and if you happen to meet him, it is said, you will have a lucky day.

We doubled back and came to a path that led into a jungle— two acres of forest primeval, quick with noisy birds and black-and-yellow butterflies. The path winds through vines and rushes, under bamboo and banana trees, by clumps of papyrus and pampas grass and emerges suddenly on the lagoon, flat and still as a dark glass under the sky.

Ducks, geese and black swans were all about, paddling over the water or prattling on the bank. On the far side, mirrored in the lagoon, stood the Queen Anne Cottage, like a vision in the wilderness. This is the house Baldwin built for the pleasure of his young third wife and his cronies of the mining, theater and sporting worlds.

It is exuberantly Victorian, a piece of white cake with red trim, a marble porch, stained glass windows and a cupola four stories high. It sits beside the lagoon amid roses and English ivy under a mighty eucalyptus and a dozen towering fan palms.

It is furnished in the plush vogue of the era, with opulent rugs, a gilt harp, a square piano, crystal chandeliers and such vivid touches as a set of carved chessmen in place on the inlaid gaming table and a peacock fan discarded in a brocade chair. The bathroom is a wonder, with dark wood paneling, pull chain plumbing and a zinc-lined tub.

The cottage was for entertaining. The Baldwins lived farther around the lagoon in the old Hugo Reid Adobe. It is also restored, but furnished in the rude style of pioneer California. The adobe was built in 1839 by Reid, an avaricious Scot who got title to the rancho, some say, by taking to wife an Indian widow to whom the governor had promised it in grant. Reid sold out and left her to die in rags.

Not only Baldwin's guests, but also his horses, lived in higher style than he and his wife did in the old adobe. His carriage house, built in 1879, shows an indulgent concern for the four steeds who drew his tallyho. They idled in stalls of cedar, redwood and fretted iron, and munched oats dropped from the loft through paneled chutes.

From the carriage house the path mounts a hill planted with avocado, fig and citrus trees and a blaze of various flowering species. Near the top stands a grove of Brazilian floss silk trees, an Alice-in-Wonderland concoction with orchid blooms and a thorny, pale-green skin like pistachio ice cream.

Heading back, we walked through the herb garden, whose plant tags bear such savory names as lime geranium, green-toothed lavender, sage and thyme, sweet marjoram, wintersweet, yellow ginger, lamb's ears, sassafras and jasmine.

The shadow on the sun dial in the herb garden told us it was time to be off to the races. On the way back to the gate we met the tour tram setting out on its morning run.

". . . This Arboretum," the driver was telling his passengers over a loudspeaker, "serves as a living plant museum . . ."

Only a few minutes later we were at Santa Anita, hearing another loudspeaker that told us, "Post time for today's race is twelve-thirty . . ."

Santa Anita is an exciting place, even for those who never play the races. The setting is superb. The great aqua grandstand and clubhouse look out over a green, blue and yellow infield, set with sparkling fountains, toward green, tree-polkadotted hills and the blue peaks of the San Gabriel Mountains. It is a view to move Cezanne.

Out front it is pleasant to walk in the paddock area, like a formal English garden with its hedges, oaks and peppers, baroque bronze statues and beds of blue and yellow pansies. At the center a marble fountain is inscribed with such memorable equine names a Moonrush, Noor, War Knight and Stagehand.

Here the visitor may see the horses eye to eye. Before each race they are led in from the stables for saddling. Then they file to the walking ring with their owners or trainers and jockeys. The noon sun burnishes the coats of the horses—bay, black, chestnut, gray and roan. Silks dazzle the eye.

"Riders up!"

Simultaneously, the jockeys mount and the thoroughbreds turn and follow their ponies out to the track. It is part of the show. Some patrons spend the day in the paddock area. They never see a race. They sit in the sun poring over racing forms, appraising the entries, hurrying off finally to make their bets.

We took a table on the Club House terrace overlooking the track and lunched on San Francisco shrimps and beer. I studied "Hebert's Handicap" while my wife considered a series of hunches. Down on the track the trumpeter appeared in his scarlet coat and breeches and blew the call to the post.

The drama begins. The thoroughbreds file out on the track and turn in front of the stands. Then they head for the gate. A four-in-hand drives up to take the judges to their posts. On the backstretch the horses prance and gallop. By now the customers all over the plant are in the final throes of calculation. Decisions are made. Lines grow at the windows.

Out in the infield the big electronic board shows the changing figures as the money wagered on each horse grows and the odds adjust.

Out at the gate the horses are in their places. There is a hush. Time and motion are frozen.

The loudspeaker barks:

"The flag is up!"

Tens of thousands of faces look up from forms and papers. The bettors fade away from the banks of windows as ticket selling stops.

"There they go!"

For a moment in the grandstand there is silence. Then, as the horses make their early moves, the cries begin to ring out, tentative at first. Now the knot of silk and horseflesh rounds the turn and explodes down the stretch, and the sound rises to a great keening chorus, shot through with shrieks of exultation or dismay. There is a crescendo as the front-runners streak under the wire, and then the mass voice subsides in a sigh. There is no other big-crowd sound quite like it.

I can take the horses or leave them alone, but it seems a waste of environment to go to the track and not experience the matchless thrill of watching your own horse, with your own two dollars on its nose, thunder down the homestretch to a driving photo finish.

We took our plunge in the fifth race. My wife bet two dollars to win on horse No. 5, a rather small bay filly with a shaky record and a green jockey. I bet six dollars—win, place and show—on the favorite. The odds were short, but the horse was a cinch to finish in the money. With a bet across the board, how could I lose?

No. 5 won. She paid $24.80. My horse ran out.

"Congratulations," I said. "How did you dope that one?"

"Well," she said, "you see my scarf? It's turquoise and royal blue. Those were my horse's colors. You didn't notice?"

Which proves, I suppose, that the legend of the white peacock is true. But not for me.

# The Huntington Library

*"I guess they were sweethearts."*
*"Yes."*

In the 1920s a story was told about a little girl whose mother took her for a Sunday outing on one of the big red Pacific Electric cars.

"Whose streetcar are we riding on?" asked the little girl.

"Mr. Huntington's, dear," said her mother.

"Where are we now?"

"Huntington Park, dear."

"Where are we going?"

"To Huntington Beach."

"Does Mr. Huntington own the ocean, too? Or does it still belong to God?"

The late Henry E. Huntington was not, after all, in competition with God, though there is no doubt he was in competition with that slightly less exalted entity, the British Museum.

Mr. Huntington spent the last three decades of his life and many of his millions creating what we know as the Huntington Library, or more completely, the Huntington Library, Art Gallery and Botanical Gardens. The treasures kept here are beyond appraisal. It is one of the great art, book and manuscript collections of the world—public or private. In 1919 Mr. Huntington put his house, grounds and collections in trust for the enrichment of the people. In 1928, a year after he died, the Huntington estate was opened to the public.

Today the Huntington Library attracts half a million visitors a year. It might be more if the name Huntington Library did not give a misleading image. The words library and art gallery and gardens can not in themselves suggest the whole experience of a visit to these grounds. True, the library itself, as apart from the other elements of the Huntington legacy, is a formidable testament to Mr. Huntington's wealth, acumen and zeal as a collector, in life and through his will.

The library building stands to the right as one enters the iron gates. It was built in the last years of Mr. Huntington's life to hold the books and manuscripts that had overflowed his private vaults. It is a massive concrete structure, somewhat forbidding despite its Ionic columns. I suppose the architects had to build for the centuries; but their work is relieved by the landscape and the sculpture. Classic bronze and stone figures of gods and goddesses; a coral tree whose blossoms burst forth from naked branches; lawns rolling out like seas.

The library holds three million manuscripts and three hundred thousand rare books. These archives, though, are the submerged part of the iceberg, open only to accredited scholars and writers. But there are half a dozen public exhibition halls in which a sample of these riches, a collection of treasures in itself, is made visible to all.

At the end of one long hall a Gutenberg Bible, open to the Book of Joshua, rests in a glass case. It is one of only forty-six copies, printed at Gutenberg's shop in the 1450s. There are even rarer works on view: the Gundulf Bible, copied by a monk about 1077, only a decade after Hastings; and the Ellesmere Chaucer, written on vellum about 1400, with a portrait of the bawdy poet himself on pilgrimage to Canterbury, "the hooly blisful martir for to seke."

There are manuscripts to inspire any redblooded American boy: A page from Ben Franklin's autobiography, with a vow to "Rise (at five o'clock) wash, and address Powerful Goodness." Thomas Jefferson's frugal accounting for expenses on his way to the Second Continental Congress ("A smith for mending pole of phaeton 2s."). Lincoln's letter to Grant ("And now with a brave army and a just cause, may God sustain you . . .").

One might spend a day in these halls, but there are two hundred acres outside, green as Eden, and the eighteenth century is waiting.

I went down the steps from the library, nodding to the bronze Diana and Apollo, and walked around the great two hundred-year-old oak and entered what is called, unfortunately, the Art Gallery. Actually, this was Mr. Huntington's home, the stately Georgian mansion he built in the first decade of this century. It is indeed an art gallery, with its precious paintings and furnishings and *objets d'art*. But I prefer to think of it still as the Huntington home, in which I am a guest. Entering its main hall I had the feeling of entering an Augustan age: eighteenth-century England, that period of surface elegance and grace and harmony, of which Dickens wrote, "It was the best of times; it was the worst of times . . ."

In restoring eighteenth-century England on his San Marino hilltop, Mr. Huntington took only "the best of times." Here and there a Hogarth face may speak eloquently of misery and oppression, but life generally was rich, gracious and beautiful. It is Mr. Huntington's concentration on eighteenth-century art, English and French, that gives his house today its flavor of life, place and time. One has no sense of museum. The house is light and airy. The windows and broad terraces look out over green gardens and a hazy valley.

The overwhelming room in the house is Mr. Huntington's personal library, an enormous chamber with parquet floors and oaken bookcases, Louis XIV carpets and the four huge tapestries by François Boucher.

The tapestries depict with astonishing exuberance the pastoral pleasures of the aristocracy in the era of Louis XV—voluptuous courtesans and powdered dandies frolicking in the countryside in their velvets and brocades. (When these tapestries were woven in the king's factories at Beauvais, Robespierre was an infant at his mother's breast.)

I could not see that the library had changed since I first saw it thirty years before. Only a day had passed. I could imagine that Mr. Huntington himself might step in from the loggia, in his white linen suit and white hat, walking stick in hand, and ask me to stay for tea.

To this house, in 1914, Mr. Huntington brought his second wife, Arabella. It was their home until her death a decade later. The bride was a lady of breeding who had lived in Paris and New York. Perhaps it was in deference to Arabella's refined sensibilities that he sought to recreate this Augustan environment. More likely Mr. Huntington was moved to furnish his own soul, after a life in the philistine rough-and-tumble of nineteenth-century American business.

He had started out as a hardware store clerk in Oneonta, New York. He was bright, ambitious and energetic. He soon caught the eye of his uncle, Collis P. Huntington, the railroad builder, whose success was exceeded only by his rapacity, a trait widely regarded in that era as a virtue. Collis Huntington took young Henry into the railroad building and management business, and the nephew seems to have proved that the blood of Thoreau and Franklin ran in Huntington veins, as well as that of Midas and Machiavelli. When his uncle died in 1900, Henry inherited thirty million dollars, including half of the Southern Pacific Railroad. He sold the SP and came to Los Angeles, where he bought up the local streetcar company and the land along the tracks and overnight became a prince of transit, power, shipbuilding and real estate.

One spring day in 1892 Mr. Huntington was a guest of the James de Barth Shorbs, who had built a home on a hill among live oaks and called it San Marino. Ten years later he bought the Shorb ranch, razed the old house and began his Georgian mansion. Then he began in earnest the collection of books, manuscripts, paintings and *objets d'art* that were to be delivered one day to the people of California as his legacy. He also began the cactus and Oriental gardens and the other plantings that made the Huntington estate one matched in Southern California only by the Arcadian realm of Lucky Baldwin.

The house today is much as it was when the Huntingtons were at home, except for a wing added as a gallery for the finest of his English portraits. The dining room is authentic Georgian. But there are exotic touches—voluptuous marble figurines of a sleeping Ariadne and a Cleopatra with the asp around her wrist. The marble mantelpiece is from a home in London's Hanover Square; impeccably Georgian. But the face over the mantel, so resolute and stern, is the wrong George: a Gilbert Stuart portrait of George Washington. Painted in 1797, it did not find its way to England for a hundred years, when all was forgiven, and then came home again half a century later.

My favorite room is the Georgian drawing room at the east

end of the upper hall. Door by door, panel by panel, it was brought to San Marino from Castle Hill, a storied mansion in North Devon. The house was gutted by fire in 1934, but the drawing room was saved. It was in just such elegant surroundings, I imagine, that the movers of Georgian society discussed the upstart colonials, and later the upstart Corsican. The portraits on the walls—the Earl of Huntington, the Duchess of Lancaster—look alive enough to come down and sit in the wing chairs beside the glowing fireplace and toast the mad king in Spanish sherry.

From the upper hall the great staircase curves down to the Main Hall, which in itself is gallery enough for one day. There is no object on the estate more graceful than the bronze Diana by Jean-Antoine Houdon. Opposite the Diana, at either side of the door into the South Hall, hang two great portraits by the English master Thomas Gainsborough. One is of Edward, 2d Viscount Ligonier, a priggish, long-faced blueblood with one hand on his sword and the other on his blue-blood horse. The other is of the Viscount's wife, one Penelope. Beautiful, proud, fiery, bold; a woman to be watched. I knew nothing of the Ligoniers, but I guessed the Viscount had been no match for Penelope. I checked my catalogue. Indeed; the Viscountess had divorced him and married another—a Private Smith of the Horse Guards. Bully for her.

For most visitors the new main gallery is the cynosure. Here they find "The Blue Boy," doubtless the best known and most beloved painting in America, and the almost equally beloved "Pinkie." It is too bad that many visitors dash through the house looking for Pinkie and Blue Boy. They ought not to be sought out, like a shrine, but discovered, come upon unexpectedly, as if one just happened to meet these charming adolescents while strolling through the eighteenth century.

Pinkie and the Blue Boy stand exactly opposite each other in the gallery, looking eternally into each other's eyes. Some current seems to pass between them, like an electric beam, enchanting all who cross it. Visitors stop and gaze and whisper, and exchange the myths that have enveloped these famous paintings.

"They were sweethearts, you know."

"Oh, yes."

"Painted by the same artist."

For fifty cents each I had bought booklets on the history of the two paintings. I sat on a bench and leafed through them. Alas. Pinkie and the Blue Boy were not sweethearts after all. He was the son of a Soho ironmonger; she was a Barrett, an aunt of Elizabeth Barrett Browning. Their stars never crossed. Gainsborough painted the Blue Boy, it is thought, in the 1760s. Sir Thomas Lawrence painted Pinkie in 1795, when she was twelve. Pinkie died that same year, a week before her portrait was shown. The next year the Blue Boy, now an ironmonger himself, and forty-three, fell into debt and sold his effects at auction. The portrait went for thirty-five guineas.

So the Blue Boy was only an ironmonger's son, dressed up in blue silks and velvets for the great painter. But he was a splendid subject; forthright, debonair, with a hint of adolescent arrogance. No doubt Pinkie would have loved him. There is that look of awakening womanhood in her fresh pink face as she looks across the gallery at the handsome lad.

A woman had taken the seat next to me.

"Such beautiful children," she said.

"Yes," I agreed.

"I guess they were sweethearts."

"Yes."

After all, as Winston Churchill wrote of another romantic legend, "Tiresome investigators have undermined this excellent tale, but it certainly should find its place in any history worthy of the name."

From the main gate a road leads down to the cactus garden. Here the spell of eighteenth-century England is utterly broken. Perhaps Mr. Huntington planned it that way. The garden covers ten acres. The path dips into hollows from which nothing can be seen but cactus; a landscape grotesque and beautiful beyond the imagining of Georgian England.

I found my way out of this wilderness and walked over the green hill to the lily ponds, which Mr. Huntington built in 1905 for Arabella, and on to the Oriental garden, yet another sanctuary for her pleasure and serenity. I walked down into the garden and around the goldfish pond with its vermilion moon bridge and past some college girls, art students I guessed, who were lying on the grassy bank, idling over their sketchbooks.

"I like Picasso," I heard one say, "and I like the Renaissance, but I don't like . . ."

I lost it, whatever it was she didn't like. I wondered if it were Gainsborough. He may be square, for all I know.

I walked back toward the main gate, followed by the muted sound of the Japanese temple gong. I decided to forgo the north gardens and the Renaissance avenue of statues and Huntington mausoleum. They would keep.

I couldn't leave, though, without looking for a remembered face. In the west wing of the library building there is a room of French sculpture, part of the Arabella D. Huntington Memorial collection. There are some busts by Houdon, and among them I found the face. It was the sculptor's small daughter. Sabine.

There she was, as I had remembered, that face of elfin innocence, joy and mischief. In this age of anti-art and the put-on, it was reassuring to see so much life and feeling imparted to a piece of stone.

Maybe the little girl in the streetcar was right. Maybe Mr. Huntington did take some things away from God. But anyway he gave them back.

# The Pike

*"Listen, I'm not going to go to the Queen Mary in my furs and jewels and then come over and walk around a place like this. Are you?"*

"I knew it. I knew the bloody Yanks would put the old Queen in a bloody sideshow." So spoke a Limey seaman (he had sailed for thirty years with the RMS *Queen Mary*) when he found out where the old ship's permanent berth would be.

The "bloody sideshow" he referred to was the Long Beach Pike, a gaudy three-block strip of games, thrill rides, chambers of horror, hot dog stands, penny arcades and tattoo parlors on the city's waterfront. Though the sailor's epithet was in the British idiom, it came as close as any Americanism to describing the Pike, which started out at the turn of the century as a boardwalk for a fashionable hotel and plunge.

And he was quite right about the *Queen Mary* being *in* the "bloody sideshow," although the Pike isn't called that in polite company in Long Beach. It isn't even called the Pike anymore. It's called Queen's Park. This new name officially replaced the *old* new name—Nu-Pike—which sprang from a former attempt at renovation. Queen's Park applies officially, however, only to a fifteen-acre portion of the Pike owned by a private amusement company which came down with the same *Queen Mary* fever that seized the rest of the city after the great white elephant was tugged into the harbor for her celebrated refurbishing. Queen's Park was conjured up from the old Nu-Pike mostly with paint and ballyhoo, and was appropriately opened in March, 1969, with the thrilling ascent of George Stokes, described as a world-famous balloonist, in his red-and-white striped hot-air balloon.

"There is no predicting where you will land," declared Stokes before his takeoff from the entrance to Queen's Park. "A balloon is at the mercy of the winds. You go where nature takes you."

Actually, Stokes was blown off course and came down in a restricted naval weapons depot at nearby Seal Beach, stepping from his balloon in tophat and tails, to the utter astonishment of the garrison.

The intrepid balloonist might have flown higher if his balloon had been filled with press releases from the Queen's Park publicity office, which hailed the park as a "bright shining star in the amusement world" and saw it "emerging as the West Coast's most successful and energetic amusement park."

In words, Queen's Park was launched sky-high. It was to become "fit for a Queen;" the equal of Copenhagen's famed Tivoli Gardens, but British "oriented," with smart shops and chop houses. In reality it didn't get as far as Stokes did. It came down where it started—on the Pike. The grandiose plans, though, may still be read in the sky.

Today the Pike is still the Pike, as it is called by the millions who have visited Long Beach since the first decade of the century, and by every boy and man who ever sailed with Uncle Sam's Navy. What renovations there have been are mostly swallowed up by the old Pike—the noisy, vulgar midway of the carny barker, the neon ferris wheel, the crazy house and the shooting gallery, the walkup dancehall and the funny photo studio (put your head in the hole, be a jackass, the folks back home will love it).

It has changed so little it seems an anachronism, a leftover of heroic America, an "American museum" as one Long Beach sentimentalist called it. The crowd has changed more than the show. There aren't as many sailors as there used to be when the boys were right off the farm. The customers are more likely to be brown or black than white, drawn in from the shifting populations of the south central plain. Even the Trip to the Moon is also called Cohete a la Luna, another is called El Pulpo and a drink called Puerto Rican Punch is sold.

But the appeal is the same. I used to rove the Pike as a boy, and the sounds and smells have not changed: hot dogs and the merry-go-round; the snap of small arms fire and maniacal laughter of the fat lady in front of the crazy house and the girls screaming on the roller coaster, all brought in on a sea breeze only faintly tainted by tidelands oil.

The *Queen Mary* herself has been added. Although the ship is a separate attraction, her new berth is directly across a narrow channel from the Pike, and she seems, as the man said, to be a part of the bloody sideshow.

To put her in the picture required a prodigious rearranging of the waterfront's geography. The beach itself was moved out, filled in, and much of it asphalted over for a parking lot. The old amusement pier, which stood out in the water and was sometimes dashed with spray, is gone. The Cyclone Racer roller coaster is gone to make way for the new Queen's Bridge. It is wrenching to an old visitor returned, and it is sure to wreak profound changes on the Pike, changes that are not yet realized.

As I walked down the Pike once more it seemed as old as my memory. I could remember nothing further back than those wonderfully frightening passages through the dark, mirrored mysteries of the fun house, the terror of the roller coaster, the crack of twenty-twos, the smell of gunsmoke and the clang of the metal targets struck by lead. Mostly the twenty-twos with their live ammunition are gone. They were too dangerous and too expensive. Most of the shooting games use compressed air and pellets now, or just an electric eye. "But those pellets can kill you, don't worry," a girl assured me. "There's a thousand pounds of pressure in there."

The barkers don't seem to pull you in the way they used to. Or maybe I don't look like a mark anymore. But a woman caught my eye.

"Come on," she called, "win a teddy bear. Just toss the ball in the hole. Two out of three, you win."

She had swung her legs over the counter and was sitting on the outside of her booth. She was middle-aged, with gray-dyed hair in a new permanent; a well-kept face carefully made up. You might see her at a bridge table in Laguna Niguel.

"How much?"

"Three balls, fifty cents. Two in the hole, you win a prize."

Teddy bears and other colored, stuffed animals of the loveable type hung on the walls of the booths in rows, the largest and most desirable being in the top row, and so on down.

I bought three baseballs and pitched two in out of the three. The woman reached under the counter and brought up what appeared to be a small shapeless wedge of cotton with a face pasted on it the size of an eight-cent stamp.

I laughed. "That's my prize?"

"That's for the first two. Try it again, go on, win a teddy bear."

I tried it again, and again got two out of three. Once more she reached under the counter. She brought up a long thin woolly yellow object, about the size and shape of one-third of a gopher snake, with two cute blue eyes pasted on at one end and a pink ribbon tied around what evidently was the neck.

"You're doing good!" the woman cried, setting up three more balls in front of me. "Try it again! Two more, you're up on the board. Win a teddy bear!"

I laughed. She smiled, just barely. It was one of those cases of she knew I knew she knew I knew. The prizes under the counter are part of the show, old as the carnival, a petty flimflam that is honest enough, in the ethics of the carny people. They are honest, in their fashion. Can they help it if people like to have a little fun?

Up the Pike a few booths a young man laid down a dollar bill and lifted a basketball, hoisting it in his palm, spinning it, getting the weight and balance of it. He was poised and graceful as he lofted the ball up toward the basket; a basketball player sure enough, a Kareem Abdul-Jabbar. The ball fell through the hoop and the net with that satisfying *snick*.

The man behind the counter folded his arms and looked away, feigning disinterest. He was used to hotshots. The player's woman stood off watching, expressionless, arms folded over what appeared to be a very small woolly pink alligator. The man shot again. He was really very good. Three out of four. Gail Goodrich couldn't do better. A winner. He looked quickly back to see if the woman was watching.

"Here he is folks!" the barker shouted, moving in to exploit this threat. "A winner! Watch how he does it! Come on there, big fella! Win a teddy bear!" A few customers closed in to watch.

Big fella tried again, and again, and once more. First time, three out of four again; then two out of four, and the last time none out of four. A blank. He had come apart under pressure. Back to the minors. He picked out a small woolly blue dog from the designated row and walked off beside the woman, not looking at her, with the dog hanging from his hand. Oh, well, it had only cost a couple of bucks and a little pride.

The old Cyclone Racer is gone. It was the greatest roller coaster, the greatest thrill ride of any kind, that I ever saw. It was very likely what they called it—"the greatest ride on the face of the earth!"

It was built in 1930 of lumber cut in Oregon, a truly fantastic wood sculpture, a famous landmark. It ran nearly forty years, taking millions of riders on a one-minute forty-second ride that knotted stomachs, drained blood and squeezed out screams that could be heard half a mile away on Pine Avenue. On the last dip the open red cars dropped ninety feet down a fifty degree angle at eighty miles an hour. Thousands of its old fans stood in line that last day in 1968 to take a last ride. The racer was torn down to make way for the bridge to the *Queen Mary*. It has been replaced by the Royal Cyclone, a more compact structure of Italian make. It does not quite impart the same sense of suicidal abandon, but it is a respectable roller coaster with some fine wrenching turns and falls.

Penny arcades are more sophisticated than they used to be, and not just because they cost a dime or quarter. Most of the action goes to war games—games named Attack, Sonic Fighter, Jet Rocket or the Invasion of Mars. Mostly they are played by teen-age boys who sit in a gunner's seat, pressing the button of electronic machine guns or bomb releases or torpedo tubes that make a deafening racket and light up explosions on the big target landscape behind the picture glass. They play at this simulated havoc with looks of orgiastic intensity, and behind them other young men gather, fascinated by the sound and flash of make-believe violence.

Two or three of the old arcades have installed back rooms marked *MUST BE OVER 18,* in which brief colored movies of pure pornography may be seen through a peep hole for a dime or quarter. I dropped seventy-five cents in one of these dark parlors and left feeling cheated; for the same amount of money somewhere else I might have won a teddy bear.

But I found one old friend in an arcade. It was the Swami. He looked the same; the swarthy face under the gray satin turban; gray, pointed beard; eyes blazing down at the crystal ball in his hands. For decades he had been imprisoned in his glass box, telling fortunes for a penny. His pink vest was faded, his shirt discolored, but his price had gone up. I tried him. Out of the slot came the same little red card with its printed message.

"Beware of a dark haired one who is jealous of your success in life and will try to make trouble for you . . . Drop another coin in the slot and I will tell you more . . ."

One thing that's fairly easy to win on the Pike is a live goldfish. The big table beyond the counter is covered with little goldfish bowls, each with its single little goldfish swimming back and forth. You throw a dime at the table and if it goes in a bowl you win the bowl and the goldfish. It's a snap. But what do you do if you win? You go down the Pike, carrying a bowl full of water, with a goldfish in it.

In time, some people say, the Pike will be torn out and the grand plans of the amusement company will be executed, with arty salons and fancy gift shops. In the meantime, however, the old Pike souvenir and curio store goes it alone, offering the world such venerated *objets d'art* as Jesus ash trays, dried starfish and Mother pillows. Their wares have hardly changed over the years except for the additions of Muhammad Ali posters and *Queen Mary* T-shirts. The Mother pillow will last as long as our boys leave home to join the Navy and see the world. Their sentiments never vary:

> *To one who bears the sweetest name*
> *And adds a luster to the same,*
> *Who shares my joys, who cheers when sad,*
> *The greatest friend I ever had,*
> *Long life to her, for there's no other*
> *Takes the place of my dear mother.*

If you back off far enough from the stuccoed front of the Lite-a-Line parlor, you will see a shingled, conical wooden cupola, ancient and peeling, in the turn-of-the-century seashore style. After a moment of puzzling I knew what it must be—the top of the old merry-go-round. But the merry-go-round rotunda is occupied now by four banks of pinball machines at which Lite-a-Line players try to be the first to light up five lights in a row, thus beating the other players and winning a few dollars in cash. Almost every seat was taken. The players played mechanically, pulling back the plungers and releasing them to shoot the steel ball into the board, game after game.

*WORLD'S MOST THRILLING AND FASCINATING INDIVIDUAL SKILL GAME,* said a sign on the wall. It seemed sad and comical that this innocent if dreary form of petty gambling had been fought in the courts for years by the city wowsers. But tough old Arthur Looff, whose father had built the first merry-go-round at Coney Island, refused to give in. He was vindicated, and died a winner at eighty-two.

The tattoo parlors are at the end of the Pike and around the corner, right handy but off the main stem. There are three, two of which call themselves the largest in the world. Their walls are covered with patterns, each with its price. They run strongly to butterflies and anchors, mermaids, dancing girls, Jesus and Mother. When a customer is being tattooed you can hear the buzz of the needle, sinister as a rattlesnake.

In the smaller of the three parlors on Chestnut a longhaired youth was sitting under a fluorescent light, naked to the waist, waiting for his first tattoo. The tattoo artist was a man of perhaps seventy; small and slightly stooped, with sparse white hair and a white mustache. He wore a smock with short sleeves and he might have been a nice old family doctor, except for the tattoos that covered his arms.

The boy looked sheepish and apprehensive, like a youth about to undergo some awful rite of manhood. Three friends watched silently from outside the rail, two youths with long hair like his, and a girl. They looked transported; nervous and unsure.

"This is the one you want?" the old man said. The boy nodded, looking at a butterfly on the pattern sheet. The old man transferred the pattern to the boy's arm. He picked up the needle and gave it a preliminary buzz.

"Let's see, have I seen your ID card?" The boy nodded.

"Oh, yes. I remember. That's good." He chuckled benignly. "Or else we both might spend some time up there on the hill."

He inked the needle and turned it on. "You're going to get lots of color," he told the boy. "Lots of color." He put the buzzing needle to the arm and slowly it began to crawl across the boy's flesh.

Back on the Pike the woman with the baseballs wasn't doing any business. "Business is terrible," she said. "I've been here twenty-five years, off and on. I was on the road for a while. It's gonna get worse.

"The *Queen Mary* isn't going to help this place. Listen, I'm not going to go to the *Queen Mary* in my furs and jewels and then come over and walk around a place like this. Are you? This is all going to be a shopping center in two years. The beach is gone. Now it's all oil wells. This stuff is all for sale."

An entire family—mother and father and children and uncles and aunts—were gathered around a booth where the patriarch, an overstuffed but dignified little man, was throwing baseballs at bottles. They spoke a lilting Spanish; Puerto Ricans, perhaps. The man's windup was very serious. He threw straight and hard. He won a prize. The carny man reached under the counter and began to explain. As I walked on they were all debating joyously whether the father was to take the prize or throw some more and go for the giant teddy.

There was a fresh breeze up from the bay. The air was good. Everywhere along the Pike the tiny colored pennants fluttered and flashed. The artificial robins were chirping in the shooting gallery with the waterfall, and something somewhere was playing "As Time Goes By."

I was looking down on all this from an orange steel capsule, suspended from a crane's boom eighty feet above the ground. There is something melancholy about all carnivals, some undercurrent of sadness in the noise. But the Pike seemed to have a special air of doom. I had the feeling the carny woman was right. It would all soon go. The world-renowned balloonist was right, too. You're at the mercy of the winds. Maybe it would be better, when it was all boutiques and chop houses and pubs, everything on your credit card.

94

But there is something elementary and honest about a midway. A man is something more than a spectator. If they fleece you, you don't mind. At least you get to throw at something when they take your money, and sometimes you win a teddy bear.

When my capsule came back to earth I bought a mile-long hot dog, to go. It's the best thing that ever came down the Pike.

# Elysian Park

*It is perhaps the most beautiful
unknown place in Los Angeles.*

In a charming illustrated book called *Tales of Los Angeles Parks,*
the artist and writer Leo Politi recalls something he saw one
day while painting in Elysian Park:

"I saw a boy, a lone boy. I watched him wandering among
the bushes and huge trees on the side of the hill. At times he
stopped; he would disappear, then appear again. Very likely
he was experiencing an exciting adventure . . ."

The boy made Politi think of Leonardo da Vinci and his
lone walks in the Umbrian Hills of Italy. There, Politi remembered reading in Da Vinci's memoirs, among the rolling hills
and towering trees, the shrubbery, the wildflowers, birds, animals and insects, Da Vinci perceived the designs and principles
that went into his life's work.

One Sunday not long ago, my wife and I were picnicking
in Elysian Park with our grandson, and as I watched him climbing up a steep trail above Chavez Ravine, slipping down a foot
for every two feet gained, it occurred to me that he was the
third generation in my family to have found adventure in this
park. That he would be a Da Vinci, I might hope. That he
would be a Smith, I was sure.

In writing about Elysian Park at all, I feel the ambivalence
of a man writing about a secret love affair. He wants to tell
the world of his good fortune, and at the same time he wants
to keep his secret to himself.

Ironically, the beauty of Elysian Park may be owed to the
fact that it has been so long neglected; not only by the city,

but by the people. Few of the city's residents have ever been there, or even know where it is. A proposed bond issue for money to bring water to its dying trees was defeated at the polls a few years ago, and in the general election of 1972 the voters approved a proposition giving the Police Department permanent use of a piece of the park, despite a clause in the city charter that says, "All land heretofore or hereafter set apart or dedicated as a public park shall forever remain to the use of the public inviolate . . ."

The amazing fact about Elysian Park is that it exists. That it has escaped the lust of land developers and the venality of politicians is a miracle comparable to the survival of the Watts Towers and the Santa Monica Mountains.

We were picnicking with our grandson, I realized, in exactly the place that a group of businessmen had decided upon, a few years earlier, as the ideal site for a convention center. It was argued at the time, and believed by many, that this development would not diminish the park, but instead produce "relocation" of its recreational facilities that would, in time, benefit all the people.

We had chosen a table in the park near a great old sycamore tree, and we seemed to be sharing the tree with a family that I guessed had come to the park from their houses in the eastside barrio. They had come in three old but highly polished cars, and there were three generations of them, at least; maybe four.

We watched as one of the young men brought a long rope from his car and threw an end of it up over a branch of the tree. Then a woman walked over to the tree with a piñata. The man tied the piñata to the end of the rope. The piñata was in three tiers, made of blue, red, white and yellow paper, and it looked homemade.

A piñata, as anyone native to Southern California knows, is a hollow object, made of cardboard and decorated with streamers of crepe paper. The piñata may be in the shape of a ship, or an animal, most often a bull, as small as a football or large as a suitcase. Inside, it is filled with treasures—candy, fruit and who knows what.

I had seen the breaking of the piñata down at Olvera Street at Christmastime, and so I knew the ritual. A child is blindfolded and given a stick. He is placed near the piñata and instructed to swing away with the stick to break it, thus releasing the treasures. First, as I had seen it, the smallest children were given a chance; then the older children; and finally, if the piñata was still intact, the adults.

I remembered that, at Olvera Street, when the piñata was lowered within reach, the crowd of children around the blindfolded batter cried, "Hit it!" or *"Dale, dale!"* in Spanish. Then, just as the blindfolded child struck, the man jerked the rope, the piñata leaped up, and the child missed, to universal joy.

Now we were going to see it done in a park, away from commercialism. Was the ritual of the piñata merely an anachronism, a quaint custom revived by those interested in exploiting ancient rites for sentimental and perhaps meretricious reasons? My cynicism quickly faded. We saw the ritual of the piñata enacted exactly as it had been enacted in Olvera Street, except that this was a family affair.

First a very small boy was blindfolded with a red bandana and given a branch that had fallen from the tree. The young man in charge of the piñata lowered it, and the children who had gathered in a circle shouted, *"Dale, dale!"* and the boy struck with the branch, but of course too late. The young man in charge of the piñata had yanked it up in the nick of time.

The little boy was retired and older children were given a chance. They were stronger; their timing was better, but the man at the end of the rope had the advantage. The piñata remained intact.

Finally the teenagers were given a turn, and with their superior wisdom they were able to anticipate the manipulations of the man with the rope. The piñata was ruptured. Its contents spilled to the grass. Apples and oranges and a few cookies and candies. The children swarmed in.

Where else but a park, like Elysian Park, I wondered, could people come together, in a setting of natural beauty, to enjoy their ancient customs? The park was the backyard they didn't have. It was a place that reassured them. They couldn't live in Bel-Air, or Pacific Palisades or Rolling Hills, but they could go to Elysian Park on Sundays, and pretend that God had them in mind, too, when He laid it out.

99

Elysian Park is only a mile from the Civic Center, and this proximity has been its curse and its salvation. Our mayors and city councilmen have at times supported and nurtured it, and at other times not only turned their backs but actually involved themselves in schemes to wound if not destroy the park.

The history of the park is as old as the history of Los Angeles. It appears in our earliest literature. When the Portolá expedition crossed the Los Angeles plain in 1769, the indefatigable Father Crespi noted in his diary that the party had camped by a river under a bluff.

"After traveling about a league and a half through an opening found between two low hills," he wrote, "we came to a rather wide canyon having a great many cottonwood and sycamore trees. Through it ran a beautiful river coming from the northwest and curving around the point of a cliff to take a direction towards the south. In the north-northeast, we saw another river bed which must have been a great overflow, but we found it dry. This arm united with the river and its great floods during the rainy season are clearly demonstrated by the many uprooted trees scattered along the banks. We stopped not very far from the river to which we gave the name of Porciúncula."

Thus, Father Crespi and his companions were the first Europeans to discover what we now call, sometimes laughingly, the Los Angeles River, and its neighbor, the Arroyo Seco, which turned out to be our first freeway.

Elysian Park may owe its survival to the fact that, in the beginning, nobody wanted it. The park's present five hundred and twenty-five acres are all that is left of the seventeen thousand acres granted to the pueblo of Los Angeles by King Carlos of Spain. This quaint custom of monarchs, granting land they had never seen and to which they held no title, was honored by the U.S. government when, at the end of the Mexican War in 1848, it took possession of Southern California.

Fortunately, the area now known as Elysian Park was regarded as useless by the pioneers of our pueblo. It was after all a mile away from the heart of things; a hard ride. It was nothing but hills and ravines, and was not a likely place to begin what was to become one of the largest cities in the world. For a long time the land was used for grazing sheep. Then in 1886 the city council, despairing of finding a profitable use for these nearby hills and canyons, decided to make it a public park. Elysian Park thus owes its existence to a king who had never seen it and a city council that didn't know how to exploit it.

It would be unfair, though, not to give credit to the councilmen, and the mayor of that time, Henry Hazard, who saw the need of the park. Hazard was a man who anticipated the ecological fervor of our times. He not only influenced the city council to declare the area a park, but he also started a tree-planting program which has never stopped.

One recent Arbor Day, I went up to the park to watch a tree planting. There were perhaps a hundred people present. There were a few speeches, but words never seem to mean much in a park. Jane Wyatt, an actress whose performance in the first *Lost Horizons* made all subsequent *Lost Horizons* merely lost horizons, made a little talk, and she quoted, more accurately than I will, I expect, a line of Ogden Nash's—"One thing we never see, is a billboard lovely as a tree." I was impressed that so few people had saved Elysian Park.

Watching the children try to hit the piñata, I found it hard to believe that this was the place they wanted to turn into a convention center. The folly of that proposition could only be understood by driving to the present convention center and trying to imagine what a devastating effect it would have had on Elysian Park.

The defeat of this ill-conceived scheme may be credited to one person—a woman who lived near the park, saw what was about to happen to it, and decided to do something about it. Her name was Grace E. Simons. She was intelligent, angry and, fortunately, competent. She organized a Citizens Committee to Save Elysian Park, and she saved it.

Ms. Simons defeated City Hall. All she did was enlist the help of her neighbors and others who understood the reason for parks. She operated under an extraordinary rule. "Tell the truth," she told her people. "That will defeat them."

Ms. Simons and her legions did not win every battle. In fact they came upon the scene a bit too late for some. Dodger Stadium took a piece of the park, and brought about a six-lane street through its most popular valley. The councilmen won that one.

But Ms. Simons and her people made enough noise to beat down an oil company's bid for a seventy-seven acre drilling lease in the park, which the councilmen were eager to grant.

Perhaps I should say something about Elysian Park for those who have never been there and will never go. It is perhaps the most beautiful unknown place in Los Angeles.

There are breathtaking overviews. From parking places on Elysian Park Road, the whole southern and western side of the city can be seen, from Signal Hill to Santa Monica. The view from Elysian Park undoes the complaint that there is no Los Angeles. The downtown skyline is impressive. So is Beverly Hills.

Late in the 1880s the magazine *Land of Sunshine* pointed out not only the beauties of Elysian Park, but also the lack of interest in it until Mayor Hazard came along.

"A matter of surprise to many new arrivals in Los Angeles," the magazine said, "is that within the remarkable advantages which the city possesses in climate and scenery more has not been done in the direction of creating extensive and beautiful parks. Trees, plants and flowers which only thrive in hothouses in the East, grow luxuriantly all the year round, and there are few days during the year when a stroll under spreading branches is not pleasant . . ."

Elysian Park seems to be a product of innumerable ironies. One of them is the fact that its roads were built, and many of its trees were planted, either by convict labor or by men needing work during various depressions. A tree doesn't care who plants it.

Elysian Park today, therefore, is not at all the rather barren bluff that Father Crespi saw. Thanks to the zeal of tree planters and the amiable climate of its location, the park has one of the most beautiful and diverse collections of exotic trees in the world. Mostly, it is eucalyptus. There are hundreds of eucalyptuses, and their scent pervades the park. There are also long rows of palm trees, gardens of sycamores, and so many exotic flowering species that even the experts don't know their names.

When the piñata game was over, I thought, well, it had been a lot of fun. It was too bad that in breaking the piñata the children had littered the lawn with strips of colored paper. I watched the families prepare to leave, fascinated by the division

of chores. The women cleaned the tables and packed the leftovers into cardboard boxes; nothing must be wasted. The men
carried the boxes back to the cars, while the little boys played
with a plastic football.

And what did the little girls do? They picked up the litter;
three or four of them, going about with paper sacks, picking
up the bits of paper from the piñata. It seemed to be a demonstration of male chauvinism, but at least, I pointed out to my
wife, it worked. The family did not want to leave the park
untidy.

I hoped that we and our politicians would always treat it
with as much respect.

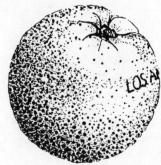

# Avalon

*The older couples stroll out to
Casino Point to look for something
lost there long ago.*

"Away with systems!" wrote George Meredith, echoing day-dreams of Everyman. "Away with a corrupt world! Let us breathe the air of the enchanted island."

Santa Catalina Island may not be enchanted in the poetic sense. It does not have the antiquity of Capri or the romance of Pitcairn or the fabled fauna of the Galapagos.

In truth, Catalina is about what you might have if you cut off forty-eight thousand acres of Orange County badlands, with downtown Laguna Beach attached, and pushed them twenty-two miles out to sea.

It is a hunk of Southern California-like geography that got its sail up and escaped the mainland one jump ahead of the land development pirates. For those of us who are left behind, it is still *away*—the quickest way away. Even if you don't own a yacht or airplane, there are ways to get to Catalina: motor cruiser, hydrofoil, steamer and seaplane.

I decided to fly. I parked my car in the public lot at Long Beach Airport one Friday morning and caught the Catalina Air Lines flight at nine o'clock. The plane was a little white-and-blue Grumman amphibian. It legitimately holds eight passengers, with a ninth riding copilot. If you are lucky and lean enough, you get that seat.

"Mr. Smith," said the passenger agent at the door, "will you please sit in the cockpit with the pilot."

I climbed into the narrow cabin and walked forward in a

crouch to the cockpit. The plane, it occurred to me, was older than half its passengers.

"Morning," said the pilot.

He was a compact man with a weathered face, windblown gray hair and a great, gray handlebar mustache. He looked as if he might have flown with Dick Arlen and Errol Flynn, in both wars.

"Morning," I said.

That ended the conversation. I scrunched into the copilot's seat and locked my seat belt, with my attaché case on my lap. That's all you need for a Catalina weekend, an attaché case stuffed with pajamas, socks and underwear.

The captain lettered something in his log with a ball-point pen, shoved the log down between the seats, spoke into his transmitter and started up his engines. In what seemed hardly more than a minute we were in the air. We flew low over the downtown Long Beach skyline. It looked remarkably like Kansas City's. I saw the *Queen Mary* in her birth, like a fat old dowager eating up the family fortune. We passed over a row of gray destroyers and a carrier or two and then looked down on nothing but water.

The pilot reached down and back, behind his seat, and gave a hand crank a few noisy turns. He was raising his wheels. We were a seaplane now, with nothing but runway below us.

I looked back. The continent was floating away. I felt a lightness of spirit known to all voyagers who leave the mainland. It is a moment of escape. A weight lifts; a string snaps.

The flight took eighteen minutes. Halfway across the channel, the island emerged from the haze like two loaves of French bread, touching end to end at the isthmus. We splashed into Avalon Bay with an exhilarating *whoosh* and planed in to the dock at the tip of the old pier.

I suppose I have flown around the world several times, one flight added to another, and this is the only airplane ride I really enjoy, from start to finish. It is quick and casual and mildly exciting, and there is something solid and reassuring about the pilot hand-cranking his landing gear, instead of pushing a button. And in less than twenty minutes you have changed worlds. You are away. Only an illusion? All the better. Who wants his escape to be anything more than that.

I walked up the pier to Crescent Avenue. It curves, as its name implies, along the crescent bay. It is probably no more than half a mile long, from the Casino at one end to the new steamship mole at the other. When you come to the end of the pier you are at the crossroads of Avalon. This is one of the agreeable surprises in traveling to Catalina, by plane or boat. When you arrive, you are there.

Avalon has hardly changed in the forty years I have known it. The town is still confined to one square mile. It lies down snug against the bay front and climbs the steep hills, like the inside of a cup, and doesn't make it to the top. I had a reservation at Las Casitas, a bungalow hotel set in the rustic flowering foothills below the golf course. It is on the outskirts of town, just three short blocks from the pier. I walked up Catalina Avenue and checked into my bungalow and walked back, taking another street.

Avalon has a look of the 1920s and 1930s. The houses mostly date from that era, small wood cottages on narrow lots, neat as the houses of retired sea captains. Their yards are no more than flower beds, but the streets are like gardens, colored with hibiscus, geraniums, begonias and hollyhocks, and every porch and eave is aflame with red or purple bougainvillea.

In an hour you are at home in Avalon; a native. If a man simply wants to get away from the system, from the corrupt world across the channel, he can sink into one of the bayfront bars like the Hurricane Cove, the Waikiki or the Marlin Club, and degenerate.

For the energetic visitor who prefers sightseeing to introspection, there are rides by boat, horse, bicycle, minicar and touring bus. I took a bus on what is called the Scenic Terrace Drive, a forty-minute run from the Island Plaza up into the hills and around the town. The bus crawls around hairpin turns and skirts unnerving precipices, stopping at points from which the entire town may be seen.

No matter how many times I have seen Avalon, the sight of it from the heights is always surprising. It always seems prettier than before, the small perfect half-moon harbor with its white boats, the Casino out on its point, the haughty old yachting clubs, the old pier, the seaplanes splashing in and taking off like toys, the palm trees and the bright bits of color on the beach.

"We're not goin' up that road there, folks," said our driver over his loudspeaker. "That's a firebreak. Had a woman on here the other day said, 'My God, driver, are we goin' up that road!' She's from the middle west, y'know. Like to throw a fit."

The tour drivers evidently are selected in part for their ability to keep up a running commentary of fact, lore and cracker-barrel humor for anywhere from forty minutes to four hours, nonstop. This patter is such a hit with the tour bus crowds that by the time the tour ends they are one big delirious family, rolling in the aisles.

We passed the old Wrigley mansion, empty but newly roofed and painted, and climbed up above the pueblo-like home of the late Zane Grey, now a museum-like hotel, and through the screen of eucalyptus could be seen the barren outback of the island, where we knew there were buffalo and wild goat and wild boar and rattlesnakes.

For fifty years this wild domain had been owned by the Wrigley interests, but recently they deeded almost all of it to a non-profit conservancy, thus guaranteeing the permanent preservation of its natural state.

"That's Marlboro country, folks," the driver said. "What's funny is we got fifteen cowboys on the ranch out in there, none of us smoke. We shot that commercial right out of the tube one night last winter, had nothin' else to do."

After the tour I dropped into the Hurricane Cove for a beer, sitting at the bar and looking out at the bay. Sailboats and cruisers were poking over the horizon from the mainland and moving into their moorings. There were maybe a hundred of them in, and more coming every hour. The big Catalina weekend was beginning.

I considered staying where I was, but the steamship whistle broke in on my peace. At Avalon, and every other small island port in the seas, the arrival of the big white steamship from the mainland is the great excitement of the day, or week, or month. It is a moment of thanksgiving and renewal for the islanders, and perhaps for some there is a bit of dread.

Like a native I strolled around the crescent of the bay and

stood on the wharf as the SS *Catalina*—all pink and blue and white—steamed in from San Pedro and tied up. It is a tricky business, docking the steamer on the open channel side of the new mole, but the captain brought it off without disaster, and the gangways came down.

I doubt if any steamer anywhere disgorges such a motley crowd of passengers. We are a casual folk. Most of them were teen-agers, over to hit the beaches and the hot dog stands until the whistle called them back.

In the four hours between arrival and departure the life of Avalon is at high tide. The mainlanders surge up and down the bay front, reducing enormous inventories of hot dogs, frozen bananas, Frosties, French fries, Cokes.

They rent boats and wet suits and take to the sea or rent bicycles and take to the hills. The young married couples with little ones rent open-air midget Austins and careen around the hills inside the city limits and the older couples stroll out to the Casino point to look for something lost there long ago.

For those who were young in the Thirties, the round white concrete pavilion with its red dome and Moorish arches is perhaps the most powerfully nostalgic landmark in Southern California. On some summer nights the vast ballroom is still thronged with dancers. But that isn't Jan Garber up there, and the boys aren't playing *Sweet and Lovely*. How could Avalon have changed so little, they wonder, and so much?

After the steamer sails, the tempo changes. Music and laughter float in over the bay from the pleasure craft. Red harbor taxis begin their rounds, hauling yachtsmen in to the restaurants and bars and back again. They will be busy till the small hours.

At dusk every day from May into September a fast boat leaves the pier with a load of passengers to look for flying fish. As the boat runs along the leeward shore a searchlight plays across the water. It not only attracts the fish, but lights them when they fly. We were lucky that night. First we saw only a fish or two, hurtling out of the water, gliding in the white beam, shining blue and silver; then dozens and finally hundreds, a countless armada of flying fishes, thrashing and leaping and skimming for dozens of yards over the water at heights of two, four, six feet, some even sailing over the boat. Fish that fly—it is a mythlike phenomenon that brings cries of astonishment and delight from the crowd.

Farther on our searchlights were flashed high up against the granite bluffs, and here and there from the heights pairs of luminous round green orbs shone back at us.

"Goats," the captain told us. "That's their eyes you see. They come down those cliffs to lick the salt off the rocks."

Early the next morning I walked down to the pancake house for a country breakfast of sausage and eggs and pancakes and then took the Inland Motor Tour. This is the big one, a four-hour safari into the backcountry, a scenic preserve of seventy-six square miles.

It is rough, stunning country, with sudden changes of panorama from misty mountaintops and grassy velds to gorgeous rocky seascapes and wooded plateaus with delightful unexpected glimpses of deer, wild pig, mountain goat and buffalo. The bus climbed from Avalon over the old inland stagecoach road, winding through eucalyptus and toyon and out among oak and cactus.

"This is real private property," our driver told us, beginning the longest tour spiel it had ever been my fortune to hear. "To get out here you have to marry a native."

Our first buffalo looked planted, like a prop at Disneyland. He stood majestic on a rocky ledge, silhouetted against the sky, as if it were his job. He was right off the back of our nickel. It was a strangely familiar sight to us who had grown up on Saturday westerns.

"That's a rejected bull," our driver told us. "The young bulls are always fighting for leadership of the herd. We got six or seven of those bulls on the island. When they lose, they wander off alone. They don't even give 'em a gold watch."

We rumbled on, leaving the defeated old bull to his solitude.

"One o'clock low," the driver called out a minute later, like Robert Taylor in a World War II movie. "I see some buffalo. Two o'clock low."

All heads turned and there they were, a herd, thirty or forty of them with half a dozen calves. The driver stopped, and we all stared out in wonder at the species we hadn't quite managed to exterminate.

Catalina's buffalo herd was started by fourteen head brought over for the filming of *The Vanishing American* in 1914. They couldn't be rounded up so were left behind. A decade later a dozen more were brought over to brace up the herd. Today the island has four hundred head.

Nobody knows for sure where the goats came from. Probably they were brought in by the Spaniards. There are thousands of them on the island. They thrive. The wild pigs were brought in from Santa Rosa Island in the Thirties to keep the rattlesnakes down. They too have prospered. For a fee the proprietors allow guided hunters to shoot pigs and goats, with gun or bow and arrow. The buffalo and deer cannot be hunted.

The tour stops at Catalina's "Airport in the Sky," a three thousand two hundred and fifty-foot strip laid down over two mountaintops; at the thirteen hundred-acre ranch where Philip K. Wrigley and his family raise purebred Arabian horses; and at the Eagle's Nest, a nineteenth-century hunting lodge in a high meadow of oaks and cottonwoods.

On the road back we were lucky. We saw an enormous raven attacking a rattlesnake, or anyway the driver said it was a rattle-snake, and we saw an arctic loon trying to take off from the surface of the Wrigley Reservoir.

"That bird came in here with wing damage," our driver said. "See him trying to take off? Nope, can't make it yet. He's waiting for his wing to heal."

I don't know if it was an arctic loon or not, but after you have seen mountain goat, wild pigs, buffalo and a raven fighting a rattlesnake, who's to disbelieve a loon?

As we turned onto the rim above Avalon and the harbor came into view we saw the steamer back at its wharf.

"Steamer's in," the driver said. "There's two thousand people hit that town since you saw it last. They come in at 11:30 or a quarter of twelve and they hit us like locusts. Then they go back at four and say they've seen Catalina."

Back at the Island Plaza the driver stopped his bus and opened the door and turned around to face us.

"Don't applaud, folks," he said. "It makes dust."

The applause was thunder.

# **Venice**

*It is a kind of no man's land,*
*given up by default and occupied*
*by irregulars and their dogs.*

In the early morning, even in high summer, our Southern California beaches are often overcast and misty, and for the genuine beachcomber, like me, this is the best time of all.

On these mornings the sky is as gray as the sea. It is hard to tell one from the other. There is no horizon, and sometimes a distant sailboat will seem to be sailing in the sky.

I have always believed that I have a special affinity for the seashore, maybe because I was born at Long Beach half a block from it; and the first sound I heard in this world, except for my own primal scream, was the thunder of the surf. That cottage is long gone, though, and today, from the spot where it stood, you can see the *Queen Mary*.

Every beach has its peculiar character and appeal. There are the broad sands to which the families flock from the inner city with their six-packs, radios and lotions; the beaches claimed by the swingers, with their portable bars and boudoirs; the turbulent coves sought out by the hard-core surfers with their elite detachment and their assumption that God has green hair and a year-round tan.

So it was to escape all these that on an overcast Saturday morning I drove down to Venice for my own communion with the sea around us. Now that I have given up waiting for the ninth wave, I find a fascination in this place which seems to be lost in time. I parked near the old Ocean Park Pier; a grand piece of wreckage it was then, like something bombed out in the war, before they cleaned it out. The sky was opal, with a hint of fire in it, and the sand was more yellow than gray.

I walked down to the hard sand at the water's edge and headed south toward the fishing pier, a mile and a half away. In an hour or two there might be ten thousand people within sight, or a hundred thousand; but for the moment I was almost alone, sharing the entire shore with a few loners like myself.

Joggers with taut faces came toward me out of the mist and vanished without a word, as if afraid a word might break their rhythm. A small boy wearing a clammy T-shirt like a nightgown was building a castle in the sand at the water's edge, keeping a wary eye on the encroaching waves. He barely noticed me, so absorbed was he in this doomed enterprise. I looked up and down the beach. He seemed to be quite alone out here at the end of the continent; a born beachcomber.

Farther on, three small girls were digging holes in the sand, like terriers. One kept running down to the water to fill a green bottle, which she then emptied into the holes, a ritual whose purpose I could not guess. Surely, I thought, these moppets weren't out here on their own. Then I saw a man standing beside a pickup camper a hundred yards inland, watching paternally.

The girl with the bottle turned and looked squarely into my eyes, a communication which I took as inviting me to speak.

"What are you digging for?" I asked.

"Sand crabs."

"Oh, yes. For bait."

"No. We just let them go."

The morning beach is sometimes littered with treasures, as if the sea made its deliveries only in the night. Here and there I came upon the carcasses of jellyfish; purplish gelatinous lumps that seemed transparent. They might be shock troops of yet another species trying to get a foothold on dry land. Given a trillion years they could make it, and find it barren and wrecked, like the pleasure pier behind me in the mist.

A boy and a girl came toward me, walking purposefully, heads down, eyes searching the sand. The boy was carrying a long rod, at the end of which was a fixture like a vacuum sweeper part. As they came close, I heard a rhythmic ping. I guessed some kind of metal detector. The boy and girl looked up, grinning.

"What are you hunting?" I asked.

"Oh . . . coins, watches," the boy said.

"Had any luck?"

"Not yet."

"We just keep trying," said the girl. I noticed that she carried a yellow gardening trowel, ready to do the digging when the male discovered treasure.

"Good luck," I said.

As I walked on, two figures jogged toward me from the distance, emerging from gray silhouettes into a young man and woman in jogging togs. The woman ran ahead of the man, evidently to give herself room for expression. Every few paces she leaped into the air and kicked out a leg in sheer exuberance. The man plodded on behind her with the grim, ashen face of the serious jogger.

Near the fishing pier a man in hip boots was working in the surf with a wire screen held by two wooden handles. He would wait for a wave to wash up to his knees, then hold the screen on the sand, screening the water as it flowed back to the sea. Then he would scan his catch and pick out the sand crabs and drop them in a bag. Unlike the little girls, he wasn't going to let them go.

The pier was crowded, doing a good business in people if not in fish. The pier is always in use. They come in the dark, and some of them stay all night. Some of them catch fish and some don't, but few who don't will admit it. I watched a woman cutting mussels up for bait. She wore dirty slacks and a faded red sweat shirt. Her face was brown and weathered; she looked tough and amiable.

"What do you catch here?" I asked. Though I like piers and have spent hours on them, I am rarely present when anyone catches a fish, and I don't quite believe in it.

"I catch corbina," she said, as if no other fish need apply.

"Really? Corbina?"

"Oh, sure. I've got 'em stacked up at home in the freezer like cordwood.

"You must be a good fisherman," I conceded, wondering what the woman's lib would think about that noun.

"If I ain't," she said, "I sure got the fish fooled."

The pier ends in a large circular platform, extending the perimeter for fishermen. Few spaces were open. It is a little cosmopolis, the end of the pier. I heard Italian and Japanese and a language that perhaps was Slavic. There were boys and girls fishing and old men and old women, brought together by a mystique that transcends the generation gap. I watched a boy fishing with a line wound around a Schlitz malt liquor can instead of a reel. His face reflected more patience than hope.

"Any luck?" I asked him.

"Naw."

"What do you use for bait?"

"I tried everything but a human being, and I don't catch nothin."

"Good luck," I said.

From the end of the pier I looked back at the low dilapidated profile of Venice, and looming prophetically beyond and to the south, the fortress towers of the Marina del Rey and its neighboring developments. Venice had fallen into decay from the vainglorious splendors of Abbott Kinney's dreams. It had been taken over by the new barbarians, as some saw them; and now it was under siege, its bohemian life-style threatened by affluence.

It was only seventy years ago that Kinney had turned a slough into a new Venice, building a system of canals with arched bridges and a central lagoon. There were genuine gondolas from Italy and genuine singing gondoliers. Stores and hotels with mock-Renaissance fronts and cast-iron Italian columns were built around the lagoon and down Windward Avenue to the sand and along Ocean Front Walk. Now the lagoon is asphalt; the canals are broken down, week-grown and scummy; half the Venetian fronts are missing, like pulled teeth, and the others are scabrous and decayed, their columns rusted. It is a funky slum, not without its charm, in which the inheritors of the vanished beatniks, disdainful of the affluent life of the nearby marina, have rooted their counterculture.

In the winter, and in the night and early morning, before the lemmings of the inner city come swarming down to the sea, there is a strange and vital community along the Venice beach front; an incongruous mixture of young bohemians and hippies, black and white, and remnants of old people, mostly Jews, who

live in tacky Victorian hotels on Ocean Front Walk, shop at
the kosher delis in between the hot dog stands, and worship
at painted stucco temples with Stars of David painted over the
doorways. An uneasy harmony seems to exist, stabilized perhaps
by the black and white police cars that creep silently back and
forth along the front.

Venice is a place where the past is still hanging around, waiting for an appointment with the future; but the future hasn't
shown up. In the meantime it is a kind of no man's land, given
up by default and occupied by irregulars and their dogs. There
is at least one dog, I would say, for every person.

It is astonishing how much human energy is expended along
this exhausted-looking front, by young and old. I found a karate
class in progress in a meeting room of the big public pavilion
at the foot of Windward Avenue. There were a dozen pupils,
some adults, some no more than eight or nine years old, all
properly dressed in white kimonos.

One little girl with long blond hair was pounding on a hanging sandbag. Snarling and barking, she delivered vicious chops
to the bag with the knife-edge of her tiny hand. Then she began
leaping in the air and giving it flying kicks, accompanied by
shrill war whoops. The bag accepted these aggressions without
a shudder.

Outside the pavilion old men were playing at bowls on the
clay courts, and half a dozen shuffleboard courts were in use.
The pace here was slower, but the intensity no less than it was
up the walk a way, at the basketball and tennis courts and the
weight-lifting enclosure, where young men with bulging thighs
and biceps tremulously lifted 200-pound barbells, for reasons
known only to themselves.

Nearby I noticed two small boys, one black, one white, sitting
side by side on a bench. What made me curious was their exem-
plary deportment. They were sitting quite still, like good little
girls in church. Then I saw that one of them held the end of
a string. My eye followed the string. It led up the sidewalk,
over a parked bicycle, and down again to the walk, where it
ended in a circle, or noose, inside which were half a dozen bread
crumbs. Crumbs were also scattered outside the noose. These
were rapidly being reduced by eight or ten pigeons. The boys

117

were trying to snare a pigeon.

I had to see it through. For two minutes I watched as the pigeons industriously snatched up every crumb, except those inside the noose. Not once did a pigeon err. The string was never crossed.

"What would you do if you caught one?" I asked the boys when it was plain that, for the moment at least, the game was up.

"Raise 'em."

"Good luck," I said, relieved that they hadn't hoped to eat one.

Two old women were sitting under the window of the card house, wrapped in hats and scarves and old wool coats and taking no heed of the shabby man asleep on the other end of the bench. I stood by the bench to look in at a huddle of old men playing pinochle.

"My husband used to play pinochle," said one of the women, "on the sand over there. In the old days. None of those men are around any more. Except Tiny. Big fat Tiny."

She seemed to be talking to me, or perhaps only to herself, but in a moment she was back talking to her friend again.

"I have to get out of that place. I don't know what's going on. A man comes to that woman's door and he goes in without even knocking."

"I thought you were going to move," her crony said.

"Well, I haven't even seen inside this other place yet. I hear it has a Cold Spot Frigidaire, but I'm not giving up *my* Frigidaire till I see it." People of her generation, I remembered, usually called all refrigerators Frigidaires—Cold Spots included.

A boy and a girl approached me with a large basket from which two nondescript kittens were trying to escape. The boy was wearing a football jersey numbered 54.

"You want a kitten?" he asked me.

"No, thank you," I said, restraining myself from adding that a kitten was among the last things in the world I might acquire.

"We had four," the girl said. "These are all that's left."

"Good luck," I said.

It occurred to me that I had been saying good luck to hustlers and entrepreneurs of one kind or another all morning.

Riders were beginning to appear on the bicycle path. It was rather new, a concrete path separate from the walk, with six lanes painted on in yellow. Some locals had protested the bike path, for fear it would bring in more people, which it did. The Venice front had been isolated when they took out the jitneys that used to shuttle down from Santa Monica with tourists and other outsiders, and now the bike paths had brought them in again.

At the end of Rose Avenue there is a small pavilion that serves as a satellite culture center. The regular weekend music festival was already going on with two men and a woman on bongos and a small crowd sitting around absorbing the beat. Nearby, enveloped by the sound, a row of four old women sat on a bench, like old sparrows in their threadbare wrappings, watching life go by on Ocean Front Walk as patiently as the two boys waiting for the pigeons to step into the snare. They had survived the beatnik generation and the hippie generation, these ancients from middle Europe, and they would probably survive their successors.

I walked back down to the sea, toward the jetty that stands out in the surf beyond the lifeguard station. Some of its great hunks of granite had been painted red with KEEP OFF lettered on in white, which of course made them all the more attractive for climbing.

I saw the boy and the girl coming down the beach with the metal detector and waited until they reached me.

"Hi," they cried, remembering me.

"You find anything yet?" I asked.

"Not yet," the boy said.

"We keep trying," said the girl, waving the yellow trowel.

I found a good rock to lean against and shut my eyes, waiting for the sun to come out and inlanders to arrive, and wondered if the woman in the red sweat shirt had caught any corbina; and if the boy who had tried every kind of bait but human beings had got a bite; and if the boy and girl had gotten rid of their kittens; and if the two boys on the bench had snared a pigeon.

You have to hustle in this life, it occurred to me a moment or two before I dozed off.

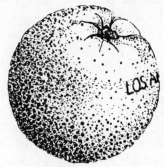

# Watts Towers

*They tried to knock it down, you know.*

In the southeast corner of the section known as Watts there is a piece of 107th Street that is cut off by old Pacific Electric tracks. It can be entered from Willowbrook Avenue, but it runs only one short block, and there it dead-ends in the rusted old tracks that slash across the neighborhood on their way to nowhere.

In most ways it is a typical Watts street: two rows of small frame houses, dateless houses that have outlived their time but are trying to keep up appearances, like old chorus girls, with paint and flowers. But this is a distinguished street, because at its dead end, on a small lot cut like a piece of pie by the old tracks, stand the Watts Towers. They are the most remarkable works of open air art in Southern California, and perhaps in the nation.

They are the work of the late Simon Rodia, an immigrant Italian who gave up women and liquor at the age of forty and spent the next thirty-three years of his life erecting these implausible monuments.

I stood in the street looking up at the towers, wondering how they might be described. Unique is a word debased by misuse, but the Watts Towers *are* unique. I could think of nothing to compare them with but the Eiffel Tower; but the Eiffel Tower is too bog, too pretentious, too geometrically severe. It bears too plainly the mark of the engineer and the drafting board.

121

We might be awed by the Eiffel Tower, but never charmed. It is the ultimate triumph of the Erector set. The Watts Towers are a wondrous poem, built in the sky by a man who was possessed by unquenchable urgings and fancies, as Columbus was possessed, and Mozart.

"I wanted to do something big," said Simon Rodia; and he did.

More than anything else, the towers reminded me of the boojum tree, which is also unique and improbable. It is found only in the wilderness of Baja California, and there is nothing even close to it anywhere else. Of the three towers, the highest is one hundred feet. They rise like upside-down ice cream cones made of lace and encrusted with costume jewelry.

A wall runs around Rodia's triangular garden, and it also bears his mark. The wall is a mosaic of Rodia's improvisations. There are panels of broken tile and panels of green bottle glass and plaques of cement in which he impressed his initials, SR, and the date, 1923, and the shape of hammer and tile cutter and the other tools of his trade, or perhaps it should be called his passion. The wall seems without design, without order. Bits of broken tile, yellow and red and blue and purple; pieces of china plates; pieces of green and blue bottles; hundreds of white seashells—all are pressed into the cement of the wall without apparent pattern; yet the wall is a masterpiece. It dazzles the eye and delights the spirit. It is all one lovely harmony.

A small black boy appeared above the wall. He was climbing in the highest tower. He balanced himself and looked appraisingly down at me. One is not allowed to climb the towers. He knew it and I knew it. He was obviously wondering whether I was going to tell him to get down. He decided I wasn't.

"You want in?" he said.

"Yes," I said, "I want in."

He monkeyed himself down and out of view behind the wall and in a moment the door in the wall swung open. A sign on the gate said the towers opened at 11 a.m. I pointed out that it wasn't quite eleven yet.

"It's all right," he said. "Come on. My sister's here."

A girl was sitting at the weathered table inside the gate. A sign said: "Adults 75 Cents." I gave the girl a dollar and began strolling in what has often been called "Simon Rodia's magic garden." I sat in the gazebo and studied the towers.

They are made of steel rings and spokes and central cores, all covered with cement, set in chicken wire and encrusted with the humble materials of Rodia's art—the debris of a wasteful society. They are connected by bejeweled spars that leap from one to the other and to the other fancies in the garden—the gazebo and the Marco Polo ship and the fountain—so that all is one interlocking structure.

Rodia was only a tile setter by trade, without any schooling at all. He owned and boasted of a set of Encyclopaedia Britannica, but nobody was ever sure he could even read. Yet he had created from some infallible inner sense of order this exquisite feat of art and engineering. For thirty-three years he worked alone, rising with his towers, coming down to fill his cement pail and climbing up again to add another bit of frosting. He used no ladders. The towers themselves were his scaffold.

Why did he work alone?

"I no have anybody to help me out," he said once. "I was a poor man. Had to do a little at a time. Nobody helped me. I think if I hire a man he don't know what to do. A million times I don't know what to do myself."

Why did he build his towers at all?

"Some of the people say what was he doing . . . some of the people think I was crazy and some people said I was going to do something. I wanted to do something. I wanted to do something in the United States because I was raised here you understand? I wanted to do something for the United States because there are nice people in this country."

In his beautiful essay on Rodia and the towers, Paul Laporte asks, "What makes the towers tick?" The answer, he suggests, is their "organic quality."

"In nature," he says, "there is a reason for everything, and there is nothing without a reason. The layout with the arcaded walls around was determined by the odd triangular shape of the lot. The lacework of the towers was determined by the need of one man creating a tall structure without the aid of scaffolding, doing all the work alone."

Even the ornamentation, Laporte points out, the bits and

pieces of tile and glass and china, was essential to provide a protective shell over the reinforced cement. "Thus," he concludes, "every part and combination of parts in these structures is a technical necessity while at the same time emerging as the character and beauty of the whole."

Other people were beginning to come into the garden. They walked around in wonder, speaking softly. People seeing the towers for the first time seem enchanted. They sit on Rodia's benches in the arbor, looking up at the towers, or stand in front of large panels of broken tile on the inside wall, fascinated as children are fascinated by their kaleidoscopes.

The girl who had taken my dollar ran up to me. "Here's your change," she said. She put a quarter in my hand. It seemed a bargain.

I overheard a man and a woman, who stood bemused before a structure covered with shards of glass from bottles that had been blue and green:

"He must have drunk a lot of milk of magnesia," said the woman.

"And Seven Up," the man said.

A wood flooring has been laid over the foundations of Rodia's little house. Only the fireplace is left, and the arched doorway, which is faced with pieces of broken mirrors. Everyone comes back for a second look at the doorway, seeing himself fragmented, abstracted, in that wall of broken mirrors.

A man and a boy were standing on the flooring by the fireplace. "This used to be his house," the man told the boy. "It burned down."

"You mean in the riots?" the boy asked.

"No. Long before that."

Not only did the house burn down. There were other depredations. Shells and glass surfaces were smashed or pried out. Fragile surfaces were defaced. The towers were in danger of falling to the vandals.

In 1959 two men, William Cartwright and Nicholas King, bought the Rodia property and formed a committee to repair, preserve and develop the towers as a community monument. It continues today as the Committee for Simon Rodia's Towers in Watts.

"They tried to knock it down, you know," I heard a man tell his wife as they looked up at the main tower. "But they couldn't. They hooked up a rig and tried to pull it down and the damn rig broke instead."

They hadn't tried to tear it down, exactly, but they tried to prove that it ought to be torn down. That was in 1959, after the committee was formed. The Philistines had condemned the towers as unsafe. The committee fought. Hearings were held. Finally, the committee agreed to pay the cost of a test.

It was a dramatic day, October 10, 1959, when the main tower was put to the test. Reporters and television crews were there. A crowd gathered in the street, some hoping the tower would win, some hoping it would fail. A hydraulic jack was used to apply a ten thousand-pound load to the tower, much more than any wind or quake would give it. It was to be a five-minute test. A minute went by. The crowd was tense. The tower leaned almost imperceptibly. And then the main beam of the test rigging began to give.

The city surrendered. The test was over. Simon Rodia's innate engineering skill was proved, and his work prevailed.

I walked out of the garden and went across the street to talk to a man who was working on a car. Had he lived in the neighborhood long? Thirty years near on. Yes, he remembered Simon Rodia. Many people on the street had been there a long time and remembered Simon, the odd little Italian with the gnarled hands and the big nose.

Simon used to sing as he worked, forty, fifty feet up, arias from operas and songs nobody in the neighborhood had ever heard anybody else sing. Funny man; complained about everything: taxes and painted women and drinking parents. But loved the country, loved America.

Rodia got along with the neighborhood children. They did business. They brought him broken bottles and mirrors and plates. Sometimes he paid them, a penny apiece for a broken plate. That was fine until the mothers of the street found out why so many plates were accidentally broken.

"He used to go off down that railroad track walking," the man said, "all the way to Wilmington sometimes, with his gunnysack, picking up things. Be gone all day, come back with a

125

sackful of junk."

He went on. "You know he even put his car in those towers there?"

His car?

"Sure. Old Hudson. He put the springs and the wheels and everything he could use."

"What happened to the rest of it then?" I asked.

He chuckled. "Buried it. Right there by the tracks."

I didn't know if Simon Rodia had actually buried his Hudson, but it seemed like a good idea.

Out in the street again I heard the Pied Piper song of the ice cream man. His truck was pulled up in front of the towers. He was doing a good business. I waited my turn and ordered a small cone.

"This here is *some* place," he said, looking with utter puzzlement at the towers. "I never been down this street before. It might be good for business. Who made that there?"

I told him a man named Simon Rodia, a tile setter. "It took him over thirty years," I said.

"Man," he said, shaking his head, "I couldn't do nothing like that, take a hundred years."

Neither could anybody else, I imagined, except maybe Leonardo da Vinci, give him an old beat-up Hudson to cannibalize and a cement pail and some kids to buy accidentally broken plates from.

# Disneyland

*A man off a riverboat don't care
a hoot what it costs to watch
a chorus girl kick.*

Some years ago, on a Southern Pacific special en route from Los Angeles to Santa Barbara, I sat in the club car eavesdropping as Walt Disney grew expansive on his favorite subject—Disneyland. He disclosed, among other things, that the monkeys in Adventureland were not covered with monkey fur, but nylon.

"We tried real monkey skins," Disney confided. "They get ratty. We found nylon's better."

That perhaps is the secret of Disneyland. It is better than the real thing.

It is the jungle without tsetse flies; New Orleans without humidity; a pirate ship without scurvy; a Matterhorn without cold; a Main Street, U.S.A., without litter.

I was one of those who scoffed when Walt Disney first talked of building a multimillion-dollar amusement park in Anaheim.

"*Anaheim!*" I said. "Who's going all the way out to Anaheim to ride a merry-go-round?"

Over the years, since it opened in 1955, I have been to Disneyland half a dozen times, usually fortified by some plausible excuse: I was taking my children; and more lately, my grandchildren; or had to go on business. Excuses are no longer necessary. Disneyland's true appeal, we admit now, is to adults. Children don't need it. Their imaginations are enough. For them, Disneyland is only another kind of reality, somewhat less marvelous than their own fantasies. Look at the faces as you wander along the thronged streets of Adventureland, or New Orleans Square, or Main Street. You see it is the adults who are enchanted.

127

Perhaps a grown man never really appreciates Disneyland until he goes alone, without children to manage and obey. It is only then that he discovers what Walt Disney always knew. The boy or girl lives in all of us.

For one thing, Disneyland has a powerfully nostalgic effect on older Americans, an effect that doesn't touch the young. And even this nostalgia is illusion. Disneyland stirs memories of an America we think we knew; but which never quite existed. It plays back our myths. There is magic in the whole effect. Try as you might, it is impossible to stay an hour in Disneyland without a blurring of the critical senses. There is nothing to do but give in and enjoy it.

Is it only chance, or is it deliberate that the visitor entering the playground first passes the depot of the Disneyland Railroad, a set piece that gives him such a stab of nostalgia that he is not likely to recover until he is back on the freeway going home? What could more effectively wrench a man of my generation back to childhood than the hiss and huff of steam and the cry of "*Board!*"

The route has been changed since I last rode the Disneyland Railroad. It now goes through the Grand Canyon and back one hundred million years into the Mesozoic Age when dinosaurs dominated the cooling earth. The train is swallowed up in a black cave, shutting out the world its passengers have left. It passes a spectacular diorama of the Grand Canyon, suitably accompanied by an ambient rendition of Ferde Grofe's *Grand Canyon Suite,* and then glides back deep into time.

Thunder and lightning; a terrible primeval screaming. Then the scene emerges from the dark. A brontosaurus—thunder lizard—wades in a swamp. He moves, his great neck thrusting his lizard head into the murky water in search of plants. All about him—in the far reaches of the swamp, on the banks, on the rocks above—his contemporaries forage and fight their losing struggle for survival. Here and there, the bones of a mighty monster foretell the doom of the species. Pterodactyls abound. I swear one damn near got in the train. Surely this flying reptile was the most hideous of creatures, with his great flapping leather wings and raw, red, crocodile face and dreadful claws.

Before long, it is evident to us in the train that there will

128

be plenty of leftovers for those unlovely vultures. Over in the wings, a grinning *Tyrannosaurus rex,* the giant meat-eating dinosaur, prepares to make short work of an armored stegosaurus. It is an awesome landscape, the diorama of the museum come to life. And entirely air-conditioned.

Like the vintage depot, Main Street, U.S.A., seems calculated to tranquilize us older visitors by reminding us of a more amiable America, before international terror and urban chaos. One needn't have lived at the turn of the century to feel nostalgia for Main Street. There is a profound sense of small town America in all of us, whatever our age or origins. Maybe it's inherited.

You can stand on a corner in Disneyland's Main Street, shut your eyes and conjure up that vanished era from the sounds alone. The steam whistle of the Disneyland; the fat harmonies of the band concert in the town square; the lovely *clip a clop a clip a clop* of the draft horse pulling the streetcar. There, surely, is a sound that has gone forever.

But finally, all the young men leave Main Street in search of adventure. Perhaps that is why Mr. Disney put Adventureland right around the corner from the town plaza—an easy escape.

I stood in line and took the jungle boat ride. I had been down that river several times before; but like the Amazon or Irrawaddy, it is always changing. Our boatman was in good form. He had a voice like W. C. Fields:

"Right out in front of us, folks, we have a couple a hun'erd crocodiles, just emerging from the depths of the river. There's old Smiley, the gran'daddy of 'em all. Come on, smile there, Smiley. Smile. Come on. He's kind a lazy today, folks, but he still has that bad habit a takin' a hand for lunch. So keep your hands inside the boat.

"Now we're comin' up on the ruins of an ancient old Cambodian shrine that was almost totally destroyed hun'erds a years ago by a devastating earthquake . . ."

I looked back. Old Smiley was smiling.

Beyond the Cambodian ruins and the monkey god, the river turns into a lagoon in which a herd of elephants are bathing. It is a scene of abandoned joy as the old bulls and cows and the playful calves frolic in the water, unaware that one day they

129

will be exterminated by carnivores like those passing among them in the small boats.

The river winds from the jungle into the veld, where we saw rhinos attacking a safari and lions feeding on zebra. Nature at Disneyland is seldom mild. Mr. Disney knew that children are savages, with savage appetites.

Once more we were in the rain forests, and a pair of big apes appeared suddenly on the bank.

"Gorillas up there!"—shouted the boatman. "These boys weigh six hun'erd pounds, got an arm spread a twelve feet. They could reach right out and yank yuh in."

I wasn't worried. I knew they were only nylon.

The Pirates of the Caribbean is one of the more outrageously theatrical adventures at Disneyland. It shows what a million dollars can do for the old Tunnel of Love. The genre couldn't be carried much further, short of running a boat through Hell. Visitors board the boats in a dark cavern on a bayou and are trundled down a chute into a subterranean chamber of ghostly tableaux, peopled by the skeletons of dead pirates amidst their sunken ships and useless treasure.

After this object lesson, the boats swim backward in time to the lusty days that went before this retribution. We sailed under the blazing guns of a pirate galleon bombarding the walls of a Caribbean port. The din was splendid. Booming cannons and pirate curses and shrieking maidens. Come the next scene, the town is taken; the fat town burghers are put to the sword and their women are sold at auction. Debauchery prevails. Slavering pirates lope around the patios and balconies in pursuit of scream-ing wenches. Rum flows. The night is rent with raucous singing. In the end, the town is put to the torch and the visitors barely escape in their little boats as flames lick at their sterns.

One can hardly imagine a more graphic representation of greed, violence, drunkenness and lechery. It is all very satisfying, and I suppose children love it as much as adults.

I had a lunch of shrimp creole at the Blue Bayou, in New Orleans. The restaurant is an open terrace overlooking the bayou from which the boats set out for the Caribbean. The atmosphere is overpowering. Spanish moss hangs low above the tables from opulent magnolia trees. The bayou broods, dark and forbidding.

The waitresses are Southern belles. Only two things seemed to be missing from the Blue Bayou. For authenticity's sake, the place needs a bit of humidity, and perhaps a bottle or two of good white burgundy in the cellar, or a mint julep.

The steamboat whistle called. Others might go on to Tomorrowland to see the wonders that lie ahead, but I was caught in the mood of nineteenth-century America. I boarded the Mark Twain at her wharf and climbed to the top deck. Again, the sounds cast a spell. A banjo played "Oh Susanna!" and I could hear the steamboat breathing ... *huff* ... *oof* ... *huff* ... *oof* ...

A small boy stood at the railing beside me. His eyes were searching the woods of Tom Sawyer Island for hostiles, I imagine. I don't know who he thought he was. But I was Gaylord Ravenal.

We did see hostiles. And then we passed a pioneer's cabin in flames. The pioneer lay on the cleared ground beside his burning home, an arrow in his chest. There was no doubt in my mind, though, that the Indians would never take the island. From the top deck of the Mark Twain, I could see that it was overrun by small boys and girls. They obviously controlled every trail and had infiltrated Fort Wilderness.

When the Mark Twain docked, I found the wharf where the raft departed for the island. A Disneyland guide, one of those piquant college girls in red vest, red tartan skirt and black derby, was reassuring an uncertain mother who was about to deliver two children to a raft named Becky Thatcher.

"There's nothing to worry about," the guide was saying. "They can't get lost."

That was good enough for me. I got on the Becky Thatcher and after a crossing of exactly thirty-one seconds we reached the island.

I have always identified with Tom Sawyer. It is something a man never gets over. If I could have had anything in the world I wanted as a boy, I believe I would have chosen an island in the Mississippi.

I plodded along a trail through the woods. Children flowed around me like wind. Finally, I came upon Fort Wilderness. Periodically, a bugle blew *charge*. There was a ripple of rifle fire from the turrets. I entered the fort and took refuge in the canteen. A young lady served me a cup of coffee and then direct-

ed me to the underground escape tunnel. "Thanks, miss," I said.
"I'll be movin' on."

I looked through an open window into regimental headquarters. Davey Crockett, the old scout, was reporting to Colonel
Andrew Jackson. A sign said it was the Cherokee Indian Campaign, 1813.

"That's not Davey Crockett," a boy said.

"Who is it then?" a little girl asked.

"It's Daniel Boone. He's on TV."

They were both wrong. It was Fess Parker.

I found the door to the escape tunnel and plunged into it
headlong. I was no more in than I was sorry. Claustrophobia
seized me. It was impossible to turn back. I was being followed.
I pushed along, grateful for the occasional lights and openings
through which I could see the outdoors, until finally, as the
canteen girl had promised, the tunnel opened and put me at
the river's edge. I headed back for the Becky Thatcher. I wanted
to get back to New Orleans and wine, women and song. Women
and song, anyway. The path rose and twisted suddenly and I
was back at Fort Wilderness.

I picked up another path, past the cemetery, and headed again
for the river, trying to keep my sense of direction. I heard a
bugle blowing *charge,* and the sharp snap of rifle fire, and
then I was back at Fort Wilderness.

I thought what does she mean I can't get lost? I'm lost.

Once back on the mainland I decided to find some entertain-
ment. The show was just starting at the Golden Horseshoe.
I went up to the balcony and found myself looking down into
the Golden Horseshoe saloon. There was a stage in the open
end of the horseshoe. Three bartenders in black vests and string
ties tended a long bar. A young lady with a tray came up to
take my order.

"What've you got?" I asked.

"Pepsi."

"That's all?"

"Yes, sir. That's all."

I ordered a Pepsi on the rocks. The show began. If there is
anything I wouldn't expect much of, it would be a girlie show
at Disneyland. By George, I had to take it back.

I won't say it was racy; but the comedian was pretty good. I caught myself laughing immoderately. Maybe it was because he wasn't allowed to be dirty. He had to be *funny*. The dancing girls were as leggy a lot as you'll see anywhere, including Las Vegas. In the finale, they came out kicking and squealing. I was hardly prepared for what I heard and saw. The boys in the orchestra pit struck up that frenzied refrain from Offenbach's *Gâieté Parisienne* and, yessiree Bob, the girls did the cancan.

Maybe it wasn't the *Folies Bergères,* but it wasn't exactly Mickey Mouse, either.

I wondered how a dive like the Golden Horseshoe could pay for such a classy show. My guess is, they water the Pepsi. But a man off a riverboat don't care a hoot what it costs to watch a chorus girl kick. Especially when she's absolutely real.

They can't make dollies like that out of nylon.

# The Lake Shrine

*A sad saint is a sad saint indeed.*
*These long faces don't know God.*

Los Angeles may have no other landmark that remains so much an enigma to passersby as the Lake Shrine of the Self-Realization Fellowship on Sunset Boulevard in Pacific Palisades.

It is seen and marveled at by tens of thousands who pass it daily in their cars, winding down the Palisades toward the ocean; it is known by relatively few. Those coming upon it for the first time in the dry hills might well be astonished. What's this? A lake? A Dutch windmill? A towering waterfall? A statue of Christ in the sky? An Indian temple?

All this is visible from the boulevard. But this is Southern California. No one is too surprised. The Lake Shrine is taken for a movie set, a mirage or an ornament for some real estate development. They drive on another quarter-mile, tires singing as they make the big curve around the lake, and then they are on the Pacific Coast Highway, rushing out to Malibu.

Like most others, I had driven past the Lake Shrine many times in the past twenty years, and never turned in, until very recently when I was invited to a friend's wedding beside the lake. The ceremony was on a grassy peninsula under the great Golden Lotus Archway, an open temple of three arches surmounted by sculptured lotus blossoms of gold leaf-covered copper. Across the grass, against a fieldstone retaining wall, stands an antique Chinese stone sarcophagus, and inside this, in a bronze coffer inlaid with silver, are enshrined a portion of the ashes of Mahatma Gandhi. It is called the Gandhi World Peace Memorial.

135

In this setting, beside the tranquil lake, the wedding party gathered, walking around the lake on a rustic footpath. The minister wore a short ocher robe over a white shirt and brown trousers. He was a bald man, and the top of his head and his face were deeply suntanned. He carried a small book and stood before a table on which a brass urn rested. He spoke with a European accent, calling us forward to stand close behind the wedding couple. He spoke the vows swiftly, his voice resonant but capricious on the breeze from the nearby sea.

"I am thine, thou art mine, that we may merge in God . . . Body, mind and soul we cast into the flame of love, to be purified into cosmic love for all mankind . . . We are united to fulfill the law of creation; and, through mutual affection, to find the infinite divine love . . . May our souls join the one spirit of God . . ."

At the end he reached into the urn and brought forth handfuls of fresh rose petals which he cast into the breeze above the bride and groom. The petals fell in their hair and on their shoulders and arms as they clung together.

"May these rose petals symbolize the blessings of God . . ."

It was several weeks before I returned to the Lake Shrine, on a Sunday morning, to attend services of the Self-Realization Fellowship in the windmill chapel, and to explore the grounds.

Just off the parking lot I entered the Court of Religions. This is an open place above the lake on which stand five low, stone and concrete monuments. each representing one of the great religions: Hinduism, Buddhism, Judaism, Islam and Christianity. The visitor at once discovers the all-embracing grasp of Self-Realization.

Though I was unfamiliar with the Lake Shrine, I was no stranger to the fellowship itself. For twenty years I have lived just across the street from its world headquarters, which occupies the old turn-of-the-century Mt. Washington Hotel and its sylvan grounds. For twenty years we have been their neighbors, unaware of them mostly, except at Christmastime, when every evening Christmas carols come rolling down over the hill from their amplifiers.

In the Court of Religions I saw a man in an ocher robe greeting visitors who had come for the early service. There are two services every Sunday in the windmill; one at nine-thirty and the second at eleven. The second is always overcrowded, so latecomers sit outside the windmill in a vine-covered patio.

The man in the ocher robe was the one who had performed the marriage ceremony. He was Brother Turiyananda, he told me. He was a swami, an ancient Indian term for a religion teacher who is in union with the Higher Self, one who has experienced God. "But swami is misunderstood so often in this country," he said amiably, "so here we are called brother, or minister."

Brother Turiyananda said he himself had performed perhaps two hundred weddings at the Lake Shrine, many of them for Christians. "They are very impressed," he said. "They are deeply moved by the way we present them to God."

He led me off toward the footpath. The court was bordered by a large rose garden and by beds of begonias and brilliant orange zinnias. We passed a small tree with a burst of vivid purple flowers and walked under an arbor of bougainvillea.

Brother Turiyananda had been here eighteen years, coming from Switzerland. His early religious instruction had been in Calvinism, which taught discipline, but which he found too stern. "Yoga is so much nicer," he said, smiling.

The lake shore is a garden that seems to bring together, like the fellowship itself, the flowers and fruits of many soils. There are cactus beds and succulents, Chinese rice-paper trees, Abyssinian bananas, golden bamboo, black bird-of-paradise, tropical fruit trees, bullrushes and beds of water lilies with yellow blooms. Brother Turiyananda had taken a personal hand in the planting and upkeep of the gardens, with certain successes and failures like any other amateur green thumb.

"I am trying to grow the lotus," he said. "I haven't yet. But I will. In India, the lotus is a symbol of the soul. It rises out of muddy waters into the light."

We came to a wood landing built over the lake. It has a roof and benches and a view across the lake to the lotus temple and to the rocky pinnacle surmounted by a white stone statue of Jesus. A waterfall starts just below the statue, tumbling sixty feet to the lake.

"Our Founder used to sit out here to meditate," said Brother Turiyananda as we walked out on the landing and looked across the lake.

The founder of the Self-Realization Fellowship was a yogi called Paramahansa Yogananda. He was born in 1893 in a poor village near the Himalayas. His father was a railway official, of high caste, but the boy, one of eight children, was drawn to the spiritual life. As a youth he became a disciple of Swami Sri Yukteswar, who for the next ten years was his guru, or holy teacher.

The young Swami Yogananda came to the United States in 1920 for a religious congress in Boston, and stayed to begin his lifelong mission in the West. He founded his fellowship in Los Angeles in 1925 and built it into an international establishment before his death here in 1952. It is headed today by Daya Mata, who was a seventeen-year-old Utah Christian when she heard Yogananda lecture and became a disciple.

Yogananda taught that God is One, the Universal Presence; that all persons are united in God, and that through meditation and the ancient disciplines of yoga, man can heighten his realization of himself and experience a real union with God. Thus he taught that all religions seek the same goal, consciousness of God. Though Hindu in essence, the Self-Realization Fellowship embraces Christ, Buddha and Muhammad, as well as Krishna, the Hindu deity, and finds inspiration in the Bible as well as the sacred Hindu writings of the Bhagavad-Gita.

"I have just one prejudice," Yogananda said, "and that is a prejudice against prejudice . . . Here we blend, because our goal is God . . ."

The houseboat was tied to the shore just beyond the landing. The early service had started in the windmill chapel and there were sounds of children in the houseboat. "This is where we hold our Sunday school," Brother Turiyananda said.

The houseboat is revered, like the landing, because Yogananda took his meals aboard it and sometimes spent the night when he was overseeing construction of the Lake Shrine. We looked into the houseboat and saw the pictures of six holy men on the wall. Sunlight came through the windows and lighted the

138

faces, making them look more human than holy. One was Jesus. I also knew the face of Paramahansa Yogananda; a dark voluptuous face, framed in straight black hair, with liquid dark eyes and a subtle smile.

"Paramahansa Yogananda was a man of great humor," said Brother Turiyananda. "He once said that a sad saint is a sad saint indeed. These long faces don't know God."

The other faces were of Krishna, Sri Yukteswar, the guru of Yogananda, himself a saint; and two others who were the *guru's* guru and *his* guru, a succession that reflected the antiquity and tradition of yoga.

On another wall of the Sunday school an embroidered prayer showed that the first paths to God consciousness need not be sophisticated:

*Good morning God, I love you so,*
*And with your help, my love I'll show*
*By trying hard all through the day,*
*To do my best in every way.*

We walked on around the east shore and I noticed that two black-necked swans were keeping at our heels with a raucous honking. Though it is not permitted, people sometimes feed the swans, the swami said, and they have become beggars. There are also a pair of white swans on the lake, given to the fellowship as a living memorial to the founder. The swan is sacred in Hindu mythology, and Yogananda's monastic title, Paramahansa, means literally "highest swan."

On the east path an occasional small sign, lettered in yellow paint on wood, could be seen half-hidden in the reeds and vines. One was a quotation from the founder: *"Everything else can wait, but our search for God cannot wait."*

We crossed a stone bridge and stood before a lovely tree, perhaps fifteen feet high, with light green shiny leaves and a clean bark.

"It is the bo tree," explained Brother Turiyananda, "from the tree of Buddha."

The tree is a direct descendant, he said, of the revered bo tree at Gaya, in Northern India, under which Gautama Buddha,

139

nearly six hundred years before the Christian era, had sat for weeks in meditation to attain enlightenment. In 300 B.C. the great King Asoka sent a cutting of this tree to Ceylon, where it flourished for nearly twenty-three hundred years at Anuradhapura. In 1957 a cutting from this tree was given to the Lake Shrine. Beside the little bo tree a sign declares:

*"It is hoped that this bo tree may grow for thousands of years, as did its forebears, reminding people of the achievement of a man who taught that others may also gain emancipation from the fetters of sensual life and gain nirvana while still associated with the body form peculiar to this planet."*

We were back at the Golden Lotus Archway under which Brother Turiyananda had performed the marriage ceremony. It was here, in 1950, that Paramahansa Yogananda had dedicated the Lake Shrine with the words: *"In this wall-less temple we worship Thee, our one Father."*

There was no need for walls to enclose God, Brother Turiyananda explained. "God is everywhere."

He looked up the cliffs behind the Gandhi sarcophagus. They rise steeply into thickets of chaparral. "We have deers up there. They come down and eat all my geraniums."

A bearded youth in a white satin robe sat cross-legged on the grass, immobile, chin slightly elevated, eyes shut. "He is not one of ours," said Brother Turiyananda. "But everyone comes here to meditate."

Near the end of the path we came to a cottage above a sunken garden and a grotto. Inside the cottage is a gift shop where one may buy Indian objects of art and copies of Yogananda's *Autobiography of a Yogi.*

When we reached the court again the early service was over and people were entering the windmill for the second service. It was to be conducted by Brother Saravananda. The ground floor of the windmill had been made into a chapel, with several rows of simple chairs. At the back a woman sat at a small organ, playing something that sounded more mystical than righteous or triumphant.

The chapel filled quickly and quietly. There were many young people. Before they sat they placed their hands flat together over their hearts and moved them up until the fingertips touched their foreheads. It is the Indian *pronam,* the swami had told me, a gesture of reverence meaning, "My soul bows to your soul."

Brother Saravananda spoke softly, but his voice was buoyant. He smiled throughout. He led a prayer to the Heavenly Father, the Divine Mother and the saints whose faces were before us, and then, instead of a hymn, the congregation sang one of the Cosmic Chants of Paramahansa Yogananda. Over and over they sang, the words falling and returning like the surf:

> *Thou art my life,*
> *Thou art my love,*
> *Thou art the sweetness*
> *Which I do seek . . .*

The chanting ended. The congregation fell silent. On and on it went, long beyond the "moment of silence" one is accustomed in the hasty rituals of Western worship. A minute passed . . . two . . . three . . .

In the silence, in the brightness of eyelids closed against sunlight, I began to feel an enlargement of my inner spaces. I sensed there were doors I had never opened, corridors I had never explored, but I have no training in yoga. I am prey to every distraction. I can not let loose of the outer world. I could hear the birds in the vines outside the windmill. I heard a swan honking across the lake. I heard the children's voices from the houseboat. I heard the whine of tires as some car came too fast down the palisade and careened around the Lake Shrine on its way to the beach.

I knew what they were saying inside the car:

"What's that?"

". . . a lake!"

". . . a windmill!"

". . . a temple!"

It is a lake, a windmill and a temple; it is a garden and a sanctuary, and to the hundreds of thousands who follow the teachings of Paramahansa Yogananda it is a shrine.

# El Mercado

*Pepsi Con Carnitas Es Superbo!*

In the deployment of great works of art and architecture, public and private, the Mexican-American communities east of the Los Angeles River, sometimes loosely called the *barrio,* have been notably neglected.

There is the educational plant of Cal State University, Los Angeles, off to one edge, but its burgeoning structures tower above the neighborhood like some utopian fantasy. The high schools are old, and half the youths drop out.

Below the college campus no office buildings rise high as they do on the west side of town, symbols of prosperity and faith in the American Way. Even the banks and federal loan companies, which are much given to the erection of higher and higher spires, have taken only a few cautious steps here and there above the barrio's two-story skyline.

The residents of the neighborhood, looking about for some works that seem to belong particularly to them, find little but the spray-paint graffiti on every wall and the sculptured angels in the vast cemeteries, whose scruffy lawns cover more ground by far than the barrio's parks. The freeways, with their soaring interchanges, are the most impressive structures in the barrio. But while they may be taken as contemporary works of art, they also make it possible for people from the other side of the river to drive through East Los Angeles without ever being *in* it.

143

Thus, most of us living in this once-Mexican land of Southern California are likely to get our ideas of Mexico and Mexicans from either Olvera Street or Tijuana, the one being as much American as Mexican, and the other being the worst of both.

In truth, the most nearly authentic Mexican atmosphere to be found in a public place anywhere this side of Sonora is at *El Mercado,* the marketplace, on East First Street—in Boyle Heights, just inside the Los Angeles City line.

*El Mercado* is all but unknown to Anglos and other Southern Californians who don't qualify for any of the several ethnic names given to the Spanish-speaking people who live on this side of the border. None of these names, by the way, including "Spanish-speaking people" and the more commonly heard "Mexican-American," are accepted as satisfactory by all; nor even by most. They are all inadequate to describe these people who are the largest Spanish-speaking community on the North American continent outside Mexico City.

*El Mercado* is a broad, yellow two-story structure on the north side of East First Street just beyond Indiana Avenue. For a stranger it is an adventure, driving out East First past *El Teatro Azteca* and bars named *El Dorado* and *Durango* and *El Leon de Oro,* and blocks of stores in old frame houses with stuccoed-over faces downstairs and old bay windows upstairs. The newest-looking building was the Hollenbeck police station, which was twenty years old, until they tore down the old Andrew Carnegie library in 1975 and built a new one. The biggest buildings are a mortuary and the red brick Home for the Aged run by the Little Sisters of the Poor.

You pass the Evergreen Cemetery, which is six blocks long, a vast dreary forest of graveyard statuary ending in the Los Angeles County potter's field with its crematory chimney, and *El Mercado* is just across Lorena Street to the east of the cemetery. It stands across First Street from a row of shabby bungalows left over from the 1920s. It stands like a palace in the neighborhood. It has no broad plate-glass facade like the usual supermarket. Its walls are made of large cement blocks, like adobes, painted yellow, with a second-story of arched windows and wrought-iron balconies.

Inside, *El Mercado* is a galleria. The lower floor is a market; not quite a supermarket, but a large store with the required cornucopia of foods, household wares and cosmetics; a bakery, a meat market and fish market, a big produce section, a flower shop and a shop of dolls and pinatas, and a cafe or two. The upper floor is a balcony running around all four sides of the building and looking down into the market. The roof is a skylight, so the entire building is lighted and warmed by the sun.

*El Mercado* is open seven days a week, nine to nine; but Saturday and Sunday are the festive days. It then becomes a meeting place, teeming and noisy with music and singing and warm with human beings eating and drinking, and when the police allow it, dancing. On a good Sunday there may be as many as ten thousand visitors.

There are many separate stalls doing business on the balcony, mostly cafes; also a barber shop and a jewelry shop and a Disco-Tek record shop that sells nothing but Mexican and Spanish records. But the big attraction upstairs is the food, the beer and the music. It is essential to add a fourth element—the language. Spanish is spoken here.

An Anglo-American like me, or any kind of American but a Mexican-American, must feel exactly like a tourist when he climbs the steps of *El Mercado* to this sunlit interior balcony on a Sunday afternoon, when the crowds begin to come in from church. Tables are set out all along the edge of the balcony and on the parquet floor at the front, above the street. The mariachi—eight or nine of them—stroll about in their costumes with silver down the legs, cornets and voices sobbing with joy and melancholy the beloved songs of land and manhood, love and betrayal, life and death.

The music is loud but not oppressive. It goes more to the heart than the ear. It bounces off the skylight and fills the marketplace below. It is a very part of the air, vibrant and alive. It is liquid and fiery as tequila, and gentle as an old man's tears. It is as stirring as "The Star-Spangled Banner" and as eloquent as the graffiti on the barrio walls.

On a Sunday afternoon the Mexicans come to *El Mercado en famille.* Many of them are not technically Mexican-Americans

145

at all, in a legal or cultural sense. Many have lived for years in the barrio, yet remained encapsulated within the old culture. Many have not been long on this side of the border. Their manners speak of the land and the pueblo, and old ways. The children are tamed and tethered, it seems, by the mere presence of the family head.

Though the music is loud the crowd is quiet, except for an occasional burst of song or cry of exuberance. The people talk softly when the song ends. They sit quietly at their tables, whole families; sometimes old people together, or young people together, and sometimes the young women are extraordinarily beautiful.

They eat the savory foods and drink the beer or the soda pop. There is much smiling and greeting of old friends. Sometimes in the late part of the afternoon, full of the mariachi and the beer, the older men grow misty-eyed, and wish to sing or dance or throw their arms about friends. There is nothing in sight to tell you this is Los Angeles, or any other place in English-speaking America, not even the sign that says *PEPSI CON MINI-PIZZA 50 CENTS.*

There are jukeboxes, for when the mariachi are silent, but nobody seems to mind if a jukebox is going at the same time as the mariachi. The mariachi play louder and their music sends out a wall, closing the jukebox music off, and the jukebox does the same. You won't find rock on the jukes, though; only things like *Asi Es La Vida,* or *El Rosario de Mi Madre.*

Ben Chayra has a small office at one corner of *El Mercado's* upstairs floor. He was born and grew up in the barrio, conceived the idea of *El Mercado,* got it financed and built against formidable odds, and now directs it as president of the founding El Mercado Investment Co.

He pointed to a large aerial photo on the wall of his office, showing *El Mercado* standing in a wasteland of cemetery and run-down houses.

"That's an overpriced ghetto," he said. "I was born two blocks from here. I went to Hollenbeck and Roosevelt and L.A. State. They yanked me in the army from here and spit me back in East L.A."

He smiled. His hair is thick and black and he wears black-rimmed glasses. His skin is dark and his teeth are very white when he smiles, which is often.

"My original idea was to bring to East Los Angeles a place where people could get together for recreation. Where could they go? This is a barren land."

He started with only the idea and $5,000 in "seed money" from an East Los Angeles businesswoman, Chiyoko Ikuta. He went to Mexico to study the famed *Mercado de San Juan de Dios* at Guadalajara, and decided to build something like it, though much smaller.

"We liked it, with all the people selling their wares and the fruits on display and the guitar music and impromptu dancing."

They set out to get financing, but nobody was interested, neither private nor institutional investors.

"This was in 1965. You just mentioned First Street, or East Los Angeles, and you couldn't get anybody to talk about a loan."

Finally they turned to the Small Business Administration which, much to their surprise, agreed to finance the project if they would sell shares and raise twenty percent of the cost.

"We did it. We sold $263,000 in shares—ninety percent of it to people living right in the area. I don't know how we did it. I don't think we could ever do it again."

The SBA came through with the rest of the money, more than $800,000, and *El Mercado* was built by Art Chayra, Ben's brother. It opened in April, 1968.

"The day we opened one old lady came to me and kissed my hand," he said, "and Father Robert blessed all the stalls—even the liquor store.

"This is a place where people love to come. Nobody down-grades them, looks down at them like what-are-you-doing-here? I still feel like that sometimes when I go over on the west side. I get a twinge. This is their place. This is their home. I like to think we have provided an oasis in the ghetto."

*El Mercado* makes no deliberate appeal to visitors from outside the Mexican community.

"We don't push tourism. It's not profitable. We don't have the room. Anyway, most of them are afraid of East Los Angeles on account of the militants. And they can't eat the food. You ever tried *trampito?* Pig snouts?"

He smiled. He was putting me on, but not entirely. He took me downstairs to a little cafe off to one side of the market. We looked into kettles of simmering *tripas de leche, cachetes, pouche* and snouts.

"You Americans," Chayra said, laughing at me, "are too fastidious."

Back upstairs on the balcony I felt more at home. The signs were Spanish, but the dishes were familiar. Carne-asada, milanesa, barbacoa, steak picado, the usual enchiladas and tamales and gorditas; and there was an especially reassuring sound to a sign that read *PEPSI CON CARNITAS ES SUPERBO!*

Each stand is tended by three or four people, most of whom seem to speak little or no English, but it is easy enough to order from the dishes listed on the signs or to point to what you want in the simmering trays. Whatever the ingredients, there is an aroma that would move the most "fastidious American" to surrender.

I ordered gorditas, which are fat tortillas deep fried and split and stuffed with beans, meat, lettuce and guacamole, and sat down to them at a table with a bottle of *limon.* Mexican soda pop, I have found, is the best.

From the table I could look down into the market at a brilliant mosaic created by the arrangements of watermelons and oranges and lemons and peppers and other colorful fruits and vegetables in the produce stands below.

The balcony was full of life. The tables were crowded. People walked around on promenade. Shoeshine boys plied their trade. Girls waited on tables reserved for patrons of stalls called *El Gallo* and *La Fiesta.* Across the table a young man who was drinking beer slowly from a paper cup wished me a *buenos dias* and began to tell me about *El Mercado* in English that was soft and musical.

"Most of the Mexicans," he said, "we miss our lands. Our customs. Our food. It makes you feel at home here. Especially the music, which is very important."

He listened to the mariachi.

"The music to which your are listening," he went on, "the

148

name is *Peregrina*. It was written by a Mexican singer who was in the south part of Mexico, where the Chichin Itza ruins are, you know? And there was an American girl, I think she was a journalist. She went there and this guy falls very much in love with her, and he's telling her—"

He listened closely again, to get the words. The song ended.

"Most of our songs in Mexico," the young man said, "they have some message. We are singing about nature, the beauty of our land, or of a woman who doesn't love a man . . ."

The mariachi began again and the young man listened until he knew the song and then began to sing. It was a song full of *amors* and *corazons* and it sounded sad. The young man smiled but his eyes were misty.

Suddenly I had that feeling of luck and warmth, almost elation, that feeling you have when you are alone in a foreign land and unexpectedly you make a friend.

I called a girl to the table.

*"Una cerveza por mi amigo,"* I told her, "and bring me another *limon."*

# Descanso Gardens

*For heaven's sake keep your eyes
peeled for a downy woodpecker!*

In recent years the Jack Smith Bird Walk at Descanso Gardens (on the second Sunday of December) has become one of the less well-known annual events on the Southern California scene.

This modest institution was launched as a joke, I suspect, by Charles Bernstein, then president of the San Fernando Valley Audubon Society, in honor of my being the only person ever to have seen a common grackle in the Los Angeles area. I am not unaware, of course, that neither Bernstein nor any other member of the Audubon ever believed my story, even though a few months later I saw a *second* grackle in almost exactly the same place—my back yard—this time walking headfirst down a tree trunk.

But any excuse for a bird walk is good enough, and at least Bernstein's little joke introduced me to the pleasures of birding at Descanso Gardens. People who go on bird walks are thought quaint, if not daft, I'm afraid; but I found that a bird walk wakes you up, turns you on, and does more for the spirit than most sermons I've heard on Sunday mornings.

It was a fine morning, the Sunday of the first walk; the kind of sharp, clear, winter day that keeps Midwesterners from going home. The walk was to start at eight o'clock. I made some coffee and dressed in birding clothes and set out over the Pasadena Freeway. Early on a bright Sunday the Pasadena Freeway can be a pleasant thoroughfare, winding up the Arroyo Seco past half a dozen pretty parks of sycamore and eucalyptus and rising toward the mountains. There are so few cars it seems bucolic.

I took Orange Grove Avenue, past the old mansions and new apartments, and dropped down into the arroyo again, skirting the Rose Bowl and Brookside Golf Course, where other early risers were already out on the fairways at their own quaint pastime.

I climbed to Linda Vista, a street like a country lane, and followed it to Devil's Gate Dam and then over Berkshire and Descanso, through miles of wooded estates in the San Rafael Hills, to the gate of Descanso Gardens. The drive alone had been worth getting up for. It was as if I had been shown an older and more tranquil Los Angeles, one that had been put away, like a fragile antique, and brought out only on special occasions.

There were a dozen cars near the Descanso gate and twenty or thirty people were gathered casually around a man in tan fatigues. He had a pair of binoculars hanging from his neck and a bird book and was talking to the group.

"I would like the group to stay together as much as possible. Talk all you want but not too loud, or you'll scare the birds. My wife, Elsie, will keep the bird list. So whenever you see a bird, call it out."

He was Bernstein. I introduced myself. He pumped my hand.

"Good! Good! I didn't think you'd come."

I assured him it was my custom to show up at all bird walks that were dedicated to me. He introduced me to the group.

"Mr. Smith is the man," he said, "who claims he saw a grackle going headfirst down a tree, although, as we know, this feat is accomplished only by the white-breasted nuthatch."

I asked them how they could be sure a grackle mightn't go down a tree headfirst when nobody was looking, but at that moment a little gray woman in a purple tweed suit laid a hand on my arm.

"There," she said calmly, "in that sycamore."

"Where?" said Bernstein. He looked along her arm to the top of the tree. He raised his glasses.

*"Is it?"* he asked himself. "Yes! It is! Glossy black, with a crest on his head. *Phainopepla.* Beautiful. We *never* see him here."

Everyone peered up at *phainopepla.*

"That's the bird our little publication is named for," said

Bernstein. "Well! This is a very auspicious beginning. Are we ready?"

General readiness was expressed. Bernstein put his hands on the shoulders of a boy who was toting a scope mounted on a tripod. He turned him in the direction of the walk and pushed him off.

"Forward!"

We set off through the gate, a ragtag company of birders, all ages, from a pair of small twin girls to a bearded old man who brought up the rear with a milking stool on which he now and then would sit a spell. Some were equipped with bird books and binoculars and scopes. Others were just out for the walk, birds or no birds.

A bird walk, I soon found out, is not as disciplined as an infantry patrol. There is a good deal of straggling and independence of effort. It is something of an ambulatory social, but conversations tend to be aborted by sudden shouted claims of bird sightings, some of them imaginary.

We turned into the rose gardens, where eight thousand bushes are set out in chronological order. They are said to trace the history of the rose from the time of Christ to the present.

I fell in beside Bernstein. He said he was a court reporter by occupation, but had been birding eight years, partly for fun, partly because of his concern for the conservation of wildlife. He led the Descanso bird walk every second Sunday rain or shine.

"I've come down here when it was just pouring, and I'm thinking, I hope nobody shows up, and darned if two or three guys aren't here with rain gear and all, and they say 'Come on Chuck,' and out we go."

"Up in that tree," someone said. "A mockingbird."

A mockingbird flew out of a tall live oak and did a stunt or two above us, then flew back, as if performing before a panel of judges in the Olympic Games.

"So we add a mockingbird to our list," said Bernstein. Elsie Bernstein wrote it in her notebook.

The air was nippy. We hurried along through the shady patches and idled in the sun. The gardens open daily at 8 a.m., but there were few other visitors out so early. It seemed to me

153

the best time of all. Descanso was a wilderness just quickening to life. In the soft morning sunlight everything seemed magnified, and the sounds of the birds and mammals were magnified in the stillness.

Descanso Gardens is best known for its flowers, especially the one hundred thousand specimens of camellia, a forest of six hundred varieties from China, Japan, England and the American South. Some grow twenty to thirty feet tall in the natural leaf mold soil and filtered light of the old live oaks. It is the largest outdoor camellia planting in the world. Besides the camellias and the roses, there are extensive plantings of lilacs, irises, azaleas, orchids, rhododendrons, daffodils and other annuals and perennials. So somewhere Descanso is always in bloom, every month of the year.

What gives the gardens their rare fascination, though, is the natural setting, the oaks and sycamores and chaparral, the pond and stream fed by the watershed and the wildlife that were there in the 1930s when Manchester Boddy bought the land, and centuries before that.

There is enchantment in the subtle blending of the cultivated with the native, a suggestion that nature can be enhanced by one touch of man, if he isn't heavy-handed. There is an idealism in the concept of Descanso that reflects the nature of Manchester Boddy, a romantic idealist who amiably sought to apply his gifts as an encyclopaedia salesman to the improvement of nature and man, as well as himself. As instruments of these aims, Boddy purchased the old Verdugo ranch with its precious oaks, and also the Los Angeles *Daily News,* with its image of Democratic liberalism, and set about with dreamy vigor to perfect the world, which then being in the throes of the Great Depression was certainly in need of it.

After the war, to get more leverage on this noble task, Boddy ran for the U.S. Senate, but lost in the primary to Helen Gahagan Douglas, who was even more liberal than he was, and who in turn lost to a very aggressive young Republican conservative named Richard Nixon. Jostled by this setback and others, Boddy soon enough sold his Eden to the county for $1,160,000 and likewise sold his newspaper, and retired to the hinterlands of San Diego County, where he died at seventy-five, having achieved at least a kind of personal utopia. He had done well enough for a young man who came to town with fifty-five dollars in his pockets.

The boy with the tripod—his name seemed to be Eric—had spotted a movement in the chaparral above the roses and Bernstein was looking for it in his glasses.

"Ground squirrel," he said in a moment, "and a red-shafted flicker. See the white patch? It's the mark of the flicker."

That flash of flicker in the bush reminded Bernstein of John Kiernan, the late New York journalist and naturalist.

"He writes in his book on birds, and I think of it every time I hear a flicker, about being cooped up in the office all winter long on the thirty-second floor of some building in New York City, writing his column, and suddenly he hears this *eey eey* and looks out, and here in these stone canyons is a red-shafted flicker, and suddenly his whole spirit is free. He lived another year."

We came to the bird observation house, a screened-in shelter looking out over Descanso's great pond. It was built several years ago by the Audubon Society and the Descanso Gardens Guild as a place where children might watch birds feeding. Ducks and other waterfowl sailed serenely over the pond. Mrs. Bernstein's list grew quickly. Mallard. American coot. Pekin duck.

"Do we have a canvasback? Yes, we do. The one with the reddish head. And here's your ring-necked duck, close in here."

"There's something in that dried brown tree, on the other side of the pond," an elderly man said quietly in my ear. "To the left, over there."

I saw it myself, a gray shape, big as a large squirrel, perched motionless in the tree. It looked like a hawk.

"It's a hawk, all right," said our leader, squinting through a scope. "He's either a Cooper's or a sharp-shinned. If he has a rounded tail he's a Cooper's. Yes. Cooper's hawk."

There was something ominous about the hawk, sitting still as death across the pond in his tree, thinking predatory thoughts.

"That's why you don't see many birds at the feeders. They keep down as long as he's around."

The feeders were set up around the house—nectar in upended bottles for the hummingbirds and varieties of seed and scratch for the larger species. A hummer, ruby-throated, suspended in mid-air inside the blur of its wings, appeared at one of the founts, feeding as we held our breaths. A beige bird with a black head dropped from a tree to the hen scratch.

"Oregon junco," said Bernstein. "He looks like a bird that somebody picked up by the tail and dipped headfirst in black paint."

We left the shelter and straggled along the walk through the California native plants garden. Here are the trees and shrubs that prospered in this arid gulch eons before it ever saw a camellia or a rose. Toyon. Ironwood. Manzanita. Coyote bush. Maybe it's because I'm a native, but I prefer these scrubby plants to the more voluptuous flowers. They're small and tough, with gnarled stringy branches and tiny leaves. The Spaniards called them *chaparro,* meaning short or small, and from this our chaparral has come.

We walked on among pines, cedars, junipers, elders, maples and redwoods. The air was scented and the birding was good. The sightings came so fast that Mrs. Bernstein was hard put to keep up.

Someone saw a wrentit, which prompted much excitement.

"It's a very small bird," the woman in purple told me, "and you hardly ever see it. You only hear its sound. It's like a disembodied voice. A bouncing ball sound. Pip . . . pip . . . pip . . . pip pip pip pippippippip."

"There, in that bush!" shouted Bernstein, more excited than I'd heard him. "The wrentit! There he goes! Oh, I knew he wouldn't stay."

The wrentit vanished. "*Very* rarely see him," Bernstein said. "You know what he sounds like? A popcorn machine. Pop . . . pop . . . pop . . pop poppop."

A flight of robins winged over us and landed on a grassy patch.

"Watch," said Bernstein. "That's one of the characteristics of robins. They take a few steps, stop and cock their heads. There's a big controversy—"

"I have a brown towhee in the scope—next to the robins."

"O.K. Brown towhee . . . so a controversy arose. When the robin stops and cocks his head, is he *listening* for earthworms or is he *looking* for earthworms? Because his vision is one-sided, you know. They did some experiments and they're still not at all positive."

"Maybe," someone suggested, "he's only trying to shake some water out of his ear."

"There! Mourning doves. On the power tower."

"Quail over there in the bush."

"That's your California quail—it is not your Gambel's quail that we see out in the desert with the big black spots and not the mountain quail with the topknot going straight—"

"Cedar waxwings! A whole flock!"

The waxwings whirled and vanished in the oak forest.

"If you'll all be quiet—we're listening to a California thrasher."

"Plain titmouse."

"Yes! A beauty!"

"In that bush, Eric. Let's get the scope on it. I see quite a bit of movement in there. Let's see. Oh—you've got a warbler there."

"Audubon's warblers—a whole flight of them."

"One year," Bernstein was telling me as we pushed on, "I heard a quail up here in this scrub oak and I told the group to wait—(there's something on the fence over there . . . scrub jay)—I told them to wait while I went to flush the quail out. I got up there—(ah, that's a lesser goldfinch)—I got up there and walked into a coyote—eyeball to eyeball. I was scared to move—"

"Pardon me," I said, "but I wonder if that isn't your grackle over there in that bare tree, two o'clock high."

Bernstein put his glasses up.

"By George!" I said. "It's going down the trunk."

He dropped his glasses. "That's your gray ground squirrel. They do it all the time."

We came to a shelter called the Redwood Rest and Bernstein called a halt. It was on to eleven o'clock.

"O.K. Let's see what birds we've listed." Mrs. Bernstein handed him her list. "Now. White-crowned sparrow, red-shafted flicker, California thrush, mourning dove, Audubon's warbler, lesser goldfinch, Oregon junco, Anna's hummingbird, robin,

157

house finch, scrub jay, canvasback, Cooper's hawk, cedar wax-
wing, pied-billed grebe, brown towhee, plain titmouse, wrentit,
mockingbird, American coot, Pekin duck and California quail."

The bird walk was over.

I felt enriched, as one is supposed to feel after one of those
"sensitivity sessions" up at Esalen. The idea is to keep your eyes
and ears and nerve ends open.

"As you walk back through the gardens," Bernstein admon-
ished in farewell, "look at the beauty of all these things, and
for heaven's sake keep your eyes peeled for a downy woodpecker."

I walked back through the oak forest. A camellia show was
going on under the trees. The specimens were set out on long
tables, a spectacular variety of opulence and color.

After the bird walk I was too famished to be detained by
mere beauty. I found the Japanese teahouse and sat outside at
a table over a pool. A girl in a blue kimono brought me hot
tea and cookies. The teahouse sits on an island above a garden
of pools, rocks and waterfalls, in a setting of Japanese black
pines, red maple and bamboo.

Like most of the improvements at Descanso, it is the fruit
of the indefatigable Descanso Gardens Guild, a volunteer non-
profit group, many of its members being women of the neighborhood. By their vigilance and vigor Descanso was rescued from
sale and subdivision.

For a moment, looking out over the garden toward the towering oaks, tranquilized by the hot tea and the sound of the waterfall, I had the illusion that there was no such thing as overcrowd-
ing and pollution and madness in the world. Manchester Boddy
had been right after all. We could all live in sweet harmony.

I drove home feeling magnified. There is more to a bird walk
than exercise. From now on, I would always have an eye peeled
for the wrentit and the downy woodpecker.

# Lion Country Safari

*In a natural situation, women's liberation is not natural.*

The sign, *CONVERTIBLES MUST BE EXCHANGED AT HERTZ*, caught my eye on the approach to Lion Country Safari's entrance, and I realized that the lions I was about to encounter would be real, and separated from me only by a thin automobile.

It happened that I was driving a convertible at that time, a species of car that is vanishing like the addax, and its plastic top would give me no more protection from the lion's tooth and claw than the zebra's hide gives him.

There were other warnings. *PERSONS ENTERING WILDLIFE AREAS DO SO AT THEIR OWN RISK . . . KEEP DOORS LOCKED, WINDOWS UP.*

The admonition to keep doors locked and windows up is repeated by the guard at the gate, and again by signs inside and on the recorded tour-guide tape. *"Don't open your windows even slightly,"* warns the voice on the tape. *"With lions, even an inch can be too much."*

I parked my convertible outside the gates. For my first safari, I had arranged to be escorted by Walter (Pat) Quinn, zoological director and former chief game warden of Lion Country Safari, the five hundred-acre African wildlife preserve in southern Orange County.

Quinn turned out to be a Tennessean with the brawny, sunburned look of the white hunter in his safari khakis. He said we'd go in his car, a hardtop equipped with two-way radio to

159

keep him in contact with his game wardens and headquarters. Before we set out he talked over the radio to his veterinary center. He sounded concerned, like a father asking about a sick child.

"You're right," he said. "It better come out. Go ahead. Let me know how it goes."

It was an eland, he said, with an infected eye. Another animal had gouged it with a horn.

"It's been festering. It's not responding to medication, so we're going to have to take it out. We've got him immobilized."

It was an eland this time, not a man, but it made me think of Hemingway's story, *The Snows of Kilimanjaro*, about the writer whose mind flashed back through his life, remembering the war and the things he had done and the things he has left unwritten as he lies on the slopes of Kilimanjaro, dying of a gangrenous leg. It had been a bad movie with Ava Gardner and Gregory Peck.

We were no sooner through the gate than the road was blocked by an ostrich. He stood in front of the car, giving no ground until we inched to a stop. Then he glared at us, like some cranky old gatekeeper demanding our credentials. We didn't blow the horn. We didn't try to drive around him. We awaited his pleasure. It was obvious that we had already abandoned our human prerogative, our insistence on sovereignty. We now deferred to the brutes whose preserve we had invaded.

The ostrich slowly straightened his neck. Up and up it went, like a periscope, with the head at the top, revolving to scan the horizon. Finding us at last of no interest, the ostrich sashayed off, reminding me of a ballet dancer walking offstage in her tutu.

We were soon among zebras and antelopes, all the graceful creatures with the cloven hooves and the quaint and lovely names. Elands and impalas, gazelles and oryxes, gemsboks, hartebeests, topis and brindled gnus. It was like the travel films we saw as children, films of the African veld so teeming with animals we never quite believed them, and thought it must have all been done with props out at MGM.

We came to a group of zebras feeding from a large hollowed-out log. Ostriches were pecking in the earth like barnyard chick-

ens. Antelope stood about. Others, familiar from zoos and picture books, stood on hillocks, outlined against the sky, or foraged
at a water hole.

"Impala," Quinn said, pointing toward a handsome antelope
with black stripes on his rump. "That's the one that does the
bounding . . . There's a pair of sable antelope up on that hill.
Beautiful. That's a rare mountain zebra over there. She's pregnant. There's a pregnant oryx up there."

It was the scimitar oryx, with its delicately curved horns, that
is thought to have been the unicorn of ancient fable. For sometimes, when he stands exactly right, the two horns are seen as
one.

We slowed to watch an ostrich who seemed to be up to something ritualistic. He was down on his elbows, waving his wings,
one at a time, like a signalman trying to stop a train. Another
ostrich stood off watching.

"He's doing his mating dance," said Quinn.

The ostrich rocked slowly from side to side in the dirt, first
stretching one great wing, then folding it in and stretching out
the other. At last the other ostrich turned and ambled off, as
if bored.

"She wasn't interested?" I asked.

"Oh, that was another male," said Quinn. "This one's just
hoping to catch a female's eye."

Up on a hillock at the top of a bony tree I saw a vulture,
enormous and magnificently ugly, like the ones that waited for
Hemingway's hero to die. The sky was a rare blue, and in the
distance the mantled peak of Baldy gleamed as white as the
snows of Kilimanjaro in the story. Sometime, I thought, I would
write a story called *The Snows of Baldy*, with all my flashbacks
in it . . .

*It was one of the things he was going to write and never did, the
time in boot camp in the war when he was in the marines and he ran
out of the barracks for the rifle inspection in the cold. The drill inspector
had taken his rifle and held it up in the dawn light with the muzzle
to his eye like a man who was going to kill himself and said, "There's
dust in your rifle, private," and flung the rifle back into his cold hands
and told him, "You sleep with that tonight and bring it to me in the
morning and I want it warm . . ."*

161

A troop of zebra trotted alongside the car. There seemed to be three mares with several youngsters and another mare waddling along behind.

"That one at the rear," said Quinn, "she's heavily pregnant."

It was a refrain. All through the preserve, except in cheetah country, there was evidence that the natural cycles of the wild had reasserted themselves here in this fenced-off veld in Southern California. These exotic immigrants had found a life-style in this subtle and benign captivity. "We've had ninety lions born here," said Quinn.

We passed under a tower up on stilts, from which a warden in a broad-brimmed hat gazed out over the terrain. We were in lion territory. To the visitor driving through, there seems to be no separation of one animal area from another. The steel fences separating such predators as lions and cheetahs from the vulnerable ruminants are hidden in gulches, not easily seen from the road.

The concealment of fences, the absence of billboards and construction, the casual presence of wildlife on every side, the flocks of birds sailing the lagoons and wheeling in the skies—all contribute to the feeling that one is indeed in wild country. It is something more than pure illusion.

Breeding and conservation of endangered species is one function of Lion Country Safari. Quinn himself, a fervent conservationist, believes that man is destroying the wild animals of the earth, not by hunting but by ravishing their habitat, and that only man can save them. Animal management of the kind practiced at Lion Country Safari, he thinks, is one way.

Just inside the lion section gate a sign reminds you *WINDOWS MUST BE CLOSED. THESE ANIMALS ARE WILD.*

The first lion we saw was a cub, an appealing little fellow, like all kittens. He was stalking a blackbird, exactly the way a house cat stalks a bird on a lawn, and with no more luck.

"He's learning to hunt," Quinn said. "The mothers teach them how to hunt. They act like wild lions here in every respect, except for the killing of the food. We provide the food."

We pulled up at a traffic jam. Three cars ahead of us were holding up to let a lion cross the road. There was also a yellow school bus with forty faces pressed against its windows.

The lion was taking his time, and changing his mind. Her mind. It was a lioness. She was not alone. There were nine lions sitting in a row on a hillock beside the road. They watched with the patient interest of cats. Then there was not only one lion in the road but three, and a jeep appeared, striped like a zebra and driven by a warden.

The warden used the jeep gently to nudge the lions off the road. Back and forth he worked, getting nowhere. He moved one lion and backed up to aim at another, only to see the first one come back and collapse in the road again like a house cat on a rug.

I saw that lions were indeed like house cats; stubborn and exasperating, and oblivious of man's dominion. They all looked placid and self-satisfied, and I had an idea that all the warnings were part of the show. If I got out of the car and walked out among the lions they would either rub up against my leg or ignore me.

"What would happen," I asked Quinn, "if I got out of the car and walked out there?"

"You'd be in trouble. You'd get killed. You'd be dead. They'd eat you up. I guarantee it. The idea that lions won't attack a man is hogwash. These animals will kill the hell out of you. There wouldn't be anything left to find but a shoe."

Beyond the ravine in which the fence was concealed, a herd of zebra grazed. There were antelope among them and others— elands, wildebeest and a pair of great kudo—on the slopes against the foothills. All were aware of the lions, and the lions were aware of them, but both knew they were separated by the fence. Nonetheless, there was a tension.

"It's a visual stimulus," Quinn said. "The lions look at them. They stalk and creep around, but the fence stops them. The zebra and the antelope, they can see and hear the lions. It keeps the pressure on them, and that's a stimulus. They breed better."

We came to a pond with an island on which, among sticks and rocks, we saw a family of chimpanzees. There were geese and coots on the pond. Storks waded, fishing. Thick flights of small birds wheeled.

Besides providing a new home for exotic animals and birds,

Lion Country Safari has also been discovered by dozens of local species. Squirrels, bobcats, coyotes have found their niches. For birds of prey it's easy pickings. The trees are full of hawks and owls and vultures. To the natural attractions, the management has added sixty thousand trees and plants.

A giraffe walked by my window, and I realized we must have left lion territory for the time being. I watched the articulation of his knees and elbows, the ripple of his muscles beneath the beautiful reticulated hide. Odd, how often the giraffe is used as a metaphor of human awkwardness. In truth he is a most graceful beast.

A string of zebra crossed the road in front of us, like a mule train in striped pajamas. They waded into a pond, scattering hunchback storks and flamingos and a cloud of blackbirds in a bone-bare sycamore tree.

We passed a herd of antelopes that hardly seemed to see us as our car moved close.

"A car's a piece of rolling metal, that's all," Quinn said. "It's no threat. There's no blood in it. Now let me show you something. See how placid they are? Now watch."

He stopped the car and quietly opened the door and stood out in the road, waving an arm. The antelope bolted.

"You see? They're wild. When they see the human silhouette—they go."

There was a rhino by the road. He was nibbling at the grass with an enormous wide mouth, like an earth scoop. Two others stood nearby.

"That's Dutch," he said. "Those two females there, they've been bred by Dutch. We hope they're pregnant."

One of the females swung her head around to look at us. Quinn rolled his window down (the head man's privilege) and called out to her with affection.

"Notchear! Gonna gitcha, old girl! Gonna gitcha! Hi, pretty girl!"

Notchear trotted on by and he rolled the window up. "She was the dominant animal in the rhino group until Dutch came in. She went around with her tail curled. It's a symbol, like if you're a general of the army you have five stars. The dominant rhino has a tail curl. Then Dutch came along. In two days he sorted out old Notchear and now she's in her proper place. In a natural situation, women's liberation is not natural."

I wondered how she got the name Notchear.

"Didn't you see that notch in her ear? We've got an eland, born in the park, goes around licking windshields all the time. We call him Windex."

A train of elephants came toward us, a big one in front.

"It's a bull elephant leading the herd?" I asked.

"Nope that's Nyla. A cow. Elephants are a matriarchy."

He shouted at the elephant in the lead as the string crossed the road in front of the car. "Hi, Nyla! Come here, Nyla!"

Nyla snubbed him, as if she'd heard his remark about women's liberation.

Though the lion breeds at Lion Country Safari, as do the addax and the oryx and the kudu, the cheetah does not. The preserve has the largest colony of cheetah outside Africa, it is said, and like the lions they are well fed and healthy. But something is wrong.

They are awesome in their grace and beauty. There is a tautness about them, as if they had not accepted their captivity, or given up their wildness. They are the swiftest of animals afoot, capable perhaps of seventy miles an hour in the short chase, quite fast enough to catch and kill the fastest antelope. But there are the fences, and there is no hunger.

Perhaps in the chain of needs and impulses there is something missing. With no hunger there is no need to hunt. With no need to hunt there is no need to survive. But if that is the secret of the cheetah, why is the lion happy and prolific?

"We don't know," said Quinn. "We've had no luck. Each park has a different program. But until we've had some success we won't know whether it's psychological, nutritional, social or what."

A pair of Marine Corps jets from nearby El Toro drew two dark lines across the sky; deadlier than any other birds of prey.

*He had come back from Iwo Jima on an LST and there was liberty in Honolulu in the spring. The gin was bad and he had fallen out of a window of the Moana Hotel onto Waikiki Beach in the moonlight and cut his chin very badly and the Japanese lady who shaved him in*

165

*the morning had to keep the razor away from the wound and there was always the chance of gangrene, but he lived and in a while the war was over and he got a letter from Harry Truman thanking him for every-thing . . .*

We pulled up into the recreational center, a compound where after the safari you can get a hot meal and go for the jungle boat ride and shop for such curios as genuine African wood carvings and posters of lions.

Pat Quinn got his medical center on the radio and asked how the operation went on the ailing eland.

"Good. Good," he said, obviously relieved.

"The eland's all right," he told me. "He's up and walking around and he's going to be all right."

And one of these days, I bet, they'll call him One-Eye.

# The Swap Meet

*I lingered over a fringed and beaded flapper dress, trying to put Joan Crawford in it.*

My wife fancies old pewter, which was my excuse for going out to the Rose Bowl swap meet and flea market one Sunday morning. But any excuse will do. There's something for everybody at a swap meet, whatever your taste, age or purse.

"I don't think there's a thing in this whole place I want," I overheard a woman saying as we filed through the turnstile into that teeming open-air bazaar that appears like a mirage every second Sunday of the month, rain or shine, around the oval perimeter of the Rose Bowl. My guess is that she soon changed her mind, unless she was immune to the appeal of old oaken iceboxes, cloche hats and flapper dresses, 1926 copies of *Delineator* magazine, phonograph records of Enrico Caruso singing *Over There* in French and English, and the sheet music to *The Pagan Love Song.*

When you're looking for something in particular, as I was, your eye tends to see over tables full of other treasures, going straight to the desired object. I hadn't been in the market three minutes when I saw the pewter mug on a table among a hundred pieces of Depression Glass and vintage dime store bric-a-brac. The table was tended by a man and woman sitting in the open door of a Volkswagen van. I picked up the mug and turned it in my hands. I have no expertise on pewter, but I can see dents and scratches as well as the next man. This mug was a wreck. It had evidently led a hard, brief life. The engraved legend was still legible:

> FIRST ANNUAL
> ISTHMUS RACE
> ELECTRA ASS'N.
> 1965
> FIRST PLACE
> SUE WILSON

What isthmus? I wondered. Who was Sue Wilson? Did she swim, or drive a motorboat across the isthmus? Or paddle a kayak?

"How much is the mug?" I asked.

"Three dollars," the woman said, smiling as if she felt a bit guilty.

I had heard that one is expected to haggle at swap meets. It's part of the fun. But I've never had any knack for haggling. It always makes me feel as if I'm insulting an honest merchant by implying he's a thief.

"Would you set it aside for me?" I asked.

"I'd be happy," the woman said. I gave her three dollars and she dropped the mug in a paper sack and put it in the van.

"My name's Smith," I said, wanting to make sure that she'd remember.

"Oh, we'll remember you," she said, smiling again.

I moved on in the stream of people, feeling I had got a good start on the day.

The shops were packed solidly around the bowl, with a teeming passageway between the two rows, as in the streets of Marrakesh. The merchants operate mostly out of battered vans or station wagons or old cars, some of a vintage as old as their wares. Their merchandise is set out on bridge tables or spread out over the asphalt or on plastic sheets or bedspreads and blankets. All meld into one continuous market.

I stopped to look down on a shop set out on a bedspread. Its wares had the look of the 1920s or '30s, and were of a variety that seemed to defy category or appraisal. I couldn't identify every article, but I recognized a pepper grinder, a kerosene lamp, a copper pan, a waffle iron, a horse collar, a set of scales, a bronzed baby shoe, a teapot, and an eagle radiator ornament.

I was struck by nostalgia. It was exactly the kind of harvest I might have hauled home in my wagon as a boy, at the end of an especially fruitful day of scavenging in the alleys of our neighborhood. Now, in the 1970s, where had all these wonders come from?

That's a mystery of the swap meets. Since the 1950s the swap meet in its several forms has been a growing phenomenon in Southern California, drawing tens of thousands every weekend to rented stadiums, fairgrounds and drive-in theaters. In two decades, oceans of things once thought of as junk have been salvaged and sold, and yet the supply is undiminished.

For a region that has so brief a history, that is traditionally bare of attics and basements, Los Angeles seems to have a bottomless capacity for yielding up the minor treasures, the not-quite antiques, the glorified *junque* whose main value is in its power to evoke the recent past.

After making sure the teapot wasn't pewter, I walked on, stopping to consider half a dozen articles set out on a small plastic square—a pearl bracelet, a toy iron, a doll, a salt shaker, a glass flower frog and a blue wooden spinning top. That was the entire inventory. Fifty cents apiece.

The face of W. C. Fields caught my eye at the next place. It was a cardboard cutout, stuck at the top of a clothes rack on which was displayed a purple velvet dress from the Jazz Age. An old fox fur hung from the neck. There was also a raccoon coat hanging on a rack under the face of Oliver Hardy. The velvet dress and the raccoon coat were on display among several pieces of furniture, including a pedal-operated Singer sewing machine and a rude chest of drawers.

"That's old, old," the seller said, seeing my interest in the chest. "The Mormons made it for a house in San Bernardino."

Farther on I thumbed through a pile of old sheet music on a long table covered with music and old magazines. A woman was going through a pile of music next to me and a man was searching a pile on the other side of the table.

"You don't see *I'm Forever Blowing Bubbles,* do you?" the woman asked.

The man began to sing: " 'I'm dreaming dreams, I'm blowing schemes' . . . I know all the words," he said.

169

"But I want to *play* it," the woman said, "and I can't play by ear. It was my mother's favorite."

One after another the old titles came up in the pile of tattered music. *Oh, How I Miss You Tonight* ... *How Many Hearts Have You Broken* (With Those Great Big Beautiful Eyes) ... *I Ain't Got Nobody and I Don't Want Nobody But You* ... *The Pagan Love Song.*

Nostalgia swept through me again. *The Pagan Love Song.* I'd heard it first at a Saturday matinee. There was Ramon Novarro's face on the cover, just like in the movie. I could still remember the words.

*Come with me where moonbeams*
*Light Tahitian skies ...*

"Oh," the woman said. "*You* know the words to *that* one."

"Yes," I said. "It was *my* mother's favorite."

A man operating out of a large van was dealing in large objects. He had an oak icebox, a Grafonola phonograph, a Singer sewing machine with pedals, a mirror in a carved wood frame from the 1920s, and a nickel-plated barber's chair with brown leather upholstering. A young man with long hair and a beard was looking at the icebox with a young woman. "That would make a good stereo cabinet," he said.

She nodded. "Yes. It's beautiful."

Two women stopped to look at the icebox. "My golly Ned," said one. "I remember when I was seven years old, we had one of those. The horse-drawn ice man used to come around. My golly Ned!"

"How much is that barber chair?" a man asked the seller.

"That's two hundred and twenty dollars. It was made in 1900. That's all nickel-plating."

"Beautiful," the man said.

"How old is that Singer?" a woman asked.

The seller shrugged. "You can't be sure."

"Sixty years old, at least," a man said. "I'll guarantee it."

I looked into the Grafonola. It was oak, and priced at seventy-five dollars. There was a Ray Noble record on the turntable. *I'll Dance at Your Wedding.*

What I really had my eye on, though, was the mirror. It was just what I needed to hang over the new bar I was building for the house. It was one of those three-panel mirrors with an ornate carved frame; the kind people used to have on the wall opposite the Maxfield Parrish print. It was marked twenty-five dollars. I wondered if I could get it for twenty.

"I notice lots of young people looking here," I said to the proprietor, avoiding the issue of the mirror. "What do they see in this stuff?"

"They're looking for something old," he said. "It's nostalgia. It's transferred from mom and pop to the kids. It's all part of the earth concept. The return to something simple. They're wearing old clothes and they're looking for old things to decorate their homes with."

I was about to ask him if he'd sell the mirror for twenty dollars, but a woman interrupted.

Do you have any napkin rings?" she asked.

"No," he said. "I don't think I have a napkin ring in the place."

Later I was looking at a glass case full of Nazi badges, emblems and other paraphernalia of the Third Reich when a small boy sidled up, peering into the case like a boy looking into a candy store window.

"Well," said the proprietor amiably. "What do you need today?" Evidently they'd done business before. The boy pointed a finger at a small stack of Nazi uniform emblems. They looked as if they might have been Luftwaffe eagles.

"How much are those?" the boy asked.

"They're two dollars each."

He thought it over, clutching some dollar bills in his fist. "Would you give me three for four dollars?"

The woman laughed. "All right." She drew three of the emblems from the case. "You know I sell good ones. Don't you buy any copies now."

I walked on, thinking about the boy's deal. He had got six dollars worth of Nazi emblems for four dollars. That was knocking a third off the marked price, wasn't it? If that kid could do it, why couldn't I?

I made my way back through the stream of shoppers to the place where I had seen the mirror, hoping someone hadn't bought it away from me. It was still there.

"What's the least you'll take for that mirror?" I asked the seller, trying to sound shrewd.

"Well, I couldn't let it go for less than twenty," he said.

Feeling slightly larcenous, I wrote him a check for twenty dollars and asked him to hold the mirror.

A woman in blue jeans, a purple University of Michigan sweat shirt and a black derby hat was tending a sea of old books and indescribable potpourri emptied from an ancient yellow school bus. I wondered not only how she had come upon such books, but how they had got published in the first place. There was a welter of inspirational titles at a dollar each: *Abide in Christ ... Three Minutes a Day ... In His Steps ... Education and the Higher Life... The Conquest of Consumption.*

She also had a wardrobe of incredible clothing laid out on the asphalt. Faded lace and velvet. Puff sleeves and ruffs. Pantaloons and buckles and feathered hats. I asked her where she had got them.

"There was this Shakespeare Club," she said, "they went out of business. Sold out. I bought it all. The whole wardrobe. I don't know anything about Shakespeare. Well, I know something about *Hamlet*. Everybody should know something about *Hamlet*. I don't know anything about this stuff except that there were some newspapers in the bottom of the box and they were dated 1928."

Besides inspiration, her books seemed to run to manuals on care of engines. *Instruction Manual for the Operation of Railroad Engines ... Austin A-40 Service Manual ... Dyke's Automobile and Gasoline Engines ... Chevrolet Passenger Car Shop Manual for 1949 Models ... Buick Wholesale Parts Guide 1954.*

"That's where I make it," the woman said. "With all these old car buffs around. They don't print these books anymore. Take steam. There's nothing current written about steam, is there?"

A Strauss waltz was emanating from a portable phonograph sitting on the asphalt by a stack of old records. "How much are your records?" I asked, thinking I might find an old Caruso.

"They're not for sale," she said. "I just like to play that stuff for atmosphere."

I stopped to look at some old toys, battered and rusted, set out on a table. A dump truck for a dollar fifty. An earth mover, ten dollars. A school bus with the faces of children painted in the windows, six dollars. A yellow cab. A good-looking cabinet caught my eye. I'm always looking for something I can use in my house in Mexico. There was a card taped to it with the words *JELLY SAFE.*

"That's pine," the seller said. "Real well made."

"What's a jelly safe?" I asked.

"Well, it's the same thing as a pie safe," she said, "except it's for jelly. A pie safe's for pies."

A large, elderly woman was sitting among memorabilia of the Roaring Twenties, picking through a box stuffed with faded dresses.

"I'm looking for lace," she explained. "You can't find real lace like this anymore. It's all nylon. I have this man out on Sunset Boulevard, he makes originals, you know? He pays good money for old lace."

Nearby a woman tended three or four tables and racks loaded with treasures from the Twenties. I lingered over a fringed and beaded flapper dress, trying to put Joan Crawford in it.

"Do you have any iron cows?" a woman asked the proprietor.

"Iron cows? I don't think so."

"How about porcelain eggs?" It was the woman, I realized, who had remembered having an icebox when she was seven years old.

"No. No porcelain eggs."

"Well, how about glass balls with snow inside?"

The proprietor rummaged through her trifles and came up with a glass ball, filled with specks of white. The customer looked into it, turning it slowly in her hands.

"Well, by golly Ned," she said.

"Look," her friend said. "Look at that old wicker sewing basket. My mother used to have one. Remember the tassels?"

The crowd was growing so thick it was hard to move through the street between the rows of shops. The sun was hot. I threaded my way back to the place where I had left the mirror and took possession. It was five feet long and not easy to handle in the crowd. I struggled back to the place where I had bought the pewter mug.

"Oh, there you are," the woman said, reaching into the van for the sack.

"I should have waited to buy that mug until I'd gone around once," I said. "I'll bet you'd have taken two dollars."

The woman looked up at the man and laughed. "Yes," she said, "I told my husband—that one's innocent."

"I'm wiser now," I said. "I got this mirror for twenty dollars."

"Yes," she said, exchanging glances with her husband. "It's very nice."

They smiled amiably and I labored on toward the gate, lugging my handcarved mirror and First Prize for the Isthmus Race of 1965.

# Marineland

*I was eyeball to eyeball with a moray eel.*

Leo Szilard, that most engaging of atomic physicists, once wrote a story (*The Voice of the Dolphins*) in which Russian and American scientists end war and poverty by following the advice of a group of dolphins, a species that, in the story at least, is far superior in intelligence to *Homo sapiens.*

Alas, just before this Utopia is secured forever, a virus epidemic breaks out among the dolphins, and they die, one by one, leaving the human race to go its paranoiac way.

Today, watching the international follies at Washington, Moscow and Peking, we might well prosper by a visit to Marineland of the Pacific, where a new college of dolphins are at their studies. They are only in the early stages of training. Because of their submerged mode of life, as Dr. Szilard observed, dolphins are ignorant of the facts of the dry world, and so are not able to put their intelligence to good use.

In his story the scientists learn the language of the dolphins and then have no trouble teaching them mathematics, chemistry, physics and biology. (Dr. John Lilly, the marine biologist-psychologist, has actually spent years trying to learn dolphin language and has said their intelligence may be equal or even superior to our own.)

Whether the dolphins at Marineland will ultimately lead mankind out of economic, political and moral chaos I don't know. It is too early to say. But already they are doing some remarkable things indeed.

175

There is no question that dolphins can be taught to play baseball, to count, to do a very graceful *pas de deux* (or *trois*), to sing and to dance what their trainers call the watusi and the boogaloo.

By the way, the term *dolphins* may include not only the smiling and playful creatures we all know and love, but also the larger, bulb-nosed pilot whale, the killer whale and, in popular usage, the porpoises. All are mammals, like seals, sea lions, walruses and sea elephants.

For years a pilot whale named Bubbles was the star of Marineland. He died. The second Bubbles, after nine years before the public, fell ill. Ironically, like Dr. Szilard's dolphins, he had been stricken by a virus. A third Bubbles went on with the show.

Whatever Bubbles you happen to see, he stars with a supporting cast of half a dozen porpoises. Their stage is the eighty-foot tank of the Top Deck Stadium, five stories above Marineland and overlooking the scenic Palos Verdes Peninsula.

Marineland covers seventy acres on Long Point, the tip of the peninsula halfway, as the sea gull flies, between Long Beach and Redondo. The view from the stadium is superb. To the west the white shacks and lighthouse of the Coast Guard stand out on Pt. Vicente like an Andrew Wyeth painting. To the east the surf foams into a string of coves and beaches and up against the rocks of Portuguese Point.

Some days the fog comes in over the point, but the sea breeze keeps the smog from regurgitating down from the metropolis, and on a good day there is a pre-Columbian sparkle on the rocks and beaches and whitecaps, and Catalina Island looks close and three-dimensional, an easy swim.

From the top row of the stadium a visitor can look out on these riches, and down at the park, with its airy plazas and big seawater tanks, like oval jewels, and be thankful that this setting has been rescued for the public enjoyment from the subdividers, whose hordes of houses and apartments march inexorably over the hills of the peninsula and down to the sea.

Bubbles was in good form the day I saw him; fifteen feet long and twenty-five hundred pounds. When the trainer came out with his buckets of mackerel, the whale surfaced with his harem of porpoises and stood in the water, head up, eyes on

176

his master, like a faithful bird dog.

"Bubbles," the trainer said, "you gonna work hard today?"

Bubbles nodded.

"Let's all sing for the people," the trainer said, tossing mackerel into half a dozen gaping maws.

The animals sang—that is, they emitted sounds. They were certainly *trying* to sing, though in truth the dolphin, musically, is closer to the pig than the bird. The pilot whale has a voice like the barking of a rubber tire against a curb.

On cue, a porpoise named Kathy squirted up out of the tank into the air like a Polaris rocket, arched over backwards and did a flip. Now how can a porpoise, which can not be manhandled, as a dog can, be taught a trick like that?

Bubbles followed Kathy, a Nureyev to her Fonteyn. He shot straight up from the tank and seemed to stand on his tail while he did a double pirouette, then slid back down into the water, straight as a fireman going down a pole, and surfaced in front of the trainer.

"What's five plus five, minus two?" the trainer asked him.

Bubbles submerged, reappeared flat out on the surface, then slapped his tail against the water. One, two, three . . . exactly eight times. Once more the tail raised up—for suspense, I imagine—then Bubbles sank into the depths, with an A in math for the day.

Five plus five minus two is a long way from $E = mc^2$. So was man a long time evolving an Einstein.

Bubbles is the sentimental favorite of the public at Marineland, but the most awesome animals on exhibition are the killer whales—Orky (from *Orcinus orca*) and Corky.

The very name "killer whale" provokes a shudder, and in fact this notorious villain is fierce indeed in his hunt for food, being not only a glutton but also a horrible gourmet. He not only devours dolphins, seals and penguins, as well as fish, but he also gangs up with others of his species to attack the largest whales, killing them only for the delicacy of their tongues.

"They're killers, all right," I was assured by Marineland's curator, "but there has never been an authenticated case of a killer whale attacking man."

I sat in the killer whale stadium watching the killers do their act. Orky and Corky had their heads out of the water, looking at their trainers, begging for mackerel.

"They're not real," a young woman in the row below us told her husband. "They must be plastic."

"No, they're real."

"Well, they look plastic."

They do. The head is like a big black plastic bulb with comic eyes and a scissored-out mouth. The body is jet black except for large white eye patches and a white belly. All told, a beautiful beast.

One of the trainers was patting Orky on the head. Orky opened his mouth, his teeth showing. He was eighteen feet long; three tons. The trainer put his head into Orky's mouth. I hoped Orky could count to ten. When the trainer withdrew, Orky rolled over on his back and the trainer scratched his belly for him.

Every time Orky or Corky did anything right he got a handful of mackerel down the gullet. Members of the dolphin family may one day seek knowledge for its own sake, but for the time being, at Marineland, the assumption is that they are motivated by food.

In training, the reward is never far behind the deed. Do it right—*pop!*—a mackerel in the mouth. The trainer also blows a whistle. The animal soon links whistle and reward. Patience is the key. Patience and the animal's own ingenuity. How do you tell a dolphin you want him to sing? You wait until he sings. Then you reward him. In time you teach him to recognize some sign or motion that means you want him to sing. He sings. Then, whistle—the instant reward—and the fish.

Dolphins are very inventive. They're always playing games. So it might be said that the dolphins think up their acts, and the trainers merely tell them, "Hey, that's a great idea," like a Hollywood producer, and throw them a fish or two.

"There's never any punishment," I was told. "No whips. No cattle prods. We may hold back on food, but we don't starve them. They know when they've done right, and when they've done wrong. They don't like to see that trainer walk away."

Down at the edge of the tank a trainer held up a sign: *SOCK IT TO ME.* Orky emerged and blew a mouthful of water at the trainer. I don't say Orky can read, any more than Bubbles can add and subtract, but it's a beginning.

At a signal Orky and Corky sidled up before their trainers on opposite sides of the tank, like taxicabs pulling up at a curb. The trainers got on their backs just forward of the tail fins, and the killer whales gave them a ride around the tank, as insouciant as horses on a merry-go-round.

After the show we went below to look through the windows of the tank. Underwater, twisting and rolling in the light from the top of the tank, the killers seemed nothing but monsters of an inscrutable creation; mindless, instinct-driven, dreadful.

I noticed a sign on the wall: *"In captivity killer whales have not proved to be vicious killers . . . Among the animal kingdom they leave that unique honor to man."*

The crowd moved on to the sea arena, Marineland's largest theater, for the seal circus and dolphin games. Dolphins may be intellectually superior, dogs may be more tractable, but no other animals, not even chimps, do tricks with such aplomb, such flair for comedy and satire, as trained seals.

These disarming animals, which are in fact California sea lions, not true seals, are gifted with faces like human caricatures, and flippers that can be used to mimic any number of human mannerisms, including the Russian form of self-applause.

We were entertained by Queenie, Peanuts and Sneezy, who balanced balls, high dived, shook hands and otherwise acted like trained seals, but also had the human chutzpa to clap for themselves after every stunt, like Ed Sullivan used to do after one of his dog acts. They finished up with style, though.

"Now Queenie will say thank you to the audience," the announcer said. "Just two words—Thank you."

Queenie slipped into the tank, swam to the audience side, climbed six steps to a platform, stretched up to a microphone.

"Ork, ork!" she barked, and slid back into the tank.

I have seen few prima donnas more gracious or taciturn.

Sea lions are a hard act to follow, but the dolphins were up to it. At the start a trouper named Splash leaped up, grabbed a rubber ball at the end of a line and pulled it down, thus raising a flag.

The dolphins played baseball with the trainers, who were at

bat. Pepi pitched, flipping a red rubber ball from the tank to the strike zone. When the trainer managed to hit the ball back into the water, the dolphins fielded it and relayed it home— Flipper to Pepi to Splash. Fielding was superior to hitting.

The ballet was lovely, the music from *Giselle,* I think. Fountains of water played over the pool. The dolphins, the *corps de ballet,* leaped high in the sun, flashing silver, arching over and diving with such grace that a human could only feel awkward and envious.

Two of them did a toe dance, holding themselves perpendicular above the water by thrashing their tails, a remarkable demonstration of grace and power. The announcer called this a watusi or a bugaloo, but it looked to me like something I saw Gene Kelly do once, a kind of stiff-backed soft-shoe with his hands in his pockets.

As charming as the shows are, I am always more enchanted at Marineland by a look into the great fish tank. This gigantic aquarium is one hundred feet long, fifty feet wide and twenty-two feet deep, and holds half a million gallons of water, figures that might mean something to anyone who keeps a twenty-gallon tank at home.

Windows look into this teeming saltwater world from four levels. At the bottom level the sensation is much like being underwater. It is as close to actual skin diving as most of us are ever likely to get.

The sunlight filters down from far above, giving a soft luminescence to all the captive creatures. In that light everything is heightened, color and darkness, the beautiful, the ugly, until it is hard to tell one from the other.

I saw a large flat fish, shaped like a coin, velvet black, with bright gold fins and an electric blue stripe around his middle, altogether an object of such simple, unimaginable beauty as to stun the senses. He floated by my window and was followed by an enormous fat grouper, a fish so bloated, coarse and gross of feature that he seemed to have no purpose but to parody the most repulsive characteristics of his distant cousin, man the glutton.

In a moment I was eyeball to eyeball with a moray eel, whose pinched face with its tiny glazed eyes and needle-toothed mouth were just human enough to suggest pure evil. A sheepshead slid up to my window and stared out. What he saw, I realized, would seem neither ugly nor beautiful, good nor bad. Fish do not make esthetic or ethical judgments, do they? I'm not sure about dolphins.

Whence this fish that looks like a sheep? Perhaps long ago a gene split and went two separate ways, one by land, one by sea.

A leopard shark swam by, perfection in every infinitesimal move. Does instinct never err? No human being, not the finest athlete, not Nureyev, not even O. J. Simpson, moves with such faultless economy and grace.

There was a flash of white and a surge of silver bubbles, and a diver in a hard helmet descended into the tank. He began to scatter hunks of mackerel from a tin box, like a man feeding pigeons in a park. The fish gathered about him—bat rays, leopard sharks, guitarfish, sheepsheads and all the others—like so many dogs and cats.

I was glad to see we are trying to make friends with these inhabitants of the deep, and to communicate with dolphins. Captain Cousteau may be right. The way we are treating the air and land, we may soon be living with them.

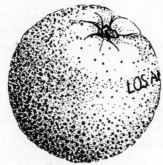

# MacArthur Park

*We used to swim in the lake.*
*It was a little pond then, and clear.*

It was a Saturday afternoon, a fresh clear day after rain. The leaves were shiny in MacArthur Park and the walks were clean. The air was nippy but the sun warmed the hundreds of people on the benches along the walks and sitting at the game tables under the eucalyptus trees.

I stopped at one of the tables where men were playing chess. One of them wore a green beret and had a large expressive face like the French comedian Fernandel. He sang to himself in a language I took for German as he studied his moves. It was a jaunty song; some folk song, I imagined. He kept his voice low, but he sang with gusto.

Next to him, a man engaged in another chess game rolled his eyes in exasperation.

"Oh, come *on*, Mark," he growled. "Shut *up!*"

"Who, me?" asked Mark, palms upturned in innocence.

"He has a nice tenor voice," said a bearded man playing opposite the man who had complained. His tone was heavily ironic.

"Enough! Enough!" grumbled the singing man's opponent, scowling down at the alarming predicament of his bishop.

A frowzy kibitzer raised a brown paper sack to his face and took a deep drink from the bottle inside.

I moved through the rows of tables. There were perhaps three hundred people at their various games. Most of them were men

183

of years; they would be called senior citizens, whether they liked it or not. But there were women, too, and a few scruffy youths of middle age. Some played chess and some checkers, but most played cards. The game was gin or pinochle, and it was played with intermittent periods of silent concentration and bursts of crusty badinage.

A man in a brown felt hat and a worn topcoat slammed his cards into the deck in disgust. "Yesterday his *wife* beat me out of a pot," he complained to no one in particular, "and today *he* beats me out of a pot."

"Stop screaming and play the game," said the man who had won the pot.

"Please! Not getting excited!" another player entreated. "Not getting excited!"

A man who looked eighty walked among the tables holding out a light blue cardigan. It looked like alpaca, and it might have been expensive once.

"A dollar fifty," the man said, not very hopefully. "A dollar fifty."

One of the kibitzers wore what was plainly a tailored suit, of a good brown tweed. His hat was a dark gray homburg, perfectly blocked. His shoes were expensive brogans, perhaps custom-made, and well cared for. He stood on an antique cane. He looked as if his chauffeur had dropped him off for a turn in the park.

But most of the people wore clothes that were ill-assorted and ill-fitting, as if they had survived from better times, or had been picked off the racks in a pawnshop down the block on Alvarado. Oddly, most of the men wore hats, either out of old habit or to shield balding pates from the California sun.

I felt a sense of community. These people were enjoying each other's company, despite the cranky dialogue, as well as the air and the scent of pine and eucalyptus and the chortling of the pigeons. There were the amenities, too, of soft drinks and hot coffee dispensed from the nearby snack bar by a jovial biddy who seemed to know all her customers by their first names.

I set out over the walk along the south shore of the lake and stopped a moment to watch two black boys fishing at the edge of the murky water.

184

"What are you catching?" I asked.

"Nothin'," one of them said, ending the conversation.

A youth in clean blue denims came up to me. He said he was from the Institute of Scientology. "Do you mind if I ask you a few questions?" he asked. "We're making a survey." He had crewcut hair, which set him apart from his generation, and carried a pencil and clipboard. I said I didn't mind.

"Do you think people work less than they did fifty years ago?" he asked.

"Yes," I said, wondering if they really did.

"How do you feel today?"

"Par."

"Would you say you're a liberal or a conservative?"

"I'm a revolutionary conservative," I said. He wrote it down and thanked me.

A man and woman were standing in front of the MacArthur monument, making a larger crowd than it usually attracts. The man said something in a Spanish that might have been Cuban. Slowly the woman read the legend on the monument to him, translating the English into Spanish.

*"Battles are not won by arms alone. There must exist above all else a spiritual impulse—a will to victory. In war there can be no substitute for victory . . ."*

Douglas MacArthur stood in front of his words in his tailored campaign uniform—battle jacket, pleated trousers and the field marshal's cap he had worn in the Philippines before Pearl Harbor. He seemed out of a deeper past than only thirty years ago.

Below him was a large dry pool that had once represented the theater of his operations in the Southwest Pacific. There were islands in it, and once they had borne bronze letters spelling out their names. But the letters had been ripped off. Only a single "S" remained. Blackbirds hopped from one island to another in a comic parody of the amphibian campaign.

MacArthur Park is a precarious little ecological system, and the miracle is that it has survived at all at the center of a burgeoning metropolis, like a small flower miraculously untrampled in a stampede. Untrampled? Well, not quite. The park has suffered a few traumas, one of them almost fatal. That was in 1934, when it was cut in two by Wilshire Boulevard; and it suffered serious damage to its identity in 1942 when its name was changed from Westlake to MacArthur in one of those patriotic excesses which break out like diseases in time of war.

For fifty-five years it had been known as Westlake Park, and then in that first dark year of the war, after the fall of Luzon, it was renamed MacArthur Park in honor of the general who was then gathering his forces in Australia. There was a one-hour parade down Wilshire to the park, with infantry and armored cars, and the mayor made a speech:

*"General Douglas MacArthur, we today dedicate this park to you. We rename it for you. You represent the kind of spirit we would like to see instilled into the very life of the community . . ."*

Even in the patriotic climate of the hour there were many who deplored the loss of a name which had suitability, charm and history in its favor. But it was a time for heroes, and the most popular song in the jukeboxes in the little bars around the park was "Praise the Lord and Pass the Ammunition."

Now the monument looked rundown and seamy. The general seemed forlorn. One had the idea he wished they would let him step down from his pedestal and fade away.

In the southeast corner of the park the lakeshore forms little lagoons which are shaded by trees, and this is where the old men and women and sometimes children come with sacks of bread to feed the ducks and pigeons and the black swans.

I passed a man who sat motionless on a bench. His eyes were shut. His hands were flattened out palms down on either side of him on the bench, the fingers spread in beds of bread crumbs. He seemed to be in ecstasy as the pigeons walked over his hands and calmly pecked at the crumbs.

A palsied and bent old man, bent so severely I wondered that his hat stayed on, was feeding the ducks, holding chunks of bread between thumb and forefinger and making them come and get it from his trembling hand. He had his favorites, evidently. Some were rejected, driven off with a curse and a raised fist, while others got the lion's share.

The main entrance to the park is at Seventh and Alvarado, and the benches along the walk in that corner were packed solid

186

on that Saturday afternoon, like the seats in the Coliseum. Most of the people were loners, sitting in the sun with their eyes shut, or reading leftover newspapers or listening to radios held against an ear. One man wore a rumpled black suit with a Ruptured Duck emblem in the lapel, the gilded button given to servicemen along with their honorable discharges at the end of World War II. I hadn't seen one that I could remember since the late Forties.

He was listening to the impromptu concert taking place on a bench across the walk. A large elderly woman in a Hawaiian print dress was singing *Carolina Moon*. Three men and a woman were playing ukeleles, sitting in a row on the bench. A man stood in front of the singer, playing a guitar. Another man was playing a kazoo. They finished *Carolina Moon* with a burst of self-congratulatory laughter and applause. Scattered applause came from the other benches. The guitarist struck a chord and ran off a few notes and the woman began to sing again, this time *Tiny Bubbles*. She sang well, with a poise and flair that echoed a life in show business, if only on the fringes. Obviously this was a regular Saturday thing, this concert, as casual as it seemed. For a few hours these people drifted together onto this small island of communion, to sing old songs full of memories, and then went their separate ways again.

Where did they come from, these park people? There must have been many more than a thousand in the park that day. Most of them, I guessed, lived in the neighborhood. It is called the Westlake district. The name MacArthur has never replaced the historic name. It is a neighborhood now of run-down apartments and hotels, once fashionable, and turn-of-the-century houses, some of them remarkably preserved. One of them, at 818 South Bonnie Brae, is perhaps the most exuberant and charming relic still left from the gingerbread era, and has been declared a cultural landmark.

The commercial heart of the district is within a radius of two blocks from Seventh and Alvarado. It is a kind of village which seems to have grown old and threadbare with its people. There has been some renewal; a few remodeled shops, a new medical building, a new location on the corner for Langer's, a deli as good as any in the city. But the district is full of life. Its people may be dispossessed, in one way or another, but they are out on the sidewalks. They meet and mix and mingle. The street caters to their needs. There are small friendly bars, pawn shops, cheap cafes, discount stores where a man can buy a shirt for $2.98, and the old Parkside Supermarket, a ma and pa size store with the fruits and vegetables out in bins on the sidewalk just as they were when I used to walk through the neighborhood on my way to school in the 1930s.

There is the California Hospital Thrift Shop, right across the street from the pornography shop, and the Mustang Club where they have live country music every weekend. You can buy old magazines for a nickel at the used-book store, which also has been there as long as I can remember. Seats are only fifty cents for senior citizens at the Park Theater, and the Handy Food Stamp Center is half a block from the park on Seventh.

In the first decade of the century the most fashionable address on the west side might have been the Leighton Hotel on Sixth Street, at the foot of the hill that rises just to the north of the park. The Leighton is still there, its cupolas giving its age away. It is a home for senior citizens now.

Wondering if I could find out how old the Leighton was, I asked a woman who was sitting outside the hotel in a blue porch swing.

"I saw this building being built," she told me, pleased at having a stranger to talk to. "It was in nineteen and three. I grew up right here in this neighborhood. We used to swim in the lake. It was just a little pond then, and clear. I'll be eighty-four in January. I'm a native. Are you a native?"

"Yes," I said. "I am."

"You are! Where were you born?"

"Long Beach."

She sat up straight and uttered a little cry. She leaned forward and held out a frail white hand.

"Well, put 'er there!" she said. "Long Beach, hey? Well, so was I!"

I walked back to the park and along the rows of benches. It was midafternoon now and there was hardly an empty seat. The concert had grown in volume. It seemed to me there were two or three more ukuleles and a red-haired woman was snapping castanets. People sitting on the benches were tapping their feet and trying to sing along.

I walked back around the lake to the card tables. There was a bite in the air now and the shadows were longer, but most of the players were still at their games, putting their cards down now and then to rub their hands.

The man with the blue cardigan for sale passed me again and gave his half-hearted pitch without waiting for a no.

"Dollar and a quarter," he said. "Dollar and a quarter."

It was getting late.

# The Bicycle Path

*Steady as she goes, mates.*

It is one of the ironies of romance in America that just as the bicycle built for two was catching on, the automobile came along, and almost overnight the bicycle was passé.

By eliminating pedaling, the automobile made it possible for a couple to save their strength for other exertions, for which the automobile also provided a comfortable arena. It was these two conveniences, more than any others, that put the bicycle in limbo for seventy years, except for die-hard cycle buffs and children. Now the bicycle is making a comeback. It isn't likely to displace the automobile, unless the day really comes when the gasoline engine as a species dies of thirst. But the bicycle is being rediscovered as a very pleasant form of exercise and recreation.

It is said that in Southern California we have more than a million bicyclists; many of them are influential citizens and a few are influential politicians. Thus, bike paths are being built along our beaches and there is talk of a citywide network.

I doubt if the bicycle built for two will ever come back strong enough, though, to be celebrated in song again. Today's woman wants to paddle her own canoe, to stray for a metaphor; most likely she also wants to pedal her own bicycle. "There is a strong indication," writes Eugene A. Sloan in *The New Complete Book of Bicycling,* "that Women's Lib has about put the male-female tandem out of business."

JACK SMITH

Also, he points out, tandem cyclists must be temperamentally in harmony. "If you're always battling about who's not pedaling hard enough, if you can't learn to coordinate getting feet in pedals, or starting and stopping, then tandeming is definitely not for you. It can put a strain on your marriage."

Still, on any Sunday the tandem is likely to turn up along one of the scenic streets marked as bike paths in some of our residential communities, and a machine called the Duo-Cycle has made an appearance at least on the bike path between Playa del Rey and Manhattan Beach. It was one of these that my wife and I drove on our maiden trial of that six-mile stretch. The Duo is a two-seater, but differs critically from the tandem. The riders do not sit one in front of the other, but side by side, in plastic bucket seats. Each has a set of pedals, independent of the other, but steering is done by means of a common handle-bar. There are three wheels and a surrey top; so it is really an adult tricycle.

We picked ours up one overcast Sunday morning at a bicycle shop in Playa del Rey. I would have preferred separate bicycles, but my wife had never learned to ride one, as incredible as that may seem for a girl raised in a town as flat as Bakersfield.

To quote the expert Sloane again: "If you're beyond the age when you think you can learn how to ride a bicycle, or if, for some reason, you cannot or should not balance yourself on one, adult tricycles might be the answer for you . . . One sees great numbers of tricycles in retirement areas . . ."

The tricycle looked safe enough, but I had misgivings as we set out over the path. Our temperamental harmony was untried. The man at the shop had told us about the clutch. There were two speeds. The person on the left could change from low to high, or vice versa, by pushing back on the pedal, as in braking. The clutch on the right side was automatic.

"At nine miles an hour," he said, "it goes into high."

"You better sit on the left and handle the clutch," I told my wife. "I'll steer."

We got in and set off down the street to the alley, which led down to the beach and the bike path. It was a typical sum-mer morning at the beach; the sky was a threadbare gray with a blue lining. Even at that early hour the traffic on the path was heavy enough to be entertaining without being dangerous. It soon became apparent that the main hazard was us.

"We'd better not both try to steer at once," I suggested as we veered over the yellow line for the second time. "I'll steer. You clutch."

"If I can't steer," she said, "what'll I do with my hands?"

"Fold them in your lap."

She folded her hands in her lap and we sailed along, keeping on our side of the path. Everyone who passed us smiled and said hello in one form or another, or shouted some word of encouragement.

"Go get 'em," cried a young woman over her shoulder as she breezed by us on her two-wheeler.

"Cute!" shouted another.

If there is any adjective I don't wish to provoke, it is that one. It was too late, though, to turn back. There was an element of pride involved; our goal was Manhattan Beach, and nothing was going to make us quit short of it—not even looking cute.

Obviously our three-wheeler was a novelty on the path. It did have a certain appeal—augmented, I supposed, by the fake leopard-skin surrey top.

"Maybe it's your cap," my wife said. "I think they're laughing at your cap."

I happened to be wearing a kepi, the kind of flat-topped military cap worn by the young Maurice Chevalier in those wonderful old Lubitsch musicals—a romantic article of attire, to be sure, but hardly one to provoke amusement.

A gentleman approached us on a racing bike—a portly chap with round face and ruddy complexion and a neat white brush moustache. He might have been Nigel Bruce. Retired colonel, no doubt. His head inclined slightly as we met.

"Good morning," he barked.

Only after he had passed did it fully strike me that he had a passenger in the basket over his handlebars. A lapdog of some kind. The colonel was obviously out airing his wife's dog.

The bike path is built on the high part of the beach, a concrete ribbon about fifteen feet wide, divided into two lanes by a yellow line. It is not all level, rising and falling with the dunes, and it meanders, which not only adds miles and interest, but also tends to curb speed. We soon adjusted to the road, pumping harder when we felt it going uphill, taking a rest when it coasted. My wife had discovered the little air horn between the seats, and it soon became her custom to answer every smile or salutation with a toot.

We stopped at the occasional pullouts to rest our legs and enjoy the scenery. The beach was coming to life. South of the marina channel jetty, in an area reserved for surfers, a few devotees of the pray-for-surf cult were hanging in the gray swells. Safely beyond the breakers half a dozen small sailboats sported about boldly in the open sea, close enough to the channel for a quick run home if the weather turned. A small plane flew low above the horizon dragging a long sign—*THE FRIENDLY SKIES OF UNITED.*

Farther down the beach the surf fishers had staked a stretch of sand. Some stood at the water's edge as if in some communion with the sea. Others sat in camp chairs beside poles embedded in the sand. It always seemed to me to be the fairest place for fishing, this no-man's land of surf between land and sea. But the rewards were small. Nothing to show for a day's skill and patience but a couple of mackerel and a sand shark, or at best a few perch.

People were streaming out from the cars to set up day camps on the playa. Every beach has its character. The playa is a favorite of families, with its broad clean sweep of sand and dozens of barbecue pits. Smoke was already blowing up toward the bike path from some of the pits, and the aroma reminded me of the aroma of ribs cooking at the Watts Summer Festival.

We pushed on into a stream of increasing traffic. It was a promenade of the kind Los Angeles has missed since the automobile took us off the sidewalks and encapsulated us. We found ourselves looking at everyone who passed, and being looked at. In our case, of course, it was partly the novelty of our rig and my kepi, and perhaps our red, white and blue bicycle shirts. Since the his and hers fad first fell on us, back in the Fifties or Sixties, I had avoided it zealously as being repulsively cute. I had bought a bicycle shirt at our local Highland Park haberdashery the day before and when I came home with it my wife had gone down and bought one like it for herself.

We soon felt at ease about our appearance. There are no dress rules for the beach bike promenade. The riders express the maverick tastes of Southern California. Evidently the garment industry hasn't caught on to the boom yet. People seemed to be dressed for tennis, sunbathing, yard work or poolside drinking. If anything was de rigueur it was the T-shirt, the most important single article of dress in our culture, along with shorts and funky hats.

A man pedaled toward us, followed by a woman on her own bike. As they passed, we saw that each had a small child riding piggyback. Other couples, like the colonel, carried dogs. Some had radios strapped to their handlebars, almost universally tuned in on Vin Scully.

The one thing these Sunday cyclists had in common was a look of gratification and goodwill, as if they thought themselves very clever indeed for having invented the beach, the sea, the sky and the bicycle, and for being generous enough to share the scene with everyone else. It was not the kind of look one ordinarily gets from a fellow motorist who has pulled up at a stoplight alongside you.

Not only were we hailed by every passing cyclist, but people sitting on benches above the beach cupped their hands to shout down encouragement or advice. *"You're supposed to pump, too!"* an old man shouted.

My wife, I suddenly realized, had been coasting, and the old kibitzer had caught her at it.

A mile or so south of the village of Playa del Rey the bike path goes under the takeoff lanes of Los Angeles International Airport. Every minute or so a big jet would appear above the palisade and fly low over our heads, screeching and trailing smoke as it labored into the skies. Their sound silenced the sea and struck everyone dumb. Lips moved silently as people shouted greetings at each other. Then in a moment the jets were gone and sound tentatively came back to numbed eardrums. These jet airplanes striking so noisily into our Sunday were an ironic reminder that we couldn't pedal out of our century. But it might be that the bicycle, which after a hundred and sixty years was the perfect end product of its own evolution, would yet outlast the jet-propelled airplane.

We made a pit stop at a beach snack bar. Soft pretzels and very hot coffee in plastic cups. Other cyclists gathered round to inspect our tricycle, the way people back in the Twenties used to gather around the town's first Dusenberg. I hadn't been the center of so much attention since I'd test-driven Studebaker's last glorious gasp—the Avanti—on the freeway.

From the snack bar we could see orange and white striped chimneys to the south, and beyond them—miles, it seemed—a pier extending out into the misty sea. "That's Manhattan Beach," said a man who had just pedaled in with two granddaughters. "About four miles."

He examined our tricycle expertly. "Used to be in South Africa," he said. "Down there, saw a fellow drive one of those things forty miles an hour."

"I haven't really let this one out," I said. "Wife's with me, you know."

As the bike shop man had said, pumping the tricycle made demands on the muscles in the thighs and around the diaphragm. Already my legs were beginning to tell me he was right. One advantage of the tricycle was that one could rest while the other pumped, but our wheels were small and our top speed hadn't been enough to blow my hat off.

All the same, freshened by the coffee, we pushed on toward the pier and were soon abreast of the towering chimneys. They belonged to the Department of Water and Power's Scattergood Steam Plant. It was the sort of installation that enrages environmentalists, and could probably never be built in today's ecological climate. But at least the department had tried to present a handsome facade to the beach, hiding the plant's entrails with plain concrete walls of pink, beige and gray. It might have been a Babylonian palace.

Back of the steam plant on the palisade sat half a dozen oil storage tanks and a big pipeline ran out into the ocean over a small pier. Beyond its end three tankers lay at anchor. The tanker is not the most beautiful of ships, nor its mission the most romantic; but to me the ugliest of ships is beautiful, especially at a distance of half a mile on a cloudy day.

The little airplane, or another one like it, was flying along the shoreline again with a new sign, the letters trailing back a hundred feet—*HOLLYWOOD BOWL MARATHON WEDNESDAY*. If the ad agencies knew what they were about, the people on the bike path and the beach that Sunday morning were the kind of people who traveled by air and might spend a summer evening at the Bowl.

A girl pedaled toward us in blue jeans and a faded purple Whittier College sweatshirt.

"It's raining down that way," she warned us as she passed.

Behind her a man was approaching fast on a bicycle with a Doberman pinscher loping along beside him on a leash.

"Hang in there," he said.

Beyond the Scattergood plant the Edison plant loomed even larger, a blue-gray tumble of functional shapes, windowless and forbidding, but more interesting to the eye, it seemed to me, than some of the termitaria that were being erected elsewhere along this precious shore.

Just beyond the Edison plant the bike path makes a climb over the dunes. Our speed slowed. We pumped harder. Suddenly the tricycle jerked and we came to a stop. "What did you do?" I asked.

"I was trying to shift gears."

"Well, you put the brake on. You aren't supposed to put the brake on when we're going uphill."

We tried pumping on up the hill, but we didn't have the power to move it from a dead start on an incline. People were whizzing by us, tooting their horns. "We'll have to push," I said.

We were pushing the tricycle up the hill when the colonel passed us again. "Steady as she goes, mates," he said. He was a retired captain, then not a colonel.

Our reward for pushing was a pleasant period of coasting which allowed me to give full attention to the volleyball courts. There are a dozen courts in the sand just north of Manhattan Beach, and beach volleyball is among the most underrated of spectator sports. It is sexually integrated, for one thing; it rings with exuberant shouts and friendly laughter; and the sight of a suntanned young sea nymph jumping and leaping about is a delight to the jaded eye.

We reached the pier at last and chained our tricycle to a

rack. You couldn't say it was raining, but now and then a warm drop splashed on my face. A small boy and girl came up and regarded our machine with looks of wonder and skepticism.

"Is that yours?" the boy asked.

"No," I said. "We rented it."

He thought it over. "Are you tourists?"

Evidently he reasoned that any adults who wore his and hers bicycle shirts and rented a tricycle must be tourists. Not bad thinking either.

"No, we live here," I confessed. "We're just trying it out."

Manhattan Beach at the pier has its own culture, which we could not hope to penetrate on a single Sunday. We looked into the Viva La Paz, whose main attraction evidently was a sound level higher than a jet airplane's. It was a dark, dank cave with a jukebox, pool table, dart board, thrift shop décor and sawdust on the floor, and appeared to be sustained by a new breed of remittance man. It was the sort of place you might spend a month or two in, but not half an hour.

We crossed the street to the Shellback, which also had a funky look but seemed to specialize in food and drink, and restored ourselves with combination sandwiches and coffee. I would have liked to have a beer, but it seemed imprudent, with six miles of tricycle driving still ahead of us. The trip back to our base was harder than the trip out. I suppose all adventurers have that experience. One has already reached the goal; the rest is anticlimax; the big thing is to get back and tell one's story.

A crowd was gathered on the beach at the foot of the jetty. I thought it might be an accident, but then I saw a girl in a peppermint stick 1890s bathing suit and another in a string bikini, and decided to park the tricycle and investigate.

"You wait here," I said. "Watch the tricycle."

It turned out to be a camera club field trip, and the young women in bathing suits were models. I walked up behind one in a green nylon bikini. She was standing in the sand with a hip thrown out in one of the standard cheesecake poses. Three photographers crouched on the sand in front of her, fussing with their cameras. One of them looked past her at me.

"Background!" he growled.

I knew what he meant. I was in the background, ruining the picture. I trudged on back to the tricycle.

The little airplane was back on the horizon with a new sign: *CUERVO MAKES THE SUNRISE.*

We had pedaled all the way back to the bike shop before we remembered that Cuervo was a kind of tequila and the sunrise was some kind of cool pink drink made with it.

By then it seemed like a good idea.

# Farmers Market

*Nothing was going good but the Depression.*

Not many of our successful institutions date from the Great Depression. It was a time of failures and endings; not beginnings.

One happy exception is the Farmers Market.

If you had to name the very low point of the Depression, you might say July, 1934.

"In 1934," Fred Beck, Los Angeles journalist, has written, "nothing was going good but the Depression."

That's when the Farmers Market began.

It was started by Earl Gilmore, who owned the land, and a busted promoter named Roger Dahlhjelm, a Minnesota Swede whose only credentials were flamboyant failures.

Dahlhjelm had sold nonexistent apple orchards in Idaho, then fled to Washington where he tried to sell the moribund Stanley Steamer. Broke again, he drifted south without a dime. He discovered Earl Gilmore's idle land at West Third Street and Fairfax Avenue.

Idle land always inspired Dahlhjelm. If it wouldn't grow apples, maybe it would grow something else. He went to Gilmore with an idea. Out in the San Fernando Valley, farmers watched their crops wither in the fields. They had no markets. The machinery of the middleman had broken down. Yet in the city people were hungry and prices were high.

Why not, Dahlhjelm proposed, bring the farmers to town and let them sell their produce on the spot, directly to the consumer? Gilmore also despised idle land. Why not?

Dahlhjelm's dream was perhaps more glorious than Gilmore's. What he envisioned was a kind of medieval marketplace, with families tending their stalls, weaving their own cloth, baking their own bread. He foresaw a bazaar as opulent as Samarkand or Marrakesh.

"This was far beyond anything Mr. Gilmore could envision," recalled John Gostovich, the present manager. "But the property was vacant. He said to Dahlhjelm, 'Go ahead and use it.' When Mr. Gilmore told you that and looked you in the eye it was a lease."

People who lived in Los Angeles in the 1930s can still remember the opening day. There were seventeen farmers in all, each with his own truck, peddling his yams or eggs or tomatoes from the tailgate. They survived that day, and came back.

One man's hard luck can be another's windfall. Other promoters had built a racing grandstand nearby on Gilmore's land, but never got it open.

"So Mr. Gilmore inherited a whole lot of lumber there," said Gostovich. "He told those farmers to help themselves. So they went and tore out the lumber and threw up some boards and some awnings, right out there on the ground. And they had some shade."

The farmers got together to do some advertising. The air was crowded with radio stations that were also hungry. They were happy to plug the Farmers Market for a lug of onions, or only a promise.

"The market struggled through till fall, and then the rains came. There was no electricity, no plumbing, no paving. They were going to quit. But a man named Magee talked them into staying. One quit. Sixteen stayed. Then one more came in, and more, and now today we've got a hundred and sixty."

To begin with, rent was fifty cents a day. If a farmer didn't have the half-dollar, he left some of his grapes or squash with Gilmore as security and redeemed them later in the day. Leases were for thirty days, an arrangement that still prevails, although some of the present tenants have installations costing a hundred thousand dollars and more in their stalls.

Like most domestic structures, the market deteriorated during the war. "When I came here in 1946," said Gostovich, "it was terribly run-down. So little by little we got Mr. Gilmore to just quietly rebuild the whole thing. The company owns the structures, the tenants own the fixtures."

Today the Farmers Market seems an anachronism. It is a kind of super-supermarket, selling everything from fondue to hammered gold, and offering an international variety of hot dishes from two dozen open-air cafes. Yet the atmosphere is of the country, and of a vanished time. A visitor has a sense of holiday, as if at an old-style country fair. The market is open from 9:30 a.m. to 6:30 p.m. every day except Sundays and holidays.

Most of the shops are family enterprises; ma and pa and the kids. Some are second generation, run by sons or daughters of the founder farmers. There is the smell and look and amiability of the old corner grocery store, where the crackers were kept in a bin, before chrome and plastic and frozen dinners.

Busy as they are, the proprietors love to talk. I was examining some enormous strawberries at a fruit and vegetable stand when the proprietor walked up.

"They must grow these in a hothouse," I said.

"Hothouse!" He was scandalized. "Heavens, no! They grow those strawberries in Watsonville, right out in God's beautiful sunshine."

"Watsonville? Isn't that a long way to go for strawberries?"

"That's nothing. Look here. Those are macadamia nuts, fresh from Tahiti. We flew in a ton. We have cherimoyas from Bogota, Kiwi fruit from New Zealand. We have Belgian endive.

"We've got some limestone lettuce comes from Kentucky. We fly it in. Only grown in two places in the United States. Terre Haute, Indiana, and Lexington, Kentucky. Has to grow in a special limestone soil. Got a flavor that's indescribable."

He gave me the tour. Red bananas from Brazil. Sugarcane from Louisiana. Garlic from France. Tiny snow apples from Washington.

"Grow those apples way up in the mountains. Ten, twelve thousand feet. They're so crisp if a lady puts a fingernail in one it snaps right open."

He finally sold me a small bunch of salsify, a European herb known as oyster plant or vegetable oyster, and gave me the following guarantee:

"Defy you to cook it and tell it from oysters."

The proprietor of a nearby stand turned out to be one Eli Meshulam, whose father had been one of the original seventeen. The elder Meshulam was not really a produce grower, but a chicken rancher. He had got into Farmers Market simply by trading fertilizer to Japanese truck farmers out in the valley, taking produce in lieu of money, and then hauling his pay to market.

"I was fifteen years old, then," said Eli Meshulam. "Mother and Dad started with Roger Dahlhjelm. So we've had three generations working here—including my wife Frances and me, and four sons and daughters."

John Tusquella can reminisce, too. Tusquella's meat shop has been a fixture of the market for more than a quarter century. It does a business of two million dollars a year. John's son Bob, who started with him at twelve cutting bacon, now has his own seafood shop in the market.

"He's got a master's degree," the father told me proudly, "and now he sells salmon steaks."

There were a dozen butchers working on Tusquella's floor. They had that extraordinarily happy look butchers have, a fact of life I have never been able to account for. Tusquella invited me into his cold room, where long rows of beefs hung from hooks. "These are hind quarters. Where all your prime steaks come from. I've got a hundred hanging in here. They age three weeks. They come from Colorado. Fed especially for us. We've been buying from the same ranch for twenty-five years."

Back in the shop, Tusquella got two tall lager glasses and poured us each a beer from a huge vat. Marvelous idea for a butcher shop. Free tap beer. Maybe that was why the butchers looked so happy.

Paul Magee runs a delicatessen, a restaurant and a nut stand. His father was the original Magee, the R. J. Magee who talked his fellow farmers out of giving up back in the bleak fall of 1934.

I met Paul Magee beside an antiquated machine that was noisily grinding out a stream of peanut butter.

"This was my grandfather's machine," he said. "He came out here with it from back East. You can't get parts anymore."

The original Magee didn't start out with a restaurant. "We were in the bulk business. Pigs' feet. Sauerkraut. Pickles. Horseradish. And then we had cooked meat selling by the pound.

"The other tenants in the market sort of started it. They'd come up with a paper plate and say 'Give me four ounces of this,' and we'd throw in some potato salad. Pretty soon the customers wanted some, and then we put a few tables out, and, by golly, the Farmers Market was in the restaurant business."

Today there are two dozen restaurants in the market, all sharing the tables placed under the trees and awnings or in the shelter of glassed-in pavilions upstairs. The aromas drifting out from these busy kitchens give the market its unique air, a savory, indefinable mixture that conjures up visions of exotic medieval feasts.

At one point I was enveloped in a cloud so seductive and tantalizing, so subtly interwoven, that I stopped and shut my eyes, trying to identify the odors. Impossible. I opened my eyes. No wonder. From that one point I could see kitchens dispensing such a variety of dishes as enchiladas, deep-fried clams, blintzes, chicken, spaghetti, roast beef, roast pork, chow mein and pastrami.

I walked on, hoping to take myself beyond the power of these enticements, only to run into a small stand where my eye was caught by a pan full of hot stuffed eggplant Parmesan, a concoction I find irresistible. I ate it at a table under a tree, watching the sparrows flutter down to pick at crumbs.

Unfortunately, man's capacity is no match for the temptations of Farmers Market. But there is consolation in the number of things that can be taken home in a sack.

One can find beautiful imported cheeses—Danish bleu, French Port Salud, Spanish sheep cheese, wine cheddar . . . Baked goods—big flat slabs of Armenian bread, San Francisco sourdough, Greek ring bread . . . Exotic cakes and candies— Swiss fudge, three-layer yellow Parisian cream cake, Panama moche, Jamaica rum torte . . . And always the voluptuous fruits and vegetables, which somehow look bigger and richer of color than anywhere else.

To the north of the market and restaurant section is a long row of stores, under the familiar clocktower, which offer most of the goods and artifacts generally thought to make life agreeable in this civilization.

Sporting goods and needlepoint, shoes and haberdashery, linens and jewelry, stationery and lingerie, pipes and knits, candles and brushes, cameras and eyeglasses, blown glass and Israeli artifacts, buttons and books and a post office, to mail it all away.

One may not find automobiles or yachts, but it is possible to buy a few thousand shares of General Motors. In one stall, unlikely as it may seem, is a branch office of E. F. Hutton & Co., members of the New York Stock Exchange.

From six o'clock on, when the bakers and cooks and candy makers are coming to work and firing up their ovens, this little corner of Farmers Market is already doing a lively business with clients who watch the changing quotations on the big light board and buy or sell with the skill and concentration of a housewife picking out a porterhouse steak or a wheel of cheese.

Most of the stores, I discovered, offer the kinds of things made for people who already have everything. This spirit is even evident in the market's pet shops, where it is not only possible to buy a boxer pup or a talking bird, but also a floor-to-ceiling cat tree and a dog's umbrella— *"Something different,"* the sign says, *"for the dog who has everything."*

Anachronism, super-supermarket, the world's biggest outdoor cafe—whatever it is, the Farmers Market brings them in at a rate of thirty thousand a day—maybe fifty thousand—and it sells a lot of pizza, T-bone steaks and yams.

In his most magnificent visions, Roger Dahlhjelm, the itinerant Swede with the broken dreams and the big idea, could hardly have asked for more.

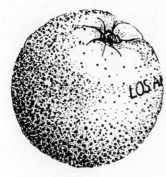

# The Watts Festival

*"You come a long way?"*
*"Yes. Quite a long way."*

Out in the hot asphalt of 103rd Street, by Will Rogers Memorial Park, a girls' drill team marched in flat straw hats, green capes, white boots and olive hotpants.

They were smart and saucy. Their leader sang out the cadence and the girls sounded off:

> *Everywhere we go*
> *People want to know*
> *Who we are!*
> *Where do we come from,*
> *Where do we come from?*
> *So we tell 'em,*
> *We're from Watts!*
> *We're from Watts!*
> *Mighty, mighty Watts!*

It was the parade of the annual Watts Summer Festival in August, and the marching girls, a unit of the Watts Labor Community Action Council, were expressing the community pride that the festival is meant to stimulate and display.

The parade was two hours long. The route was lined six deep with watchers. There were tiers of faces, from the small children on the curbs to the tall men in the back with smaller children on their shoulders. There were the old people out front in chairs, and the teenagers, jeering amiably or shouting "Right on!" And few of the faces I could see were white.

207

In one way, Watts is like Heaven. Everbody talkin' 'bout it ain't agoin' there. Watts is also like Hollywood. It is more a symbol than a place, and what Watts symbolizes may depend on what part of the elephant we have hold of in our blindness.

Watts is a word in the language now: synonymous with ghetto; synonymous with the August riots of 1965. It means poverty, oppression, violence and despair.

But every year in August, every year since Watts got the world's attention by setting itself on fire, Watts has put on its summer festival and offered itself as a symbol of creative energy, hope, joy and pride.

There are five days of carnival, dance, theater and sports, and a feast of gospel, rock, soul and jazz. The climax is the big parade on the final Sunday afternoon.

For visual and emotional exuberance there is no spectacle on the Southern California scene to compare with the summer festival, and yet, unfortunately, it remains largely undiscovered or ignored by the white community outside south central Los Angeles itself:

It could be fear that keeps the whites away. There was a shooting in 1967 at the park, the kind of incident that gets remembered. It could be ignorance. Or perhaps it is only indifference, the most regrettable reason of all.

Though I went down to Watts as a reporter in the immediate aftermath of the 1965 revolt, which is what the people of Watts have come to call it, I had never gone to the festival until the summer of 1970. Watts, I realized then, was farther from where I lived than fifteen miles. It was five years away, the time it took me to get there. Five years of talking about Watts and never going there, except once or twice to see the Towers.

That first year I didn't go to see the parade, but just drove down one hot night to walk in the park and look at the people. *"Look at the people,"* Bernie Casey had written in one of his poems, *"one person at a time."*

I parked that night on Central Avenue a block or two north of the park across the street from the faded orchid facade of a boarded-up liquor store on which had been spray-painted the admonition:

## GET OFF YOUR KNEES PRAYING TO BE WHITE

There was a midway set up in the park, and the scene was surreal in the summer night. I was reminded of carnivals on hot summer nights in the San Joaquin Valley when I was a boy. There was the Ferris wheel, lighted with a thousand bulbs, turning slowly in the dark sky above the upturned faces; the smell of hot dogs and mustard; the ice cream truck playing *Casey went out with a strawberry blond* . . .

But the experience seemed richer and deeper in Watts. Neon and strobe lights glared and flashed; rock bands sent out waves of noise like sonic booms, and scattered bongos sounded like tribal drums in the night. The air was succulent with barbecued ribs and sweet potato pie. The night was sensual and gaudy, like a brown nude painted on black velvet.

There were not many white people in the park that night, either, and a young black boy fell in with me as I walked, the way boys do when they want to make friends. He wore a billed cap hanging at a cocky angle off the side of his head.

"They's a lot of people here," he said.

"Yes," I said. "A good crowd."

"They's more people here than live here."

"Yes. There must be."

"You come a long way?"

"Yes," I said, "quite a long way."

I bought a hot dog and a sweet potato pie that night from a girl in a booth. "If you like it," she told me, "you come back."

I did go another summer. I went on the last Sunday of the festival, in the daytime, to look at Watts and see the parade.

For a symbol, Watts isn't much to see. It was once called Mudtown, back before World War I, and according to a writer of that era it was "a tiny section of the deep South literally transplanted." A retired Pasadena businessman named C. H. Watts had a ranch in the neighborhood, and when it was annexed to the city of Los Angeles in 1926 the name stuck, a name whose meaning today has nothing to do with its forgotten donor.

The main street of Watts, in a civic sense, is 103rd Street, beginning at Will Rogers Memorial Park and ending a few blocks to the east with the sadly dilapidated old Pacific Electric depot and the yellow brick home of the Watts Writers Theater.

In between are the branch library, the branch city hall, the police and fire stations, and a few shops and stores that survived the fires of 1965 or have crept in since.

A few blocks to the southeast, Simon Rodia's Towers rise out of this flatness, exotic and improbable. They stand beside the rusted PE tracks at the dead end of a street which seems to deteriorate before your eyes, except for the Watts Towers Community Art Center next door. The art center, though starved for money, churns with ghetto creativity, like a volcano in a dead land.

The streets where people live offer their own stark testimony to the struggle of Watts for self-respect and survival. Mostly the houses are old and broken and askew; they have gone to seed, along with the brown weeded yards they sit behind. But some are mended and painted and cared for with obvious pride, and there are blocks that seem to lie in the balance between renewal and decay.

The parade was to start at one o'clock and by noon the park was thronged with people in a festive mood. It was more of a Mardi Gras crowd than one ever sees elsewhere in Southern California. I had never seen a crowd so beautiful and flamboyant. In their dress, in their shouts and laughter, in their movements and their faces there was a humor and a self-conscious exuberance not seen in the crowds at the racetrack, lost in their calculations, or the crowds at the Coliseum, racing from the exits for their cars.

Except for the jet planes shrieking intermittently overhead, on their descent to International Airport, it would have been hard to place this scene in metropolitan Los Angeles, or anywhere else in that mythical land once known as white America.

The heart of the festival, from the way the crowd went, was the little alley of jerry-built plywood concessions on the inner parking lot of the park. They were mostly food stands or boutiques selling handmade jewelry, bongo drums, modish Afro clothing, wigs, or posters and mementos of such black heroes as Malcolm X, Muhammad Ali and Martin Luther King.

Soul music poured out of the little booths from radios, carried on clouds of smoke from oil-drum barbecues. The odors of cooking ribs and ham and chicken were so rich and succulent that I imagined myself salivating like one of Pavlov's dogs.

Beyond the street of booths I saw a crowd in front of a stage and I walked over to find out what was happening. A man I had seen before was being interviewed on the stage, a very handsome, graceful man. He was Elgin Baylor, the Laker superstar, then at the end of his remarkable career as a player.

"What does Watts mean to you?" the interviewer was asking Baylor. "You—a successful man, who's always been able to make it, a man who has not been tremendously bothered by poverty. What does Watts mean to you and how do you relate to Watts?"

It was a question a man could not easily answer, out there in the sun, with cooking ribs and soul music on the air, but he had to try, because there were a hundred young faces out there, looking up expectantly, and a hero couldn't just disappear.

"Well," said the man who had made it, "I've been really poor myself. My family was very poor. Really, everything I've made, I had to work hard. I was fortunate enough to have some ability to play basketball and sort of get out of it that way, out of poverty, get an education and everything else.

"Right here," he said, looking out at the faces, "there's a lot of people not fortunate enough to have that opportunity, and I think this is—you know—terrible. Because when I was in college lots of guys had as much ability as I did, as much talent, some of them had more. But I was just one of the fortunate ones, one of the very few that was able to make it. And this is so prevalent here, it happens here, you know, because there are a lot of talented, creative people here in this community, and it's awful that none of this has been exploited.

"If people would just come to this community, to see what kind of talent they have here. This festival is a fantastic thing. We're so low on funds, and to put this on by ourselves, I don't think it could be done anywhere else, except here in Watts . . ."

The crowds were drifting to the sides of the park to see the parade. Across 103rd Street boys perched in the limbs of trees as thick as sparrows. They sat on the roof of the Mobil gas station at the corner, and across Central Avenue they sat on

211

the roof over the Clark barber shop in front of the big sign
saying *Al's Pool Room and Beer Bar.*

The parade started on time, with the Teen Post Band in white
and maroon out front. Muhammad Ali, the almost-champion
of the world, was to have been the grand marshal, but he had
cancelled and Sammy Davis Jr. had taken his place. There were
cries of approval as Sammy Davis came along in an open Cadil-
lac, wearing an African-style robe and necklace.

"We *fo* yuh, Sammy!"

"You Number *One,* baby! *A*lways dependable!"

"Right *on,* brother!"

There were other public figures, major and minor, and the
usual district politicians and community leaders, but in Watts
the heroes are not made at the polling places. The cheers went
to Sammy Davis Jr. and Rosy Grier and Jim Brown, the great
halfback and sometime movie star, whose raised clenched fist
aroused the younger women to shrieking adulation along the
route.

There were a few floats in the parade, brave but makeshift
floats that would never make it to the Tournament of Roses.
Their theme was work, family, education, and one had a banner
with some words by James Baldwin:

*"We cease to hold each other the moment we break faith with one
another. The sea engulfs us, and the light goes out."*

But the great truth of the festival parade was in its youth;
regiments of young people; children and teenagers and young
adults, boys and girls, marching and chanting, strutting and
enjoying themselves. They represented schools and clubs and
civic self-improvement organizations, all related in some way
to the effort of the black community to work together in their
own cause; and their pride in their unity and skill and in their
*looks* was unmistakable.

Their uniforms were mostly simple and looked as if they might
have been homemade, with much denim and khaki and plain
cotton dyed light orange or green or yellow. No Music Man
had come to Watts and sold them a carload of gold braid and
epaulets. There was a flair in the costumes, a style that was

a long way from John Philip Sousa and Main Street America. Its origins were in the jungle and the plantation. One group of youths, marching for the ubiquitous W.L.C.A.C., wore jeans and khaki shirts with black fists on the back; another wore green ponchos and white duck pants and big straw planters' hats. You wouldn't be likely to see so much done with so little in a dozen Rose Parades.

After the parade the crowd surged back into the park to hear the music and feast on ribs and sweet corn and chicken, and a few looked into a street of booths, set up by various social service agencies working in the south Los Angeles ghetto. Their signs and literature were a catalogue of the ills and needs Watts knows; help for pregnant girls, help for jobless boys, help for the mentally ill—help, help, help . . .

"Winter, summer, spring or fall," said a voice from a sound box in one of the booths, "all you gotta do is call. You got a friend."

A young man in a booth run by the U.S. Naval Shipyard wanted to tell about it. "We're trying to acquaint people here in Watts with job opportunities," he said, "in naval shipyards, because, man, the naval shipyards want to see some of our people come down there from Watts and work, so they can get some money and put it back in this community and build it up . . ."

Another young man was explaining the Trade Tech Mobile Advisement Center, a service of Los Angeles City College.

"We been in the supermarkets and the shopping centers. We talk to 'em, give 'em a push down to the school, and once they get to the door, the counsellors take over and fit 'em in . . ."

I was drawn back to the street of concessions by the promise of something to eat. I stood in line at a booth called Jerusalem Soul Barbecue, a name of such charming eclecticism that I couldn't resist it. I ordered barbecued chicken and a girl served it up on a paper plate and drenched it in dark red sauce.

"If you like it," she said, "you come back."

I had never been sure what was meant by *soul food.* Now I know. It is food that goes straight to the soul. The chicken was very good barbecued chicken, but the sauce was soul food. I went back to the Jerusalem Soul Barbecue.

213

"You're back," the girl said. "How you like that chicken?"

"Right on," I said. "I think I'll try a sweet potato pie."

Sweet potato pie goes straight to the soul. It is a rich and satisfying experience.

There are many things I don't understand about America, and one of them is how it is possible to grow up in this country and not know a thing about sweet potato pie.

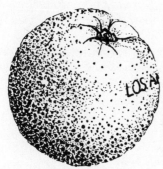

# Rodeo Drive

*"Does it have a price?" I asked.*
*"Yes. Everything is priced.*
*It's two and a half million."*

It might be argued that what holds western civilization together—more than credos, cartels and a common faith—is a very small number of streets that offer the finest goods our culture has to offer.

They are the Via Veneto in Rome, the Champs Elysées in Paris and Fifth Avenue in New York, among others, and now, finally, our own Rodeo Drive in Beverly Hills.

To stroll along Rodeo Drive today is to be reassured that our civilization has not fallen wholly into the hands of the proletariat. There is still a level at which the elite may feel comfortable and unthreatened, at which the most refined tastes may be indulged, the most sybaritic yearnings satisfied; and all it costs is money, which keeps the riffraff out.

To compare Rodeo Drive with the Champs Elysées is perhaps stretching it a mile or so, to say the least. Rodeo Drive does not happen to begin with an Arc de Triomphe and lead past the Grand Palais and the Renault automobile agency to the Jardin des Tuileries. All the same, it has become in recent years a very chic street, where one can pay anything from thirty-eight dollars for a vial of Gucci *parfum* to a fortune for a work of art.

Oddly, Rodeo Drive was sort of a dark horse in the Beverly Hills sweepstakes; a slow starter. Only a few years ago it appeared that any one of several other north-south streets had a

215

better chance of emerging as the most soigné street in town, but the others seem to have become commonplace, if not tacky, while Rodeo has grown into seductive maturity as suddenly as Colette's Gigi.

This transformation has taken place in the three short blocks between Wilshire Boulevard, where the street is anchored by the elegant Beverly Wilshire Hotel, the Brown Derby, Brentano's and Bonwit Teller, and Santa Monica Boulevard to the north. It is an avenue of luxuries; but, on the other hand, it is not barren of necessities. Rodeo Drive could sustain life, if one didn't mind the cost and didn't mind repairing his or her own shoes, doing his or her own laundry and living on tinned pâté de foie gras and that sort of thing from Jurgensen's.

It may be significant to note that there are about as many jewelry shops as apparel shops on Rodeo Drive, and the windows aren't full of cheap wedding rings, either. In Braun's Fine Jewels, for example, I saw a bracelet in the form of a coiled cobra, with diamond eyes, and a butterfly brooch with jade wings and diamond eyes and feelers. (They might have been rhinestones; you could fool me.) There were no price tags, of course. That would have been vulgar. On the other hand, the jewelry at Van Cleef and Arpels is evidently too precious for window display. It is shown in photographs, on models.

Most of the stores and boutiques are offspring of prestigious parents in Rome, Paris, London and other capitals of the fashion world, not to mention such monied American cities as Dallas and Houston, and each of them displays these points of affiliation proudly on its doors in gold leaf, giving the impression that the important cultural alliances between the western nations are not made by parliaments, presidents and kings, but by such establishments as Bally (exciting sportswear for ladies and gentlemen ... London, Zurich, Paris, Houston, Troy, Mich.); Van Cleef and Arpels (New York, Palm Beach, Paris, London, Geneva, Monte Carlo, Deauville, Cannes); Hermès (Deauville, Cannes, Monte Carlo, New York, London, Rome, Tokyo); and Courrèges (Paris).

The tone of the street is kept by even the smallest shops. Frank Hoffer's tailor shop identifies itself only with a discreet window sign: *BESPOKE CUSTOM TAILOR FOR MEN*. What a fine

Edwardian ring that word *bespoke* has. It means the same thing as custom, so I suppose its use in Mr. Hoffer's window is redundant; but it conjures up visions of Saville Row, for which a bit of pretentious redundancy is a small price.

Luxuriant swatches of plaid suiting are displayed in the window—merino wool, cashmere, mohair, camel's hair—straight from Barclay's Woolen Co., Ltd., 13 Saville Row, London, along with magnums of Laurent Perrier champagne and a bust of Apollo Belvedere.

The fine plaids and the word *bespoke* reminded me of the Cockney cabbie who saved up all his life for a bespoke suit, and when at last he stood in front of the tailor's mirror and saw himself a gentleman, he wept and wondered, "Why did we have to lose Indja!"

My feeling of being in a Tory establishment deepened when I entered the London Shop. The facade had been remodeled into what I took to be a Georgian style, with a coat of arms over the door and a red carpet leading off the sidewalk. The window was a treasure of silk scarves and cravats, walking sticks, belts and braces, and presiding over this haberdashery was a photograph of Winston Churchill in a velour chair, cigar in hand.

Just inside the door I was met by a six-foot-three-inch Beefeater, but he turned out to be a cardboard cutout. I suppose it would be too expensive even for the London Shop to have a genuine Beefeater hanging about.

Oriental rugs lay here and there over the red carpeting. The chairs for customers were red velvet. Back in the shoe store hung portraits of Queen Elizabeth II and the Duke of Edinburgh, and just behind the cash register another picture of Lord Churchill, with a passage from the most stirring of his wartime speeches:

"Let us therefore brace ourselves to our duty, and so bear ourselves that if the British Commonwealth and Empire lasts for a thousand years men will still say, this was their finest hour."

A red plaid number in a rack of sports jackets caught my eye, and surreptitiously, not really wanting to attract assistance from one of the gentlemen salesmen, I checked the price tag. It was $235. I hurried on over to the cravat display case, on

217

which a small card stood, as if to reproach me: "The lowest price," it said, "is not always the best bargain."

Up the street I went into Gucci's, after checking its foreign alliances first in gold leaf on the door. New York, Palm Beach, Paris, Chicago, Firenze, Roma, Milano . . . It sounded all right.

I thought I might buy silk scarves for my daughters-in-law, but they turned out to be a bit more expensive than I felt I wanted to pay at the moment.

"How about perfume," suggested a young saleswoman who had come to my aid. "This comes with a little atomizer," she said, showing me a small vial that had the familiar green and red stripes, a Gucci benchmark. "You keep it in this little *pouchette,* and when you take it out, everyone can see you have a Gucci. And it's only thirty-eight dollars."

As it turned out, I decided against buying the perfume, but I was not unrewarded. I had learned the word *pouchette,* meaning, I inferred, a small suede pouch or sack.

As I say, Rodeo Drive could sustain life, but there is only one grocery store—Jurgensen's. The Jurgensen stores are not grocery stores in the limited sense of our supermarkets, but as they call themselves, "gourmet importers and purveyors of specialty groceries, wines and spirits."

Among the gastronomic adventures laid out in the window was a line of Chalet Suzanne soups—romaine, gazpacho, red consommé, vichyssoise—whose flavor was described as "delightfully unidentifiable." There were also tins of quail eggs, chocolate-covered baby bees, fried grasshoppers and Strasbourg liver pâté with perigord truffles. There are shut-ins in Beverly Hills and environs, I am told, who buy all their groceries from Jurgensen's, by telephone.

Though sidewalk space is at a premium, the merchants of Rodeo Drive have done what they can to give it the desired look of sylvan-urban charm. Flower boxes and potted trees soften many of the storefronts. Mr. Guy, at Brighton Way, has planters all along the front; Cafe Swiss stands in the guise of a chalet behind six small cypress trees; Elizabeth's Pastry Shop and Tea Room has converted itself into a sidewalk cafe by squeezing two round tables and four chairs into a seven-by-four-foot space out front. (Elizabeth, by the way, is Elizabeth La Belle, a New

York girl who danced twelve years with the Rockettes at Radio City before coming west to open up her tea shop.) And all along the sidewalk at intervals of forty or fifty feet are Indian laurels planted by the city of Beverly Hills.

But the whole street offers only one other sidewalk cafe, the front court of the Daisy, on the east side, with a dozen tables under a gnarled old tree that adds to the patron's sense of being outdoors by dripping dead leaves into the soup du jour.

There are fewer restaurants than jewelry stores on the street. Besides the Daisy and Elizabeth's tearoom, there are only the Brown Derby, Cafe Swiss, the Luau, one of those ersatz Polynesian longhouse places with palm trees and a waterfall out front, and Chez Voltaire, adjoining the Beverly Rodeo Hotel.

Jerry Magnin's seemed to be specializing in safari clothes, including a large stock of shirts from China. The Chinese shirts, of a light cotton in green or tan, were as little as fifteen dollars, but similar shirts from Paris, which seemed not that much different at first glance, were sixty dollars.

"Why the difference?" I asked a saleswoman.

"Oh, the material. The tailoring."

I had to agree. There was some elusive quality in the French article that set it apart. One could march in a people's parade in the Chinese shirt, or actually go on safari, I suppose; but for a cocktail party or lunch at the Daisy, one would prefer the French.

Hunter's Bookstore holds down one corner at what is called Little Santa Monica Boulevard, providing another kind of nourishment from that provided by Jurgensen's. "Ten years ago," one of Hunter's people told me, "Rodeo Drive was nothing but small doctor buildings and little stores. Now it's *the* street."

On the opposite corner Carrol & Co., the V.I.P. Shop, purveys "Wardrobe for Gentlemen." The ambience is British, with coach lamps out front and pictures of Fletcher Christian and other members of the *Bounty* crew in the windows. Inside, the gentleman shopper is made to feel at home by paneled walls, models of sailing ships, English sporting prints and other objets d'art suggestive of London clubs and Sussex country houses.

My mood swung instantly back to France, though, when I entered Eres. There was a poster in the window with a vivacious

219

young woman advertising the *Jardin de Paris, touts les soirs,* and the store inside was divided into sections identified as Place de l'Opéra, Avenue de Champs Elysées, Boulevard du Montparnasse and so on.

"I suppose your collection is French?" I asked a saleswoman.

"Not really," she said. "Just our sweaters and T-shirts."

I looked at a pale green crocheted skullcap, thinking my French daughter-in-law would love it, but it was thirty-six dollars. Not that I considered that an excessive price. *I* certainly wouldn't try to crochet one like it for thirty-six dollars.

One might expect the humblest shop on the street to be Williams-Sonoma, which sells pots and pans and other cooking hardware. However, *its* pots and pans are for "gourmet cooking," a sign made clear, and I saw a young woman in the window arranging a set of gleaming omelet pans with the esthetic care of M. Zarekeivan arranging pieces of antique silver in his window down the street.

Simplicity was the tone of Amelia Gray's windows, where two manikins in angelic white lace evening gowns stood in individual mirrored showcases: woman, the cynosure. Next door Edwards-Lowell, furriers, were also content to let a single garment say it all. It was a full-length white coat, draped over a circular bench under a crystal chandelier at the center of the store. I walked in, quite sure that I couldn't possibly be mistaken for a customer.

"Can I help you?" a woman said.

"What kind of fur is that?" I asked.

"Brown shadow mink," she said.

"Could you tell me the price?"

"Just a moment." She went into an office and fetched a man who turned out to be Merrill Lowell, the owner and designer. Mr. Lowell was in a slightly liverish mood, having just heard on the radio another attack on the fur industry by the "fake fur" people, whom he accused of masquerading as protectors of endangered species.

"They renew this attack every year about this time," he said, "at the start of the cloth coat season. Actually, the furrier is as interested as anyone in protecting endangered species, if only to protect the raw materials of our trade. I'm a frustrated veterinarian myself. I love animals."

Lowell said he was pleased with the Europeanization of Rodeo Drive, but he would like to see it go one step further and adopt the siesta. "I'd like to see the merchants close from one to three-thirty in the afternoon and then stay open to seven. People would have their main meal at noon and then a later dinner. That's much more healthful."

The idea of a siesta seemed to have improved Lowell's mood and I asked the price of the brown shadow mink.

"That coat," he said, "is four thousand . . . (pause) . . . nine hundred . . . (pause) . . . and fifty dollars . . . and it's draped very badly." He walked over to the coat and deftly rearranged it.

The most expensive merchandise on Rodeo Drive is not to be found either at the furrier's or the jeweler's, but at the Wally Findlay Gallery (Paris, New York, Chicago, Palm Beach), where I was stopped just inside the door by a Degas street scene. From where I stood I could also see a Renoir portrait, a lily pond by Monet, a pastel study of a mother and two children by Cassatt, and, at the back an eight-by-fourteen-foot panel by Cézanne.

A bearded young man who turned out to be Thomas Phelan, the manager, said the Cézanne had been kept in the artist's family until its first public showing in 1974. It was a scene in the woods near Cézanne père's estate at Aix-en-Provence. "He painted it when he was twenty-one," Phelan said, "to prove to his father that he was an artist. That's Émile Zola there in the middle."

"Does it have a price?" I asked.

"Yes. Everything is priced. It's two and a half million."

On the other hand, it turned out, I could have the Cassatt pastel for only two hundred and fifty thousand dollars. "That was a study for an oil which President Johnson bought for the people of the United States," he said. "It is now in the White House."

Claude Monet's water lilies were priced at eight hundred and fifty thousand dollars. "He painted that in 1904, when he was experimenting with shimmer, the play of light."

"Do people really come in and buy such things?" I asked.

"We have yet to have someone come in and snap one off the wall," he said. "Oh, paintings at twenty, thirty, forty thousand—yes, that has happened. But pieces this large of course take a little more time and finesse."

Giorgio's (ladies' and gentlemen's apparel) has a corner entrance on Dayton Way with coach lamps and a white and yellow striped awning. There is an espresso and spirits bar at the center of the store, a haven, evidently, for late afternoon shoppers. It had the air of a small club, with autographed photographs of movie stars from Norma Shearer to Telly Savalas, and a backgammon board set out beside the fireplace on a table between two chairs.

"Good morning, sir," said a man in a steward's jacket. "Would you like a cup of coffee?"

"Indeed I would," I said.

"It is an illustrious honor," he said, a bit theatrically.

"You have an elegant way of speaking," I ventured as I sipped the coffee.

"It is sincere, sir."

"Thank you," I said when the coffee was gone. "That was very nice."

"Your pleasure is paramount, sir. It has been a prestigious honor."

If the Europeanization of Rodeo Drive seemed transient and illusory, it gained validity when I looked across Wilshire to the Beverly Wilshire Hotel, with its Italianate facade and its pretty red, white and blue awnings. It looked substantially and genuinely old world, and perhaps, I thought, it had had an influence on the changing image of Rodeo Drive, through sheer force of character.

I crossed Wilshire to the hotel and lunched in Hernando Courtright's El Padrino Room on artichoke hearts and white wine and was ready for siesta.

# Busch Gardens

*To these birds here, a big old black housecat might as well be a leopard.*

If Adam and Eve had hired a gardener, got rid of the serpent and put in some Budweiser on draught, their Eden might have been as nice a place to visit as Busch Gardens.

Anheuser-Busch, the people who created Busch gardens out in the middle of the San Fernando Valley, had the benefit of God's experience. Their paradise is so well run that the flamingos are breeding, the resident vultures are happy, and human visitors are flocking in at the rate of two million a year.

The Biblical Eden, it is supposed, was created in the desert by the flow of water from the Euphrates. Busch Gardens was created in the arid San Fernando Valley by the flow of Budweiser, Busch and Michelob from the nearby brewery.

Following an old family tradition, the present Augustus Busch had the seventeen and one-half-acre gardens built alongside the company's new plant. Thus, what might have been thought a community eyesore became an oasis. Busch Gardens is a well-kept jungle; a labyrinth of islands, lagoons and waterways, resplendent with rare trees and exotic birds and set with three pavilions where the company's product is served free.

Most visitors begin with a Skyrail tour of the brewery. I found it a heady adventure, not to say yeasty. The little cars, hanging from their monorail, climb to a height of eighty feet as they run around and through the plant. The eye enjoys a view of the valley from mountain to mountain, and the nose is piqued by the aroma of boiling malt, herbs, hops and grain.

223

Giant windows are built into the walls of the plant, so passengers can look down into the works. We glided by one vast room where two rows of enormous steel vats seemed to march off into an endless distance.

"This is the storage room," our motorman informed us. "Those are lager tanks—one hundred eighty-eight of them. Each tank goes fifty feet into the wall and holds thirty-six thousand gallons of beer. If a man drank one gallon a day it would take him ninety-nine years to empty out one tank."

At that provocative thought, cries of appreciation arose from the passengers in our car.

We rolled through the bottle and can plant, where three thousand bottles and cans a minute were being filled and capped and packaged by immaculate automation.

"It is estimated," our motorman said portentously, "that this year alone, this plant will serve the thirteen western states over eight hundred million glasses, bottles and cans of beer."

The plant tour ends with a red carpet walk through a warehouse and down a ramp into the gardens. The transformation is instant and illusory—from Midwestern brewery to tropical atoll.

The setting is pure Joseph Conrad, without the humidity: the flat mirror of the lagoon; the coral islets alive with pink birds; the flights of bamboo and clouds of flowering trees; the cries of parrot and macaw; and the white river boat idling at the dock.

Our boatman was a suntanned blond youth in a dazzling white uniform with gold epaulets. The electric boats run over submerged tracks, but our man made a show of steering at a mock-up wheel. Like all his fellows, he knew the names of the birds and plants, and also the hazards of the twenty-minute cruise.

"Please keep your fingers in the boat," he warned. "Our macaws can snap a broomstick with a single bite. I've seen 'em do it." I'd heard the same warning on the river at Disneyland; but here, evidently, it wasn't any joke.

The boat travels three-quarters of a mile, but the sense of distance is greater as it runs narrow passages, circles small islands, rounds the three pavilions and probes a gorge and a mini-sierra. At the outset we passed a small tree, utterly naked of foliage, with half a dozen gaudy birds in its branches. They scolded us. Macaws, our boatman told us.

The macaw is rude, smart and comical. He denudes trees just for the hell of it. He looks like a military drum major and makes a sound like somebody scraping your backbone with the top of a beer can. He is the most intelligent of the parrots and lives to be seventy-five, if he's lucky.

"To the right," our boatman said, "is the Brazilian floss silk tree." This is a strangely beautiful tree, with an umbrella of delicate pink flowers and a green-bark trunk well toothed with the thorns the Creator visited upon Adam for eating the forbidden fruit.

"We are now entering the Palm Island area."

We cruised into a small lagoon whose banks grew giant and dwarf bamboos, a coral tree, date and fan palms and thickets of pampas grass. From an islet on our port side a pair of toucans eyed us. These odd birds are two-thirds beak, and like all exotic birds look artificial. It is hard not to suspect that the birds of Busch Gardens, like the fauna of Disneyland, are made of nylon and electric components.

We circled Michelob Terrace. Visitors sat at tables under umbrellas, sipping beer as they looked out across the lagoon at an island full of flamingos. An iridescent-blue Chinese pheasant pecked along a bank. Sandpipers and small white ibis scratched about. A black Tasmanian swan crossed our bow.

We thrummed on, passing under a bridge from which two blue-and-gold macaws glared down at us. Giant philodendrons grew on the banks, along with umbrella grass, a Mexican yucca, a weeping pittosporum and papyrus reeds, like lion tails blowing in the breeze.

We emerged into the main lagoon. Here the three-room Budweiser Pavilion, enclosed and air-conditioned, stands over the water. Visitors sat on ice cream parlor chairs, sampling beer from paper cups and looking out at swans and copper-colored ducks, an island aflame with flamingos, a gaggle of snow geese and a lonely old weatherbeaten pelican with one wing gone.

From the main lagoon we could see the entrance to the gorge—a rocky peak, like the needles of Fiji, with three ungainly feathered monsters perched on its pinnacle. "King vultures," our pilot told us ominously.

All year long, night and day, the vultures haunt that particular point, he said. What keeps them there, I wondered, as we passed in their shadows, looking up into those red pitiless faces and unfathomable eyes.

Macaws, flamingos and sacred Egyptian ibis in the middle of the San Fernando Valley a man might believe; a gorge, no. But there we were, like Lewis and Clark, pushing upstream under sheer walls of gray stone.

The gorge, we learned, is made of featherstone, a volcanic foam that weighs a fifth as much as granite and can easily be shaped. It is so light it floats, our boatman assured us, and must be anchored to the bottom of the lagoon. We purred under the Busch Bavarian Pavilion, whose three open-air platforms reach out over the gorge from a height, and again my taste buds picked up the spicy bite of hops on the air.

Then the gorge fell away, and our boat entered the cascades, a canyon that conjures up the water sounds and pine smells of the High Sierra. The boatman shut our motor, and we listened to the water gushing and tumbling over the rocks under the pines. I knew it was heresy, but I thought of the Olympia ads on TV—the ones that say, "It's the water!"

We came out in the main lagoon again.

"We're just in time for the bird show," my wife said.

"Bird show?" I said. "I'd rather been looking forward to a beer."

The bird show is staged every hour under a big Moreton Bay fig tree in front of a shaded amphitheater. I don't believe I had ever seen a bird show before. They are much like a dog show, except the dogs are birds. It is remarkable what macaws and cockatoos can be taught to do. A macaw named Cecil, for example, gave children in the audience a kiss by taking their noses in his beak.

"We've never lost a nose," the trainer said.

Beebee, a red, blue and gold macaw, tucked her head under and turned somersaults. A cockatoo named Gus pushed another named Eunice in a red wagon. A big fire and rescue act was the *grande finale*. Gus, or maybe it was Sam, rescued Eunice, or Edna, from the upstairs window of a burning castle, while Ed put the fire out and Robert ran Old Glory up the flagpole.

It takes three to six months to train a show bird, the trainer said. At the moment, he was training an Australian sulphur-crested cockatoo named Clyde to ride a bicycle over a tightrope.

Busch Gardens has close to a thousand resident birds, plus an uncounted number of drop-ins who discover the easy life and good pickings and decide to hang around. Some are a nuisance and some are a menace.

"We have a falcon in the gardens right now we're not too happy about," I was told. "He's already killed some birds."

There is also the problem of cats. That is one of the reasons that the macaws are rounded up every day at dusk, on broomsticks, and taken in for the night.

"The cats come over the fence after dark. To these birds here, a big old black housecat might as well be a leopard."

Another reason the macaws are taken in is to keep them from tearing up the trees.

"They'll strip a tree. It's what they do in the balance of nature. In the jungles, with all that moisture, the plant life grows too fast if the birds don't keep it down. So in *that* environment, they're a balance. But here, where the gardens are more or less man-made, we have to fight that balance."

Some of the resident birds have pinioned or clipped wings—those that tend to fly away, or are very rare and valuable. Most of them, though, not only stay in the gardens but hardly ever venture from their own small perch or territory. I asked about the vultures.

"Oh, those birds can fly away all right. Why do they stay put? We feed 'em. Horsemeat. Every day. They only need to leave their nesting area in search of food, and we supply that. They're a lazy bird, too."

The gardens' food bill is forty thousand dollars a year. That's for the birds alone. The daily handout is prepared in a spotless kitchen in the birdhouse. It includes grapes, bananas, raisins, apples, carrots, beets, spinach, corn, cottage cheese, hard-boiled eggs, cod liver oil, wheat germ and even garlic, plus a vitamin-packed nectar and a special diet to keep the scarlet ibis and flamingos in good color.

On the way back to the pavilion we stopped to chat with some of the talking birds that are kept in cages near the Penguin and Otter House.

I tried to communicate with a Java mynah bird named Big Bill. A sign on his cage said he could repeat such phrases as "Hi, how are you?" "Polly want a cracker" and "George, I am going to watch TV." It said he could also laugh and whistle at girls.

"Hi," I said. "How are you?"

He ignored me.

I tried "Polly want a cracker?"

"Hi," he said. "How are you?"

"I'm fine," I said. "How are you?"

He whistled.

We beat our way back to the Busch Pavilion, up in the gorge. We got cups of beer and took a table out on one of the platforms over the water. A black-necked screamer was fishing in a pool. A white stork with pink legs and black wing tips stood one-legged with his mate on a rocky bluff. I thought I saw a snowy egret. Down the gorge a way a great crowned crane spread his golden crown.

Across the lagoon a waterfall tumbled from a height of forty feet. It churned the lagoon white, blew up a cloud of spray and filled the gorge with a light, exhilarating thunder.

I remembered what the boatman had said. "You are looking at the largest man-made waterfall in the San Fernando Valley."

The moment was idyllic. I knew how the vultures felt. Why fly away? I put down the rest of my beer and sighed.

"We better go on home," I said. "A man could go to seed out here."

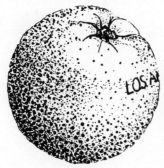

# Pierce College Farm

*"What is it you get from hogs that you can eat?"*
*"Bacon and eggs!" a boy shouted.*

The yellow school bus trundled over the farm road past fields of alfalfa. It was packed with first and second graders and was driven by one of those intrepid women who seem able to handle these clumsy vehicles and their restive loads in any kind of crisis.

I had taken a seat on the aisle near the front and immediately found myself under the intense scrutiny of a small boy on the inside seat. A pink card with the number 1 was pinned to his blue windbreaker. He held a brown paper bag in his lap.

"My uncle has a farm," he said at last, evidently having decided I was fit for conversation.

"Oh?" I said. "Where is it?"

"Back East."

"Where back East?"

"I don't know. On the train it takes a day to get there."

I didn't know how far "back East" you could go on a train in a day, but it reminded me that when I was about this boy's age I had told my teacher that my family came from back East, and when she asked me back East where, I said "Colorado." It was a long time before I could understand why she laughed.

We who live here in Southern California by the seashore, ringed in by our mountains and deserts and beyond them the Rockies, are so dramatically isolated from the rest of the United States that anyplace beyond the Colorado River is back East.

This particular morning I was sharing with the children on the bus an experience that is regarded as an American child's

229

birthright, but one not always realized. We were going back
to the farm. There were perhaps forty children in the bus and
I would have been surprised if any of them had ever been on
a farm before.

These children were from South Pasadena, right across the
freeway from where I live. We were all city people, and we
knew that eggs and chickens and milk all came from the supermarket.

Actually, our farm wasn't back East at all, but west. We were
setting out on a guided tour of Pierce College's working farm
on the four hundred and twenty-acre campus near Woodland
Hills, in the southwest corner of the San Fernando Valley.

One of the virtues of a metropolis is that is has wonders that
most of its inhabitants have never seen, harbors they have never
explored.

If you take the Winnetka offramp from the Ventura Freeway
and drive north half a mile or so, you will see on your left the
spacious campus—a spread of low rolling hills with scattered
one-story buildings around a mall a quarter-mile long, and in
the deeper hills to the south the fields and pastures and structures
of the farm.

Pierce College was started shortly after World War II as an
agricultural school. The San Fernando Valley, some people may
remember, was then still more farmland than suburb. The great
postwar building boom was just gathering its breath to blow
the farms away. When the doors opened back in 1947 there
were two hundred and eleven students who had never heard
of data processing and some of the other subjects on the present
curriculum at Pierce.

The college changed with the valley. It is now one of the
eight Los Angeles Community Colleges, offering two-year pro-
grams in the liberal arts, journalism, nursing, horticulture, business, data processing, accounting, real estate and secretarial services to nearly eighteen thousand students.

But meanwhile the agricultural sciences department has
stayed. The farm prospers, selling its beef, eggs, milk and wool
at market prices. Since it is the only agricultural school in the
Community Colleges system, students transfer from other dis-
tricts of the city to learn farming, and many come from other

counties. From Pierce, some go into farm work, some on to higher education in agricultural science or veterinary medicine.

To share the farm with children of the city, and to keep alive the college's identity as an agricultural school, the free guided tour program is offered throughout the year. There are tours not only of the farm itself, but of the nature center and natural history museum. There is also a Braille trail for the blind.

I took the tour on a weekday morning, waiting for the school bus at the farm's retail store with Ina Geller, of the Pierce communications staff, and Ron Wechsler, a graduate who came back as a member of the agricultural sciences faculty.

A sign over the counter of the farm store listed the specials of the day: pomegranates, quinces, limes, tangerines. There were also large plastic bags bulging with raw wool from the farm's last shearing, an event to which schoolchildren are annually invited.

"It's such a lovely spring rite," said Ms. Geller. "So charming. We go up to the sheep pasture and there's nobody there at first, and then in half an hour there are children all over the place."

I wondered who bought the bags of wool and what they did with it.

"Oh, women from the community. They card it. Start from scratch."

The store is open to the public, and while its prices are competitive, not lower than those of markets in the community, it is much patronized by residents who like the idea of buying fresh produce from a farm store.

"You see," said Ms. Geller, opening a large refrigerator door, "our eggs are special."

She lifted an egg carton with the label "Quality Eggs from Hens with a College Education." "We have three thousand chickens who do their best for Pierce," she said.

The store is in the Agricultural Industries Building, and I saw that the bulletin board in the hallway had different kinds of notices from those you might find on the bulletin boards at other community colleges.

*FOR SALE: English hunting coat. Bright blue. Stands out in a show ring . . . Arabian stud service . . . Wanted: Indian runner duck hen . . . For sale: Palomino mare . . . For sale to good home: Goat female . . .*

231

By the time the bus came, three young women from the agricultural school had arrived to lead the tours. The student guides are trained by the college community services office. "So what the children learn about cows is accurate," said Ms. Geller.

We climbed aboard the bus with the children and set out for the pigpens, which were to be the first stop on the tour. It was on this brief trip that I sat next to the boy whose uncle owned the farm.

That was the end of our conversation for the time being, though, as we soon reached the pigpens and the excitement was too great to permit idle talk. The other groups disembarked and the guide for Group 1 held her group on the bus for a briefing. I decided to stick with Group 1.

"OK, everybody," she said. "Look up here. Before you get off the bus there are three things I want you to remember. One, wait till your guide quits talking before you ask any questions. OK? Two, never run ahead of the guide. Some animal could get out and there might be trouble. Three, don't touch any animal unless we say it's OK. You might go home with four fingers."

"You shouldn't hit pigs, either," a boy volunteered from the back of the bus, "because they could bite you." When no one challenged this statement, he rushed on. "Horses could kick you and you could lose a leg."

"We hope," said the guide, "it won't be that dreadful. By the way, my name is Patti. You're my group. You're going to stick with me. OK? All right, let's go."

We climbed off the bus and crowded up at a pen in which half a dozen or more young pigs—pink, white and russet colored—were rooting and shoving each other about, and feeding at will from a bin whose food drops they operated with their snouts.

"All right," said Patti, without ceremony, "these are hogs. What is it you get from hogs that you can eat?"

"Bacon and eggs," a boy shouted.

"Well, bacon, yes. The eggs come from chickens."

"Sausage."

"Sausage. Right."

Patti pointed out that footballs are called pigskins because they used to be made out of pigskin, although most are now made out of plastic.

"I have a plastic football," a boy said, which seemed to verify, in part, at least, the information just imparted.

"How many of you," Patti asked, "think pigs are stupid and dirty?"

From the hand count, I estimated that two-thirds of Group 1 thought pigs were stupid and dirty, a percentage which, by projection, I found myself able to apply to all schoolchildren in South Pasadena and very likely all in Los Angeles.

"Actually," said Patti, "pigs are really pretty smart. They're one of the smartest animals we have here at Pierce. They learn very quickly."

She pointed out the water fountain in a corner of the pen. There was a metal bowl and above it a faucet which was operated when a pig pressed his snout against a lever. Now and then a pig would trot over to the fountain and get a drink, nonchalant as a child using a fountain.

"Actually," said Patti, "pigs like to stay clean. The reason they roll in the mud is to stay cool. Pigs can't sweat, the way we do when it's hot. So they roll in the mud."

From the pigpen she led us down a road and up a hill a ways to a fence beyond which we could see sheep grazing. "What do you see up there?" she asked.

"Cows," a boy said.

"You're looking the wrong way. Those are sheep. Those woolly ones, higher up. What do we get from sheep's wool?"

"Coats," said a boy.

"Yarn," said a girl.

"That's right. Every spring we give the sheep haircuts. It keeps the sheep cool and we get wool. The female sheep are called ewes, and they have lambs. We're lucky, because they usually have twins. What do we call the father sheep?"

"A billygoat."

"No. That's a goat. Father sheep are called rams."

"Rams!" a boy exclaimed, evidently making the connection for the first time between the male sheep and the Los Angeles member of the National Football League. "I *like* the Rams!"

We walked back down to the pigpens and stood in front of

a barn-like structure marked FARROWING BUILDING. Patti asked if any of her group could read the sign. It was too much for them.

"Does anybody know what farrowing means?"

I was hoping her eyes wouldn't find mine, because it had occurred to me that I wasn't quite sure what farrowing meant.

"OK," she said. "Farrowing building is a big word for pig nursery. What happens in here, the mother pigs, the sows, have their baby pigs. If you're lucky we'll see a father pig in there, too. He's called a boar, and he weighs eight hundred pounds and can be very mean. So don't go messing around with a boar."

We followed her into the farrowing building, walking between rows of farrowing crates in which enormous sows were suckling their litters. It was a maternal scene not different in its elements from those of any species, yet in those inert slabs of flesh on the one hand and the shoving, noisy offspring on the other it was easy to see the inevitability of the pig's fate as a metaphor for human sloth and greed.

We were lucky. The boar was inside—a big red fellow who seemed to stand unusually high off the ground on long legs. This height was a new strain, Ron Wechsler said, bred into the animal to make him more efficient. It also looked as if it might make him faster on his feet and more dangerous.

"Boars are very dangerous. You have to watch yourself every minute. Pigs will *eat* people, you know. If you're working around a boar and fall down and get knocked unconscious, for example, you're in real trouble."

The little boy hadn't been exaggerating, then, when he said it was a bad idea to hit a pig.

We got back in the bus to go to the dairy. I sat in the same seat and the children sat in their same seats, in which they had left their bags of lunch. The boy on my left resumed the conversation. "My uncle's barn burned down," he said.

"Yes," I said, "that always seems to happen."

The girl in the seat in front of him had twisted around in her seat and was regarding me with a persistent, unrelenting inquiry that defied appraisal. Filial? Maternal? Merely curious? She had soft gray eyes, freckles on her nose and two pigtails tied with white bows.

"Did you bring your lunch?" she said at last.

"No, I forgot," I said.

"You can have half of mine." She opened her sack and withdrew a brown bread sandwich, wrapped in plastic. "You can have half of this." She reached in again and pulled out two brown chocolate cookies of the kind called brownies, I believe, also wrapped in plastic.

"You are very kind," I said.

Pierce has eighty head of dairy cattle, brown Swiss and Holstein, which produce seventy gallons of milk a day, most of which is purchased by Carnation. The cows are milked by machine, but in power shortages, or when the machines aren't working properly for some other reasons, some of the ag students are rousted out of bed at three o'clock in the morning to do the milking by hand. "The cows can't wait," Wechsler said. "They're milked twice a day, at four a.m. and four p.m. We adjust the clocks to the second. Five minutes before milking time, the cows will already be lined up and waiting."

Patti led her group to a pen where several Holstein calves were getting used to the world on spindly legs. Their white spots were as white as milk and their black was a clean jet glossy black.

"They're beautiful," exclaimed a little girl, expressing the truth of it precisely. A good case might be made for a Holstein calf as one of the most beautiful and appealing animals in nature, though it is not their destiny to be glamorous.

There seemed to be no bulls about. "All our dairy cows are bred artificially," Wechsler said. "One reason for that is that dairy bulls are extremely dangerous. You can never go into a pen with a dairy bull without some kind of protection."

At a pen holding a brown calf, Patti allowed the children to feed alfalfa to it through the fence. "But keep your fingers together," she warned, "so she won't mistake your fingers for alfalfa."

From the dairy we rode in the bus past alfalfa fields and green pastures to see the beef cattle. Pierce has about two hundred head. Steers ready for market are sold to the public through a local slaughterhouse. "There's a waiting list. We can't keep up."

235

Flocks of pigeons and sparrows wheeled in the air above the pastures, now and then landing like a black carpet on the green. "Birds are a real problem. The pigeons get into the mangers and cause disease problems and the ducks walk right down the furrows and eat the seed as soon as it's planted."

From the fence we looked out on the pasture at the scatter of cattle. "If you look hard," said Patti, "you can see the mother cows feeding the calves."

She gave it to the children plain. "When a steer gets to weigh about a thousand pounds he goes to market, and that's what you get at MacDonald's."

"You mean french fries, too?" said a cheeky lad.

The barn was at the top of the hill, overlooking the whole farm. Clarence the Brahma bull was outside the barn in his pen. "He likes to show that he's strong and mean," said Patti, "so be careful. Can you notice something about Clarence that's different?"

"He's got a hump."

Patti also pointed out that Clarence had flop ears and a wattle. She led us into the barn and Wechsler got into the pen with Clarence and drove him into a stall inside so he could be seen up close. He was a fine beast, with a magnificent head and large glossy eyes. He kept sponging his nose with his tongue, making it glisten.

A cow poked her head through a window and Patti introduced her as Clementine. "I guess she's Clarence's wife," she said. "We used to say she was his girl friend," Patti said in an aside to me, "but then she had a calf, and the children said she must be his wife."

On the way down the hill we stopped to look at the goats. "Do you really feed them cans?" a boy asked. I guessed it was the same one who had asked about the french fries. There's one in every class.

"Once when I didn't used to come to school," a girl said, "I used to have two billygoats." She had blond hair and wore a yellow sweater and was holding a bouquet of alfalfa. "One was a girl and one was a boy."

There was nothing left but the chickens. The college chickens are white leghorns and are also a paying part of the farm, along with the hogs, the dairy and the beef cattle. "Each hen lays one egg every twenty-eight hours, or six eggs a week," Patti told us. "No matter what you do, however you try to bribe them, they won't produce any more. Also, the eggs these hens lay are not fertile. No matter how long she sits, they won't hatch."

The commercial layers, she pointed out, lead an easy life. "All they have to do is eat, drink and lay eggs. Now let's go see some chickens that do lay fertile eggs."

We moved on to a pen inhabited by hens and roosters. Everyone noticed at once that most of the hens had raw spots on their backs from which the feathers had been picked. Some had bigger patches than others, and these seemed to be the smaller ones.

We were looking at the victims of that barnyard phenomenon known as the pecking order. The biggest and strongest hen pecks the next biggest and strongest, and on down the line to the littlest and weakest hen, which has nobody to peck.

"It's a good thing people don't have feathers," said Patti. "Oh," she added as the hideous possibilities really reached her, "wouldn't that be *terrible?*"

She pointed out that the roosters were the larger chickens. "They're the ones with the big red combs and the big wattles under their chins. That's partly what makes them a rooster."

I felt she had faltered somewhat on the definition of roosterism, but there were no questions.

The tour ends at a little park directly behind the Agricultural Industries Building. There are picnic tables and carved animals to play on. Group 1 joined the others in the park and altogether they began to set up a shrill chant:

"We want lunch! We want lunch!"

"This group," one of the teachers explained, "is very lunch oriented."

Ms. Geller asked me to have lunch with her in the college cafeteria and I was going to say that I already had an invitation, but I saw the girl with the pigtails chanting "We want lunch!" as loud as the rest, and I realized she had forgotten me.

I had a soufflé. It was made with college-educated eggs, I was told, and it was quite good. I kept wondering, though, what was in the little girl's brown bread sandwich.

237

# The J. Paul Getty Museum

*A helicopter was hovering over the garden and he was quite sure the man looking down from it was Mr. Getty.*

Two thousand years from now, when archeologists from other planets are digging in the earth's ruins, they will be profoundly puzzled, I expect, by the discovery of the J. Paul Getty Museum.

For here, on the coast of Southern California, where American civilization will have reached its zenith, they will turn up the stones of a splendid Roman villa, evidently destroyed by earthquake and the nuclear wars of the twenty-first century.

Assuming that by the time our scholarly visitors unearth this treasure they will already have worked out the chronology of earth man's successive cultures, they will be obliged to conjecture that somehow, just at its highest tide, Roman civilization planted a palatial outpost on this distant shore.

From the fluted columns, the Doric and Corinthian capitals, the tiled mosaic floors, the bronze and marble sculptures, the layout of peristyles, loggias, temples and cubicles, they will conclude that the villa was built in the first century B.C., perhaps by Julius Caesar himself, who could easily have subdued the local savages.

I'm not sure they would be any less bemused, though, if they were to learn that the villa was not built in the first century but in the twentieth, and not by a Caesar but by an American billionaire who lived in a fifty-five-room Tudor mansion in Surrey Place, London, and among other things occupied himself by writing homiletic essays on money, virtue and success for *Playboy* magazine.

239

If anything that cost seventeen million dollars can be called
a whim, the Getty museum is the whim of J. Paul Getty, the
oilman who is said to hold so great a portion of the world's
wealth that it would be impossible for him to liquidate without,
so to speak, breaking the bank. It is also impossible for the
ordinary man to grasp how much money a billion dollars is,
but you get some feel of it when you first see the Getty museum
and remind yourself that the man who built it and owns it,
every stone, has never even seen it, and maybe never will.

The museum stands on a wooded hill above Santa Monica
Bay, a quarter-mile up from Pacific Coast Highway. The stone
road climbs through towering eucalyptuses and evergreens that
quickly shut out the city, so that when the museum suddenly
looms ahead, there are no surrounding structures to make it
seem incongruous. It is no trick at all to imagine you are indeed
approaching an ancient villa.

It is a necessity of our times that the villa stands over an
underground garage, but its entrance is surely the most magnificent garage entrance in the modern world. Nothing but
chariots could ever before have been driven through such stately
gates.

From the garage an elevator rises to an airy loggia with Corinthian columns. This opens into the Peristyle Garden, which in
itself is worth the expedition. The garden is perhaps a hundred
yards long, planted about a great reflecting pool that runs almost
its full length, blue as the Bay of Naples. There are bronze deer
among the shrubs and trees, bronze wrestlers, a wing-footed
Mercury resting, and at the far end of the pool a bronze youth
napping supine in the sun. On either side the garden is enclosed
by deep porticos with Doric columns, terrazzo floors, ornate
wood ceilings and walls painted to give an illusion of other
structures and landscapes lying beyond the villa.

There seemed to be a mile of hedges, and a gardener told
me they were varieties of Japanese and English boxwood. There
were borders of purple campanula or bellflowers; a ground cover
of chamomile (an herb valued by the ancients for tea and baths);
pink Dianthus; daffodils and irises around the pool; bay trees,
oleanders, pansy beds, English ivy. All of them were plants that
could have been found in a Roman garden. Even the pink roses
were an ancient variety, unchanged through the centuries.

At last I approached the facade of the museum itself, feeling as if I might be met at the great bronze doors by the master of the house, some rich merchant, most likely, down from Rome for a weekend of revels among his slaves and houris at the villa.

I sat for a moment on one of the semicircular stone benches at the far end of the garden. It is right here, I suspect, that most visitors will find out whether they like the Getty museum or not. Perhaps for scholars and students of art, the collection inside will be decisive; they will be immune to Mr. Getty's fantasy. But for most of us, it will just be a question of whether we are enchanted by the structure; whether we buy it.

I found it easy to buy. As everyone perhaps knows by now, the museum is an imaginative re-creation of an actual house, the Villa of the Papyri at Herculaneum, which was buried by volcanic mud when Vesuvius woke from its long sleep in A.D. 79, obliterating the little resort town on the Bay of Naples and its larger neighbor, Pompeii.

The few survivors fled into the sea, the mud soon hardened into rock, and it was almost seventeen centuries before the buried Herculaneum was discovered. In 1709, workmen sinking a well in a monastery garden struck what turned out to be the upper tier of the town theater. A little more digging exposed precious marbles, and soon an inscription that identified the site as Herculaneum.

The scent of treasure quickened the cupidity of nearby princes. The looting began; but it was slow work, tunneling through rock, and it was forty years before another stroke of luck, another well shaft in another monastery garden, intruded on a colored marble floor. It was a garden pavilion of some fabulous villa. For the next fifteen years the villa was explored and looted. Its plan was mapped meanwhile by a Swiss engineer; but his work was unfinished, and the villa remains underground and not fully known to this day.

It was the villa's treasures that brought it fame. Besides the fine marble floors, it yielded an abundance of bronze and marble busts and statues, many of which are now in the museum at nearby Naples. Modern scholars were even more interested in the many books of Greek and Latin, written on rolls of papyrus, which were found in the villa's library. From this literary cache came the modern name—Villa of the Papyri.

The carbonized papyri were partly readable, and were found to be mostly philosophical, especially Epicurean. Many were the works of a certain Philodemus, who lived in the first century B.C. and was a protege of Lucius Calpurnius Piso, the father-in-law of Julius Caesar. Thus it is thought likely that the villa was owned by Piso, and that Philodemus was his star boarder.

It was this buried villa, with its revelations and its mysteries, that inspired the Getty museum. It was the romantic fancy of J. Paul Getty to reconstruct the villa on his hill above the Malibu, and let the critics be damned.

Damned they were. When the museum was opened to the public in 1974, the critical reaction was reminiscent of one of those winter thunderstorms that sometimes break over the Bay of Naples itself, quite out of keeping with its sunny reputation.

Though most everyone was respectful of Mr. Getty's art collection, and grateful that it was to be shared, there was general disdain for the house he had built to keep it in. At best, they called it kitsch, and the exiled billionaire was upbraided for blowing millions on a dubious re-creation of a structure designed for another place, another time, by an architect two thousand years in his grave. Noblesse oblige? Preposterous. It was arrogance. It was vanity carried to the point of folly if not madness.

They certainly had a point. Here was Los Angeles, trying to rise above its comic image as one vast breakaway movie set, where nothing was what it seemed to be, and now our richest patron had built a sand castle for his second childhood and set us back two thousand years.

On the other hand, as I sat there on that ancient stone bench, I surrendered to the illusion. The sky was blue. A slow wind came up from the bay, moving through the surrounding screen of pine, eucalyptus, sycamore and cypress. The bronze youth dozing in the pool was a slave; he would soon be wakened by his master's whistle. It was a nice day in Herculaneum, summer of '79.

Finally I climbed marble stairs under the eight fine Corinthian columns of the facade and entered the marble vestibule, which in turn opened into an inner garden. This garden would have been at the center of the villa's life. There are four small fountains at the corners, a long central pool with five supple bronze maidens, and a surrounding peristyle of forty columns topped by Ionic capitals. What other thoughts could such a garden inspire than epicurean?

I wandered on through the museum, not following any guide, but more like a man enjoying his house. I had the feeling I was in a villa, not a museum, and I liked it. These would have been the bedrooms, saloons and workrooms of Lucius Piso and his household, including, no doubt, a complement of guests who drank too much and stayed too long.

I was drawn first into the Hall of Aphrodite, the Greek love goddess whom the Romans called Venus. Here she was in all her postures, the classic ideal of woman—a bit large in the hip and small in the breast, by contemporary American standards, but endowed by her Pygmalions with a soft enveloping graceful power; Aphrodite crouching, Aphrodite adjusting her hair, Aphrodite with a dolphin—the Venus Mazarin, so called because she once belonged to Cardinal Mazarin, the brilliant minister of Louis XIV. Her head, right arm and a breast had been restored, her label said, probably in the eighteenth century. I may have just imagined it, but I thought her eighteenth-century Mr. Higgins hadn't quite got it.

But no one had tampered with a Greek head, from about 100 B.C., which had a smashed nose and other mutilations. Yet she was lovely, as if the mind supplied what the eye could not see. I would not have wanted her restored, any more than I would like to see arms on the Venus de Milo.

The Hall of Aphrodite opens into the atrium—an airy, vaulted chamber in which it must have been a serene delight to sit with a bottle of Asti Spumante, or whatever the cellar held, with a vista through one hall to the west porch and garden, and through the inner garden with its bronze maidens to the east porch and garden. In the atrium itself water trickles from a bronze boar's head into a shallow marble pool; a marble Aphrodite waits in an alcove; sunlight falls softly through an opal ceiling.

Nearby, in the small Gallery of Colored Marbles, are a dozen sculpture portraits of Roman people: a plump matron, folksy and mischievous, who might have come from Dickens; a young lady, prim, aloof, perhaps disappointed; a youth, intense, restless, troubled; a happy girl, solid and good; an old black man with eyes that have seen it all; a lovely girl, serene, wondering, full of promise; a headstrong mother; a beautiful spoiled child; a plain girl, strong and responsible; a bearded man with deep lines and penetrating eyes. They seemed more real than the movie stars in our wax museums. I had a feeling that when I left the room they would all start prattling about me.

The nearby Temple of Herakles, or Hercules, as the Romans called him, holds perhaps the best-known piece in the collection, and one for which its owner is said to have a special feeling. It is the Lansdowne Herakles, a statue of the young god-hero with lion skin and club. The temple is a small, round, high-domed room, lighted only by a shaft from on high. Hercules stands in this bright shaft—powerful, unafraid, full of good works.

Though possibly inspired by an earlier Greek work, the Hercules was carved by the court sculptor of the great Roman emperor Hadrian, and was found in his villa at Tivoli. It was later acquired by the Marquess of Lansdowne, and presently bears his name.

"Herakles was not only a model of human achievement," says the museum guidebook, "but the subject of philosophical interpretation and hence an appropriate model for a Roman emperor or an outstanding American businessman."

I'm not sure I grasp the logic of that thought. The Lansdowne Herakles reminded me more of the young Victor Mature than of J. Paul Getty. But in time, I suppose, when Lansdowne is forgotten, it may become known as the Getty Herakles, and our visitors from space will wonder who *he* was.

Lucius Piso, being a man of affairs, must have had an office in the villa; anyway, it has one now, and there I found Stephen Garrett, who runs the museum for Mr. Getty, at his desk. He turned out to be an amiable, witty Englishman, and capable of being amusing about the most serious subjects, such as why his employer chose to reconstruct an ancient villa.

"Actually," said Garrett, speaking with an engaging emphasis, like a chap from early Evelyn Waugh, "Mr. Getty doesn't *like* modern architecture. You see?"

I nodded.

"This may be *reprehensible*," he went on. "It may be short-*sighted*. But he doesn't *like* it."

Mr. Getty had always been interested in the classical Greek and Roman periods, Garrett was saying. By a happy chance, as it turned out, he had lived for a time in Naples, near the site where this very villa, or its model, had been discovered.

"He thought a classical building would provide an appropriate environment for his collections, and would have the appearance of a work of art itself. He felt that by doing a restoration of the building, he would have something to offer to people who might never *get* to Italy, never *get* to Herculaneum or Pompeii, never walk or stand in such a building as this."

As for the critics, they all wore blinders. They could only see one right way.

"My own view," said Garrett, "is that there are a *number* of alternatives. Many museums are dreary, cold, barren—as places to be *in*. They're not fun. This is a perfectly tenable alternative.

"Our experience is that people like *being* here. It's the *ambience*. Having walked up that garden and come into the vestibule they're in a highly pleasant frame of mind. And many of them, when they leave, will tell one of the guards, 'Please thank Mr. Getty for me.' "

Getty built the museum near his Spanish-style mansion on a sixty-five-acre site he bought in the late 1940s. In 1954 he opened some of the house to the public, by reservation, to show a part of his collection. But this arrangement was inadequate for collection and public both, so he added the villa. From the start, it attracted more visitors than it had room for.

I wondered how long it had been since J. Paul Getty had been "home," so to speak.

"Eighteen years," he said. "But of course, he could pop in anytime. Just a few weeks ago one of the gardeners was terribly excited. A helicopter was hovering over the garden and he was quite sure the man looking down from it was Mr. Getty. Actually, I went out to have a look."

"It wasn't Mr. Getty?"

"No, it wasn't. But I wouldn't have been at all surprised. Not at *all*."

After absorbing the ambience of antiquity in the lower floor of the villa, it seemed anachronistic to go upstairs, where the museum keeps the Getty collections of decorative arts and Renaissance and Baroque paintings. They hardly seemed the sort of things one would expect to find in Lucius Piso's attic.

All the same, it is a princely collection, and a graphic lesson in what an American boy can acquire with hard work, thrift and a bit of luck. More fortunes than one are represented by such pieces as Rembrandt's nonsaintly *St. Bartholomew*, Peter Paul Rubens's *Four Studies of a Negro's Head*, Gainsborough's portrait of *Anne, Countess of Chesterfield*, and Conaletto's *Arch of Constantine*, to name only a sampling.

The upstairs is drawn into the lower house by the upper spaces of the atrium and the inner garden, and from a small balcony the visitor can look down into the little temple where the Getty Herakles stands.

He seemed to me to be alert, as if listening for some expected sound. Perhaps a helicopter?

On the way out I paused for a moment to speak to one of the guards. "When Mr. Getty comes," I said, "please tell him thanks for me."

# Santa Monica

*Title to the ocean, the sunset, and the
air is guaranteed by God.*

It all comes to an end at Santa Monica—the whole vast shining
incredible land—in a merry-go-round.

Standing one day on the bluffs in Palisades Park, I was reminded of the old story about the two ladies from Iowa who
had stood in perhaps that very spot, gazing upon the Pacific
Ocean for the first time.

"Well," one said, "it isn't as big as I expected."

And from the palisades above Santa Monica Bay, the Pacific
Ocean really doesn't look so big. It is such a neat, well-composed
view. It seems almost two dimensional. those pretty sailboats
out there are only painted on, by Dufy, most likely. And the
whole picture needs a frame.

More than any other place in Southern California, the Santa
Monica bayfront perhaps best fulfills the fantasies of the inlanders on their first pilgrimage, despite the disappointment of
the lady from Iowa.

The beach is broad and tan and scattered with sun-browned
people in bits of dazzling color. Small boats nod at their moorings or glide back and forth inside a crumbling breakwater.
Sumptuous homes and beach clubs with tennis courts and swimming pools sit at sand's edge, just inside the highway. To the
north this vision ends in the dark bulk of Point Dume; to the
south, in the voluptuous silhouette of Palos Verdes Peninsula.

Altogether, it is probably what the unravelled Eastern businessman has in mind when he finally decides he's "got to get
out to the Coast."

247

In such places as Scott City, Kansas, it is thought that Hollywood has a seashore. Cary Grant lives on it. America ends in a green park, overlooking Cary Grant's house, the beach, the sea and the beautiful people.

It is all quite true.

Palisades Park stands a hundred feet above the highway and the beach. It runs for a mile, like a green ribbon, between the city of Santa Monica and the sea; a narrow strip, no wider than Ocean Avenue, which separates it from the city. It is poised precariously on the palisades, fenced off from the edge of the eroding bluffs.

The park begins at the old pier on the south and goes north to Inspiration Point, which has been made somewhat less inspiring in recent years by the rise of a nine-story apartment hotel whose two top stories are given over to the lodging of its tenants' cars. Thus the cars have a better view than the people, an arrangement which seems to be the ultimate apotheosis of the automobile in our culture.

A board walk runs through the park under splendid palms, cypresses and eucalyptus trees, passing several minor points of interest, including two nineteenth century cannon aimed preposterously out to sea, as if on sentry duty in our eternal vigilance against the Yellow Peril.

About midway in the park a path has been cut in the face of the bluff, leading down to the highway. I took it down and walked along the highway past the beach mansions, then trudged across the sand and walked back toward the pier on the hard wet beach at the edge of the surf.

This is the mildest of encounters with the sea, without peril even for people who aren't suitably dressed, or undressed, for the beach. The surf is tame, partly due, I suppose, to the broken down old breakwater, valiant to the last. There is no likelihood of being speared by a surfboard or carried away by an unexpected wave, though the unwary are sure to get their shoes wet.

The Santa Monica pier is antique. Naturally many people want to tear it down. Naturally many people want to leave it up. At best, it is on reprieve. It has an embattled look, somewhat misshapen and askew. It creaks and groans on its weathered pilings, and supports a ramshackle row of shops, fish markets, galleries and cafes. At its shore end it is ornamented by an enchanting old merry-go-round.

It has stood there throughout the century, this Victorian play-house, while generations of concrete buildings have come and gone. The little horses of the carousel are exuberantly sculptured, obviously of Arab blood, with wild eyes and flaring nostrils. The old organ pounds and clangs and wheezes as if trying gal-lantly to finish this one last song before expiring. A sign tells its story:

"Welcome friend. The music you are listening to is coming from one of the oldest organs in the country, built in 1900 . . . Constantly playing for seventy years. The merry-go-round has the happiest record in the U.S. The horses were imported from Germany and are all hand-carved. There are no two horses alike. Your grandparents and mom and dad probably rode this ride when they were children. All the great actresses, and their chil-dren, too. Come aboard, close your eyes and listen to the music . . ."

This was the first merry-go-round my own sons had ridden. We had lived in Venice then; the older boy was three, and I remembered with what emotions I had put him on his horse and let him go it alone. Very probably, it had occurred to me then, this had also been *my* first merry-go-round.

As he whirled around, gripping the post till his knuckles whi-tened, his face suffused with an unutterable joy, a scream inside him that would not quite burst out, I composed a song in my mind:

*O what a thrill to be three*
*When the band begins to play;*
*My heart is filled with glee*
*As I go my merry way . . .*

Not very good, but neither is some of John Philip Souza's stuff, when you reduce it to the printed page.

I detached myself from the pull of the merry-go-round organ and walked out on the pier, looking into an "art gallery" awash with pop posters and urns and statues of chalky white Venuses and elongated cats; a gift shop offering such marine novelties as dried starfish, driftwood and abalone shells; a penny arcade, its pennies inflated by time to dimes and quarters; a shooting gallery; a palmist who was out to lunch.

Fishing is free from the end of the pier, and there is always a hardy group of fishermen out there, whatever the hour and the weather. Pier fishing draws all kinds: children, old crones, teenage girls, couples with infants. I saw one young mother diapering a baby while her husband watched his lifeless line with serene detachment.

Though I don't fish, I have haunted piers most of my life. It is my conviction that nobody ever catches anything, so there must be some other motive, deep and elusive, for staying out there all day in the wind and sun.

I saw an old man sitting on a bench, watching some small boys fish. His benign face was weathered, his hair and eyebrows grizzled. He wore khaki pants, sweat shirt, worn tweed coat, tennis shoes and an ancient captain's cap.

"Does anybody really ever catch anything?" I asked him.

He grinned up at me, then went back to watching the boys. "Oh, yes," he said. "They catch lots. I caught me a big halibut, right over there. Weighed thirty-nine pounds.

"Oh, ho, Tommy!" he shouted at one of the boys. "So you've decided to use bait today! That's a good idea!

"Something got hold of a boy's line yesterday. Pulled the whole thing in—pole and all. Somebody said it must have been a shark. I think it was a big stingray. Sharks don't come in here this time of day."

Suddenly there was great excitement. A man pulled in a small halibut, flat and mottled, with a finny fringe.

"Oh, he'd make a good breakfast," the old man said. "Just fry him in butter."

He looked out at the breakwater, a ragged dark line, like the back of some enormous sea monster. It had been made of great blocks of granite, many of which had tumbled into the sea.

"Fishing hasn't been so good here, though," he said, "since they built that new breakwater."

"New?" I said.

"Well, new in Thirty-three, it was. I been fishing here since Twenty-eight."

The view inland from the pier is as pleasant as the view from the palisades—the opposite side of the picture postcard. Behind the beach the palisades run for a mile or two—the visible end of the continent—pinkish-brown cliffs, agonized by the centuries. The park runs along their top, a thin green line, and beyond that the row of structures on Ocean Avenue—some brand-new white towers, some peeling old houses from the age of elegance.

Below the pier in the water near the shore, a school of surfers floated on their blue, red or yellow boards like water bugs. Umbrellas of brilliant hue polka-dotted the beach; pink and brown flesh and scraps of cloth covered the sand like fluorescent confetti.

It seemed incredible that only a hundred years ago there was nothing here but land, sea and sky. An Easterner, writing years later of a visit he made to this shore in 1869, recalled that it was "an unpeopled waste—no light (dressed) brigade of sportive bathers charged the angry surf; neither keel nor oar vexed the breakers that broke on the desolate shore."

Juan Rodriguez Cabrillo and his crew were the first white men to see Santa Monica Bay, on their voyage of 1542. Then two hundred and twenty-seven years passed before Gaspar de Portolá and his soldiers camped at a spring above the bay. It is said that one of Portolá's men named the place Santa Monica, likening the spring water to the saint's tears for her wayward son, Augustine.

It was another century before John P. Jones, a Nevada senator, and Colonel R. S. Baker, a cattleman, who had bought the old Mexican land grants, formed a township, filed maps and started selling lots. The sale was held on a hot July day in 1875. They hired Tom Fitch, an orator and auctioneer of note. Hundreds of people buggied down from Los Angeles to hear Fitch and to see the ocean. Both were magnificent.

Fitch promised that anyone who bought a lot in Santa Monica would have the Pacific Ocean as a backdrop, with a daily sunset of "scarlet and gold" and "a bay filled with white-winged ships."

He went on to say that the title to the land was guaranteed by his employers, but the title to "the ocean, the sunset and the air is guaranteed by God."

The chamber of commerce still makes that claim today. They boast also that Santa Monica's climate is matched only by that of the French Riviera and two small strips on the west coasts of Africa and South America.

South of the merry-go-round are the volleyball courts. They are used exclusively by the very young, good-looking and sun-tanned, of both sexes, who play the game with a fierce animal energy, leaping high, lunging through the sand, tumbling head over heels and bellowing Tarzan cries of triumph or dismay. Bronze thighs and biceps twitch and ripple as the contest see-saws.

On the sidelines other youths, equally flawless, take their ease beside lissome young females in bright bikinis, together worshipping their youth, the Lord's wisdom in providing two sexes, and the blessed sun.

Only a hundred feet on down the promenade another generation is at its games: Old men on benches at long tables, bent over chess or checker boards, their seamed faces knit, their concentration as intense as that of the volleyball players, though at much less cost in physical exertion.

Walking back past the merry-go-round I stopped to read the weathered sign over the entrance:

"Merry-go-round apartment house. The only apartment house in the world that has a merry-go-round and an organ. In the morning the guests awaken to the tunes of the organ and all day they go about their duty with music in their ears. When they are ready to go to bed music helps put them to sleep . . ."

I looked up. Indeed there was a second story. Curtains and other signs of occupancy showed in the windows.

What a wonderful thing, I thought as I drove back to the heart of the city, to live one's life at the beach above a merry-go-round.